CW01512050

# RITUAL OFFERINGS

# RITUAL OFFERINGS

*Feeding Your Spirits — Empowering Your Magick*

Edited By:
*Aaron Leitch*

NEPHILIM PRESS 2014

# Ritual Offerings

Edited by Aaron Leitch

Copyright 2014 to Nephilim Press and the individual
Authors and Artists featured within this work

ISBN: 978-0-9987081-2-6

No part of this publication may be reproduced, stored in a retrieval system, or transmitted in any form or by any means, electronic, mechanical, photocopying, recording or otherwise, without the prior permission of the Publisher.

# Contents

# *INTRODUCTION:*
## MAGICKAL OFFERINGS IN
## WESTERN OCCULTISM

*Aaron Leitch*

"Then will [the spirits] demand of you some sacrifice or courtesy if you wish to be served and obeyed promptly. You shall reply that sacrifice is not to be made unto them, but rather unto the only God."

"For the enchantments whereof the evil enchanters and sorcerers make employ, are in no way wrought by the true method, and they only have power to execute their end in proportion to the tributes, sacrifices, and pacts, rendered in return, which latter evidently bring about the loss of the soul, and very frequently that of the body as well."

"...for in employing [the spirits], if you make unto them the least submission, the slightest prayer, or honour, you are rendering yourselves their slaves, and they are in no way submitted unto you."

[*Book of the Sacred Magic of Abramelin the Mage*, Book II (Chs. 17 and 26) and Book III, "Essential Remarks Upon the Foregoing Symbols."]

he quotes on the previous page are perfect illustrations of the Western attitude toward offerings and sacrifice made to spiritual beings. Ritual offerings have been regarded as base and low forms of magick, used only by "the other guy" who simply can't hack the magickal arts without signing his soul over to one or more demons. The assertion is that an offering made to a spirit is tantamount to worshipping it, or at the very least giving over your personal authority to it; if the spirit demands a sacrifice in order to work for or with you, then it is demanding to be in control. Even today I encounter would-be magicians who proclaim — with full dogmatic authority — that one must *never* give anything at all to a spirit, nor allow it to ask for anything.

Yet throughout history and across the globe, the making of offerings and sacrifice has been foundational to both occultism and religion — including the Bible upon which texts like the *Book of Abramelin* base their own authority. It was practiced by the earliest tribal shamans and continued well into the era of the Temple religions — including the religion of Israel — until both Judaism and Christianity abandoned the practice, considering it "too pagan." The rest of the world continued to make use of offerings and sacrifice (of various types), and still do to this very day. How, then, did the practice become taboo here in the West? It all began with theocracy. In the ancient world, religion wasn't a matter of personal choice. Every nation had its own patron deities, its own official priesthood, and its own state-sponsored religion. There was no dividing line between religion and politics; if you were a citizen of the state, you were by default an adherent of the national religion. Therefore worship and sacrifice to the national gods were, essentially, acts of patriotism. You were worshipping and feeding the god who ruled and protected your nation and your people.

To offer these things to a foreign god, then, was an act of treason. You were supporting the god of some other people — who may in fact be counted as enemies of your own government. Therefore, the theocratic authorities declared it illegal to offer sacrifice/tribute to a foreign deity.

We can see this in the books of the Old Testament. The kings, priests, and prophets of Yahweh waged a never-ending war against the gods of their neighbors. The worship of Phoenician deities such as Baal Hadad and Astarte by the people of Israel were a continuing threat to the political sovereignty of the state. (If your people join a foreign religion, they effectively become supporters of that foreign nation.) And so the neighboring gods were demonized — quite literally — and any sacrifice made to an entity besides Yahweh was viewed as worship of that entity and declared a sin and an act of unbridled evil.

By the time the Roman Catholic Church had risen to power, this attitude had reached a fever pitch — with the Crusades and Inquisitions (both of which began in the twelfth century) intended to destroy non-Catholic cultures, religions, and occultism. All forms of shamanism and witchcraft, including offerings made to ancestors or spirits, were declared illegal. If you were caught engaging in such "satanic" practices, you would be arrested, forfeit all of your worldly possessions, and possibly tortured before execution.

"Witchcraft" (the craft of working directly with spirits) became something good people simply did not do — and thus we find a slew of mystical texts from the medieval and Renaissance eras (like *Abramelin*) attempting to distance themselves from more ancient pagan practices. They decry ritual offerings and sacrifice as something to which only the lowest of black magicians resort. In other words, "My magick is pure and holy, but *the other guy's* magick is evil!"

# Magick as Psychology

After the Renaissance, the 17th century brought the Age of Enlightenment (or Age of Reason). With this came another proverbial nail in the coffin for the "Old Magick": Western society was discovering the scientific method and sought to divorce itself from old "superstitions." Remember, too, that any practice hinting at witchcraft could still get you arrested or at least ruin your reputation, and the Church often viewed early scientists as little better than (or equal to) witches themselves. Therefore, it is no surprise that scholars, astrologers, mathematicians, chemists, and doctors (all vocations with historical roots in the occult) wished to distance themselves from the old ways as much as possible.

Occultism certainly continued to exist through this time, but it became a very intellectual pursuit. Its students inherited, from the Greeks, a philosophical view of spiritual beings: that the gods and spirits didn't "exist" as objective entities in their own right, but were simply metaphors created by the ancients to describe lofty concepts or the forces of nature. Over the next several centuries, the Hermetic Qabalah, alchemy, astrology, Tarot, and other intellectual occult pursuits gained in popularity. This period also saw the development of Freemasonry and the sudden appearance of Rosicrucianism. The focus of magick slowly shifted from working miracles in the outer world to rectifying one's inner Self.

The Age of Reason also led to the birth and development of psychology, and thus ultimately to the psychological model of magick, which presupposes the spiritual entities we invoke are merely archetypal images we place over our own instincts and psychological complexes. Jung, in particular, is highly regarded among occultists who view magick in this way. The Golden Dawn's teachings (late 1800s to early 1900s) often reflect this psychological model, as do the writings of Aleister Crowley:

> "The spirits of the Goetia are portions of the human brain.
> Their seals therefore represent [...] methods of stimulating or regulating those particular spots (through the eye).
> The names of God are vibrations calculated to establish:
> (a) General control of the brain. (Establishment of functions relative to the subtle world.)
> (b) Control over the brain in detail. (Rank or type of the Spirit.)
> (c) Control of one special portion. (Name of the Spirit.)"
> [*The Initiated Interpretation of Ceremonial Magic*, Aleister Crowley]

This attitude has been held in high regard for the last one hundred years. It has affected every system from the Golden Dawn to Thelema, Wicca and Neopaganism, Chaos magick and countless manifestations of modern Hermeticism and Rosicrucianism.

For those who have adopted the psychological view of magick, most of the practices of the Old Magick seem like silly superstitious babble: robes sewn with thread spun by a virgin, lion-skin belts, midnight trips to crossroads, spirit feasts, holy water, meticulous timing of rituals, weeks of confession and prayer, etc., — all of these sound like pointless distractions from the psychological standpoint. (And, in fact, many modern magicians have worked to remove all of them from their spells.)

If the gods, angels, and spirits are just aspects of your own psyche, then the ancient protocols for approaching them make little sense. Why would you need to feed and care for them? Why be concerned with offending them or driving them away (since they are within you at all times)? If I cook a meal and offer it to a spirit, then take what's left and toss it into a river, aren't I just wasting both food and my time? And, most importantly, why should I view magick as anything more than a form of occult psychotherapy? This has been the mindset of modern magick for the past several generations.

# The Spirit Model of Magick

However, don't think for a moment that the Old Magick is dead and gone! It may have gotten some pretty bad press in the West, but the older methods of magick are still alive and well in the world today. Just a few examples: There are African Traditional Religions (ATRs) such as Santeria, Palo Mayombe, and Voodoo. There are indigenous folk traditions in Africa, South America, Australia, across Europe and Asia, and several types in the U.S., including Hoodoo (in the south) and Hexcraft/Pow-wow (in the north). Not to mention Native American shamanism.

In every one of these cases, Christianity came but was unable to over-throw the old ways. For these people, the new religion was simply added to what they were already doing, and Jesus was merely another guardian spirit to call upon in times of need. Therefore, the Old Magick was never lost in these places. Sometimes it is practiced in secret behind Christian trappings (as can be seen in Santeria), and other times it is practiced quite openly — giving rise to a kind of "Catholic witchcraft" as found in Africa and South America. These people saw no conflict in setting up an altar and making offerings to a saint or archangel as easily as they would to a pagan deity. To this day the *novena* — originally a nine-day Catholic funerary observance — is a standard method of working magick in such cultures. An altar is erected, offerings are made, and the saint is beseeched to offer spiritual assistance.

What unites all of these traditions, and sets them apart from mainstream Western thought, is the so-called "spirit model" of magick. As opposed to the psychological model, the spirit model views gods, angels, spirits, ancestors, and other entities as very real beings. The art of the shaman (or witch, conjuror, etc.) is ambassadorial by nature: He approaches his patron gods and familiar spirits in order to negotiate on behalf of his family or community. The people need help in the real world, not philosophy. They need results-oriented magick that makes things happen. They desire protection, health, prosperity, happiness — all of which the gods can provide *if* the shaman can convince them to intervene.

The protocols involved in that art are therefore vastly important: how to properly summon the spirits, communicate with them, gain their respect, and convince them to work for and with us. It is important to know what will attract them and what will offend them and drive them away. And, most important of all, it is necessary to know how to properly and safely build life-long working relationships with them. The offerings we make to these spirits — and *how we make them* — is a large part of how that is accomplished.

For the past two decades, these concepts have been making inroads back into the West. Religions like Santeria and Voodoo are no longer off-limits to Caucasians. Even those who stick with Western systems (such as Solomonic mysticism) are turning toward indigenous folk traditions like Hoodoo, Hexcraft, Brujeria, Palo-Mayombe, Native American Shamanism, and others for lost occult teachings. And, perhaps for the first time in centuries, it is (slowly) becoming acceptable to view and work with the spirits as real persons rather than convenient fictions.

However, the movement is still young, and those students who desire to explore the Old Magick find very few resources. The greatest majority of modern Western occult texts are based upon the psychological model. Therefore, you will be hard-pressed to find a manual that teaches the proper methods of ritual offering. Sure a few books — mainly of the Neopagan persuasion — might suggest you leave leftover wine and cakes outside for the faeries. And offerings to the dead/ancestors are quite common when Samhain (Halloween) rolls around. But for the greatest majority of the time, offerings are either passed over entirely or reduced to a metaphor like everything else.

At least until now. This book is intended to fill a gap in our modern magickal knowledge, providing a "how-to" manual for making ritual offerings to spirits that *actually exist*. It is not within the scope of this book to prove the existence of the spiritual, nor to convince anyone who believes otherwise. However, most (if not all) of what you read in this book is written from the standpoint of the spirit model of magick. The authors I have gathered are the top names in their fields, and they view the spirits as quite real. While we do not intend to denigrate the psychological model for those who find it useful, we are unapologetic about our desire to see things differently and explore older ways of working with the spirits.

# WHY RITUAL OFFERINGS?

Nearly every author in this book has reported that their magick was "supercharged" by the inclusion of ritual offerings in their spells. Likewise, their students have responded with similar results. Spells that used to take weeks to produce results suddenly happen overnight. Summoned spirits that used to appear weak or far away suddenly become strong and very much present. Talismans begin to have their effect much faster. Why should this be the case?

Because spirits are important to your magick. Today it is quite common to see spirit work listed as a "type" of magick: To accomplish your goals you might choose (for example) a talisman, a spell, an incantation, *or* summon a spirit. However, this is not how magick was viewed in the ancient world. Spirits were not merely an option, a tool to be utilized when the magician deemed it necessary. No, spirits were the very heart and soul of all magick.

That talisman you consecrated has a spirit attached to it, who accomplishes the intended goal. The incantation you used worked because the spirits heard it and acted upon it. You were not alone when you cast that spell; your patrons and familiars were present and *casting the spell with you*. And what about spirit summoning, like we see in grimoires such as the *Key of Solomon* or the *Goetia*? Those are methods of first-contact with the spirits, who will then teach the summoner how to do proper magick with things like — you guessed it — talismans, spells, and incantations.

In all of the above, spirits are the common factor. It is the shaman's relationship with the local spirits that makes his magick work so impressively. He knows how to attract them, gains their respect, and uses ritual offerings to feed and empower them so they can protect the tribe.

Some still choose to view spirit-feeding as a symbolic act — a kind of earthy sympathetic magick whereby we use food to activate otherwise non-physical (spiritual) currents here on the physical plane. Others, like myself and many of the authors in this book, feel the Western gods, angels, and spirits have gone without feeding for far too long; thus, if you feed them as part of your magick, they respond in a big way. No matter how you choose to interpret it, the *knowledgeable* use of offerings will produce impressive results; they will "supercharge" your magick.

But why does it work? Do daemons, angels, and gods — who have no physical bodies — need earthly food in order to survive? Absolutely not! The archangel of the Sun, for example, hardly needs food from us in order to keep the Sun shining. The god of the sea needs no fish from you to keep the tides moving. The entities we work with in our magick are embodiments of natural (or even cosmic) forces. They exist, and will exist, so long as the machinery of the universe keeps running.

However, if you're going to call these entities down here to our earthly plane of existence, then the rules change. You are pulling them *away* from their natural habitats and asking them to offer assistance with physical problems — be they health, wealth, love, battle, or what-have-you. In order to accomplish miracles for us, the spirits need energy (or life force) from right here in the physical plane, and they depend on us to provide it.

I suspect one of the largest factors in failed magick today is the lack of energy transfer. Sure we put our own passions and energy into our spells, and we usually burn candles and incense — both of which are offerings in their own right. But is that enough? For instance, would there be enough energy in a taper candle and a stick of incense for a spirit to translate into a new home for you? Or a new job, or to heal a disease, etc.?

The vital fact that your familiar spirits need energy in order to accomplish your desires is missed by too many modern magicians. How often have we performed spells or summonings, demanded what we want, then banished the beasties away without further consideration? Even if a spirit desired to help us after such a rude encounter (which is unlikely), from where should it draw the necessary energy to make something manifest in the real world? If you increase the raw energy (life force) available to the spirit, you increase the likelihood that it can produce results and produce them faster and more efficiently.

Besides the need for energy, there is also a social reason for making ritual offerings: fairness and respect for the spirits involved. Consider the arrogance required to summon a powerful spirit or angel and demand (not ask for) what we desire, without so much as an offer to make payment for the work done! Western occultism — drawing largely from biblical dogma — assumes the mage should have ultimate authority over the spirits, and they should jump to his commands merely because they fear him.

This kind of thinking arises from the Western belief that offerings equal worship, or that an agreement made with a spirit to pay it fairly for its work is somehow a bad thing. The magician is not presented as an ambassador negotiating with the spirit world for help in the physical; he is presented as the all-powerful "Image of God" to whom the spirits must bow on command.

However, I can assure you no spirit is going to rush to serve you due to some "fear" of your power. They certainly will not leap to serve you if you heap threats and hostility upon them. Even if they did, they wouldn't be able to accomplish anything on your behalf without the necessary energy. And, since only they can tell you what they need, that means learning how to negotiate with them — to make a deal. Yet if there is anything more infamous in Western occultism than ritual offerings, it is the dreaded "pact with a spirit."

# Pacts with Spirits

If I call a contractor to work on my house, he's not going to take the job if all I have to offer are commands and threats. He wants to be treated with respect and *paid for his services*, or he's going to find himself another client. Your patron and familiar spirits feel the same way, and offering to compensate them fairly is a major part of earning their respect.

A pact is often defined as "selling your soul" to a demon in return for favors. However, the truth is that a pact is merely a covenant — a contract. Any time you agree to pay a spirit for its services, you've made a pact between the two of you. This is hardly dangerous all by itself. It only becomes dangerous if you allow the spirit to dictate the terms of the deal.

Just as if you were negotiating with a contractor for a job, you have to go in knowing what you are willing to spend. The contractor, who should be more knowledgeable about his craft than you, can give you an estimate, tell you what supplies he requires, and might even tell you the job will be more expensive than you planned. Therefore, you negotiate until both parties are satisfied with the deal. But if the contractor suddenly changes the terms, or demands more than you feel is justified, *you* have the right to fire him and find yourself a better contractor. As the client, you are ultimately in charge of the relationship. Forget that, and you can be easily swindled.

This dynamic is no different for spiritual helpers. It is certainly appropriate to negotiate deals with them. In fact, as we will see in this book, certain occult texts suggest making a small offering during a spell with promises of even larger offerings on successful completion of the work. What the larger offerings should include (or how they should be offered) can be suggested by the spirits. Keep an open mind, leave aside arrogance, and allow the spirit to tell you what it needs to get the work done. It may need more than you planned, or it may need its offerings done in a particular way or in a particular place (etc.) — and my rule of thumb is always:

What the spirit wants, the spirit gets — *within reason.*

This means you should give the spirit what it needs to do the work but not allow it to dictate the deal to its own advantage over yours. You can negotiate deals within reasonable limits, but your familiars should never *demand* anything of you. (Respect runs both ways, of course!)

A spiritual entity is like any other living being: It wants a home, sustenance, care, and companionship, but it wants to expend as little effort to get them as possible. If a spirit can wrangle those comforts from you without having to make good on its own promises, it certainly will. Thus, you cannot allow the spirit to gain control of the relationship, insisting upon more and more from you, refusing to work until you pay up, etc. Most especially, you must *never* allow a spirit to demand more than you are comfortable with or willing to pay. Know your own boundaries and what you are willing to offer, expect the same respect you show the spirit in return, and do not hesitate to tell a spirit "no way" if it asks for something like your neighbor's cat!

You will find the spirits are willing to work within your boundaries (if your boundaries are also reasonable). These guys want the offerings you are providing and want more of the same in the future. It is not in their best interest to be greedy, lazy, destructive, deceitful, or stubborn — because if they are, you will simply stop calling them and make the offerings to someone else. They know this, and that is your greatest tool in the art of taming otherwise wild spiritual entities. *Always* stay in charge of the deal![1]

---

1 I strongly urge you to read Gilberto Strapazon's essay *Offerings in Ceremonial Magick and ATRs (Risks and Influences)* for more on the dangers of allowing the spirits to gain control of a relationship.

There is so much more that could be said about building working relationships with spiritual entities. Establishing your patrons, house gods and familiars, erecting altars, the importance of intermediary spirits and ancestors (to name only a few examples) — all vital to understanding and making use of the Old Magick in our modern world. Any one of those subjects could fill a book on its own! However, this present book will focus upon the primary subject:

# A "How-To" Manual for Ritual Offerings

As it was conceived, the heart of this project was this introduction and the essay called *Liber Donariorum: the Book of Offerings*. The latter is intended as a practical guide for ritual offering: what to offer, how to make the offerings, what to do with them when they are done, etc. It includes tips, advice, warnings, and protocols to make your practice safe, respectful, and efficient.

Plus, it is not tradition-specific — you can make use of this manual regardless of the type of magick you use. From Golden Dawn ceremonies to Wiccan Sabbats and Esbats, all the way to simple hoodoo/witchcraft spells — if you wish to approach the spirits of your tradition as real and objective beings, this manual will tell you how to do it properly.

I should also mention that much of the information I present in *Liber Donariorum* comes from Western sources. I have, in this introduction, taken a stance that offerings were abandoned in the West, but that is not entirely true. While they were abandoned by the early Golden Dawn and pretty much everyone who followed, we find they are still present in many of the old grimoires. The *Key of Solomon* itself includes them — in fact, I will cover that material — and you will find references to offerings, sacrifices, and spirit-feasts in many other grimoires. (These are the very books the author of *Abramelin* denounced.) These practices can be traced to the oldest Western magickal texts — such as the Greek Magickal Papyri and the Arabic *Picatrix* (both primary sources for the Solomonic tradition). It is from these ancient Western sources I have drawn much of my own practice, along with healthy doses of what I've learned from Santeria, Palo-Mayombe, and Voodoo.

However, I want to give students more than just a simple how-to manual. I also want to introduce you to the philosophies behind the practice — the "why" to go along with the "how." I want you to see how spirits are approached in different traditions, why they feel ritual offerings are important, and even how they believe offerings work. To this end, I have gathered together some of the most respected magicians in modern occultism — especially those who are known as Old Magick practitioners and/or who view the spirits as real persons. Each one will write from the standpoint of a different tradition — Western and Eastern, modern and ancient — so you might come away with a fairly complete understanding of this subject.

**Zadkiel**, in his *Elements of Making Offerings*, provides his own how-to manual for making spirit offerings that both supports and expands upon *Liber Donariorum*. Of special import is his discussion of using divination to communicate with the spirits — a vastly important subject, as it is ultimately up to the spirits to tell us what to offer to them and how to offer it.

**Brother Moloch**, in his *Ancestors and Offerings*, outlines a practical method of working with your ancestors. He covers establishing and maintaining a shrine for your departed loved ones, how to properly interact with them, what substances should be offered to them, and even a practical ritual you can use for the purpose.

**Frater Ashen Chassan**, in his *Whispers From a Skull*, shares his adventure in obtaining a new familiar spirit, bound to a human skull, who has become his constant teacher and magickal companion. He describes the nature of such spirits and the relationship between them and their human masters. He explains in depth the lessons that spirit has given him about the proper way to make offerings, what to offer, how to establish spirit altars, etc.

**Frater Rufus Opus**, in his *Back Yard Path Toward the Summum Bonum*, outlines the nature of Genii Loci (local spirits) — familiar spirits you can find right in your own backyard. How to find them, communicate with them, and make offerings to them for the purposes of establishing relationships.

**Sam Webster** drew material from his doctoral thesis (*The History of Theurgy from Iamblichus to the Golden Dawn*) for his essay *Offerings in Iamblichan Theurgy*. Sam offers a later Hermetic view of offering and sacrifice, linking different kinds of sacrifices to different levels of manifestation or attainment. Physical offerings, such as described throughout this book, are the first and most basic type. But he also describes sacrifices of word, sign, and gesture (which make up the basis of magickal invocation) as an intermediate form of offering, as well as offerings of pure mind/energy that can only be made by ascended masters.

Think offerings are entirely missing from modern Hermeticism? Think again! **Chic and Tabatha Cicero** have provided an incredible (and *very* involved!) Golden Dawn ritual of offering to the Goddess Ma'at and the Forty-two Assessors of the Hall of Judgment. In this rite, no less than *forty-two* individual offerings are placed into a fire in conjunction with the famous Negative Confession found in the Egyptian Book of the Dead. I would consider this ritual something the faint of heart should avoid. And before you read it, I would suggest reading Sam Webster's essay on Theurgic offerings — as you will see many examples of them in the Cicero ritual.

**Nick Farrell,** in his *Offerings in Roman Deity Magic*, explores the subject of offering and sacrifice as it was understood (and in some cases is *still* understood) in Rome. Different kinds of offerings are described as well as different types of spirits to receive them. He also discusses the necessity of getting the Gods "on your side" to ensure success of your endeavors. He ends with an example ritual he has personally used to invoke the Mother Goddess of any nation to guide and protect its people.

**Jason Miller,** in his *Severed Head Cakes and Clouds of Dancing Girls*, takes us away from the West and into the offering practices of the Far East. Drawing largely from Tibetan *Vajrayana* tradition, he explains the origin and use of *tormas* — bloodless offerings that stand in for more ancient animal and human sacrifice. He covers traditional baked tormas, re-usable "toy" tormas, and even tormas (and other offerings) made entirely by visualization. Also of special note is his discussion of offerings made to harmful and hostile spirits — a practice that is nearly unknown in the West, but which should be taken far more seriously.

**Denise Alvarado,** in her *Ritual Offerings in New Orleans Voudu*, explores the philosophies and practice of offerings in her tradition. She discusses the difference between "sacrifice" and "offering," covers the protocols for working safely in graveyards, and then gives instructions for offerings to three specific

Voudou loa: Marie Laveaux, St. Expedite, and Black Hawk. This is a wonderful illustration of how different spirits may require different offerings (or manners of offering), how different things might offend them, etc.

**Gilberto Strapazon** gives us *Offerings in Ceremonial Magick and African Traditional Religions (Ideas and Practices: Risks and Influences of Integrating ATR)*. This essay is a departure from the others in this book, because it focuses upon the "downside" of working with spirits and making offerings. By no means should the student assume this practice is "safe" — in fact, there are very real dangers in working directly with spiritual entities, and those dangers greatly increase when you attempt to appropriate rituals and techniques you don't understand from foreign cultures. Plus, having been a member of the ATR communities in his country, Gilberto has seen what can go wrong when aspirants begin to let the spirits call the shots. I suggest you read this essay more than once!

*Zorge,*
Aaron Leitch, August 2014

# *Liber Donariorum*:
## the Book of Offerings

## Aaron Leitch

My offering, and my bread for my sacrifices made by fire, for a sweet savour unto me, shall ye observe to offer unto me in their due season. [Numbers 28:2]

# PREFACE

everal years ago, thanks largely to the ubiquitous presence of visual
social media, I decided to do something I had never dared attempt
before: I took photographs of my offering altars and posted them on
my blog. The first was from an invocation of the archangel Iophiel[2] — one of
my patrons and house gods. I included some biographical information about
the archangel, the ritual I had used, and a rather lengthy section explaining
how I had prepared the food offering to him. Plus, of course, *plenty* of pictures.

Afterward, I was poised to defend the practice from those who adhere
to the Western psychological models of magick. That is, those who believe
magick is all in the mind, that angels are just images we place over our own
instincts and mental complexes, and who therefore would see a food offering as a superstitious waste of both effort and food. However, I was actually
shocked by the feedback I received.

People loved it! Even if they didn't quite know why, there was just something about that beautiful altar and the feast laid out upon it that spoke to
something very deep within them. They wanted to know more: How did I
know what to offer? How long should it be left on the altar? What should
one do with the food once the ritual is done? In other words, what they were
seeing called to them, but they had no clue how to go about it.

So, I began to answer their questions to the best of my ability. I also
continued to upload photos and write-ups of further offering rituals — to
archangel Michael (Sol), archangel Sachiel (Jupiter), even archangel Samael
(Mars) — so people could see how different planetary offerings worked for
different spirits.[3] I tried to teach the protocols I had learned — from the ATRs
(mainly Santeria and Palo- Mayombe), from the Solomonic grimoires, and
then directly from the spirits I was feeding.

---

2   See my blog: http://aaronleitch.wordpress.com/2011/05/12/invocation-of-archangel-iophiel/
3   These are also posted to my blog: http://aaronleitch.wordpress.com/tag/offerings/

In all cases, the information I provided was appreciated. A few even went ahead and followed my lead — much to the approval of the angels or spirits involved. (Iophiel has received offerings around the world now, thanks to my blog posts about him. That helps me, too!)

However, it wasn't enough. It was no problem to guide a single student through making his or her offerings, but I really wanted to archive the information in a single source that everyone could use. Such a manual needs to cover all the basics: what to offer to whom, how to prepare it, how to offer it (for different affects), what protocols must be followed, how to properly dispose of the leftovers, and more. Because this information has been largely lost in the West, it is necessary to provide a manual to guide the beginner through the basics.

So I have created this manual to be that very guide. My hope is that this document will spread throughout the Western occult communities — regardless of any individual tradition — and have a significant impact on how we work with our spirits.

# SOME THEORIES ABOUT OFFERINGS

In the introduction, you learned why we should make offerings to our patron and familiar spirits. I discussed spirit feeding and payment for services rendered. I also stressed the need for energy transfer in your spells — so the spirits have what they need to do the work you've requested — as well as how to build a working relationship with an entity based on personal safety and mutual respect.

But what do we know about *how* the spirits consume the food offerings we give to them? Frankly, the answer is "not much." For all the work we do with them, humans have very little understanding of what spirits are made of and precisely how they accomplish their work. Or, in the case of this essay, exactly how a non-physical being consumes (energy from) physical food.

However, that doesn't stop different traditions — and even individuals — from developing their own theories on the matter. The essays that follow in this anthology will certainly explore many such theories. For now, though, I would like to offer a few simple ideas to get us started:

First, let me offer my own theory. I suspect a spirit consuming a food offering is something of an alchemical process. In alchemy, the prime material is first broken down (called *solve*) to its most basic elements — often through processes with names like fermentation, maceration, or putrification. In short — the material rots, or at least that process is simulated. Then the desired chemicals are extracted from the decayed matter, purified of their impurities, and re-combined (called *coagula*) into a new and perfected substance. This is how alcohol is made, and how plants are turned into medicines.

I suspect the *solve* process is also how spirits consume energy from offerings. Once you serve the food, it immediately begins its own process of breaking down into its basic elements. (I have found that food offerings left on an altar tend not to literally rot, but more on that later.) As the food dries out, evaporates, is consumed by fire (in some cases), or otherwise deteriorates, it undergoes chemical changes. These "transformations" from one physical state to another provide the energy consumed by the spirits.

Of course, my theory is not the only one — or even the best one. When I asked about this subject on my Solomonic forum, I received some rather inspired answers which I feel are worth sharing:

Ochani Lele is a Santero with decades of experience with ritual sacrifice in the Lucumi religion. He sees offerings as a method of releasing the life force present in all things:

> "Everything has *ashe* (*prana*, life, power, etc.) and food is no exception. Everything has different 'types' of ashe, and ashe in varying amounts. There's no difference between lighting a candle, lighting incense, saying a prayer, or offering food. Just as a ceremonial magician might use sandalwood incense on one occasion or a green candle on another, sometimes spirits or orishas or gods want the ashe inherent in food instead of a candle, or incense, or what-have-you."

Brother Moloch is a sorcerer and initiate of the Haitian Vodu religion. He views offerings as something in which the spirits (in this case, spirits of the dead) find comfort and enjoyment, reminding them of what they once enjoyed in life:

> "The Saints walked the earth at one time and they liked what life had to offer: good food, smoke, drink, sex — the pleasures life had to offer. They miss these things and enjoy it when we indulge

them in it. We eat to sustain our bodies whilst they eat for the pleasure it brings them. [When] I invite a Saint to dinner, I don't give it a slab of bloody meat on a plate — hell, I wouldn't eat that so I wouldn't expect a guest to. Would you? No. I cook the food and offer it cooked which is how they like it."

Rufus Opus is a Hermetic magician and Solomonic practitioner. His view — influenced by biblical literature — is based on smell. It strikes me as very similar to Brother Moloch's view:

"In the Old Testament, God wanted his offerings cooked too. It said the smell of the burning fat was pleasing to the Lord. I think it's interesting that the smell was what was important. In Revelations it talks about how the incense in God's temple was 'the prayers of the Saints.' The smoke rises as it is released, heading up towards the heavens. The scent itself is the invisible essence of the offering. I think it's apparent to us here that the spirits aren't physically consuming the offering, so they just assumed it was the scent that pleased them, the invisible essence. All the words for 'spirit' seem to be based on the word for 'breath' or 'wind.' You can't usually see breath or wind, but you can feel it and see it affect the material realm. Makes sense that the unseen movers would eat the unseen essence of a thing."

I don't see any of these theories as "correct" at the expense of the others. I think all of them have a solid point to make and should be taken together as a larger picture.

Let us now leave behind conjecture on why spirits want food or how they go about eating it. Now, we shall learn how to put all of this into practice:

# THE PRACTICE OF RITUAL OFFERING

An altar (or table) decked out with offerings is more attractive to the spiritual creatures than one without them. It is an important part of gaining their attention, as well as letting them know you are worth their patronage.

- A standard practice is to make a small offering during the spell itself, while promising the entities a larger offering upon successful completion of the work. This places you in a good position as the "client" — the initial offering is only enough to gain the spirits' interest, allowing you to negotiate an acceptable deal for full payment later.

- It is perfectly acceptable to ask the spirits what they would like (or what they require) in exchange for their work — including what to offer and how (or where) to offer it.[4] The spirits' wishes will overrule anything in this manual, as long as you always remember:

- The deal must be reasonable (on both sides) and acceptable to both you and them. And *always* stay in charge of the deal! If a spirit continually asks for more and more for the same amount of work (or less), or asks for something unacceptable, you are under no obligation to keep working with that spirit. If it refuses to meet you in a reasonable agreement, or is otherwise deceitful, harmful, or refuses to work, dismiss it and summon another. In time you will find those spirits who are well suited to you and willing to work with you in an equitable manner.

- It is also important to avoid making regular offerings to the spirits, including your familiars. Each offering should be made as payment for a specific service performed. In this way they will always be active and eager to earn their keep. As it is written in the *Book of Abramelin*, the spirits are industrious creatures and must not be coddled like pets.

  On the other hand, a spirit who expects to be fed on a schedule will be less inclined to work and may become a lazy glutton. Your only option then is to withhold food until they agree to work, which is counterproductive and certainly *not* the kind of hostile relationship you want with them!

---

4 Due to space restrictions, I have not included information about divination and spirit communication here. Some people are natural skryers and can simply converse with the spirits directly. Others need to use a divinatory tool, such as a pendulum, sortilege, cards, or geomancy (a much-underrated Western system of spirit-communication!). What you use will depend on your own natural talent, and *what the spirit desires/requires you to use.* Zadkiel, in his *The Elements of Making Offerings*, discusses the vital importance of divination to your spirit work.

- In the case of your patrons and house gods, you will not likely be setting them menial tasks, but instead asking for general blessings and spiritual support in your undertakings. You may wish to feed them once a year on their established feast or holy day. In these cases, a single large offering during the invocation is enough; though follow-up offerings to show gratitude after a successful undertaking — or just general good luck in life — is not to be discouraged.

- Other exceptions to this rule would be offerings made to your ancestors and your personal head-spirit/guardian angel — for whom you can make regular offerings without harm. However, such regular offerings should be kept very simple (such as fire, water, and incense), and special or more elaborate offerings given only as thanks for specific work accomplished.[5]

- In much the same light as above, you want to avoid overfeeding your spirits for any single task. For most day-to-day needs (help at work, extra money, aid in finding a new vehicle, problems with the neighbors, etc.) a simple offering will suffice; fire and water, incense, bread and honey will most often do. Larger offerings can be made for more urgent situations (such as healing or other emergencies), launching a new business, moving into a new home, etc. Remember that animal flesh (such as steak or chicken) is a *very* big deal and should only be given when *a lot* of energy is necessary and the need very great.[6]

- If you are feeding your house guardians and patrons once a year, they can be given a large offering including animal flesh. The smaller standard offerings can be given at any other point through the year.

- If you are working with an entity for whom we have historical information — such as a Greek God or a major Archangel — do not neglect to research the traditions that have honored him or her in the past. Look for foods, plants, and animals that were sacred and/or offered to

---

5   See Brother Moloch's *Ancestors & Offerings* for more on this.
6   Forgetting this fact is why ancient cultures found themselves slaughtering thousands of animals at a time to their over-glutted gods.

them in ancient temples,[7] determine if they had an established feast day, specific prayers or devotions, statues or icons, etc. Incorporate these into your offerings where possible.

# Standard Offerings (for all Spirits)

In many cases — especially when working with a new spirit — you will be unsure what to offer. Or perhaps you'll find yourself in a situation that does not call for an elaborate offering and need something simple yet effective. Fortunately, there are certain items which can be offered in all situations:

## Water

*Always* include water in your offerings. Fresh water from a river or spring is best, but tap water will do in a pinch.[8] Or you may use water that is in sympathy with the spirits:

- Rain water for aerial or storm spirits.
- Sea water for undines or sea spirits.
- River water for river spirits.
- Spring water (water from underground) for earth-bound and chthonic spirits, and the dead.
- Some traditions infuse planetary forces into water by leaving it outside overnight where it can "soak up the rays" from a given planet in the nighttime sky. (Or, for Solar water, leave it out during a sunny day.)

## Fire

This usually comes in the form of candles — which means the wax is also an offering.[9] Properly colored paraffin candles (both tapers and seven-day) are

---

7    A wonderful resource for this is *The Continuum Encyclopedia of Animal Symbolism in Art* by Hope B. Werness. It is not easy to find in hard copy now, but significant portions of it can be found on Google Books (where it can be searched by keyword): http://books.google.com/books?isbn=0826419135

8    In Brother Moloch's essay *Ancestor Offerings*, he suggests allowing tap water to sit in a bowl for twenty-four hours before use, to allow the chlorine to evaporate.

9    In the Solomonic tradition, blessings and an exorcism are spoken over the wax before the candle is used. See the *Key of Solomon*, Book II, Chapter 12. Otherwise bless the candles

commonly used; however, natural beeswax candles are always preferable. (Best if you can get it directly from the beekeeper.)[10] If you do not know the color that is sacred to the spirit[11], you can use white for celestial spirits and black for nature or chthonic spirits.

- A candle used as an offering should be allowed to burn away completely.
- Another way to offer fire is to pour a small amount of rubbing alcohol into a metal libation bowl. Set it on your altar and light the alcohol for a wonderful blue flame.[12] Please carefully consider your safety!

This is about offering fire itself. Burnt offerings (which are materials *consumed by* fire) will be covered later in this manual.

## INCENSE
This is more popular in some cultures than others. Here in the West its wide-spread use is likely thanks to the influence of the Catholic Church. It is essentially a kind of burnt offering: Plant material sacred to the spirit is reduced to ash — preferably in a consecrated censer — so it will release its pleasant odor. That scent will further attract and empower the spirits.[13]

## BREAD
I try to avoid using over-processed white sandwich bread and go for fresh loafs of French or Cuban bread instead. Or bake it myself.

## HONEY
It is almost always a good idea to include honey in your offerings, as it has the effect of sweetening the spirits' disposition toward you. Get the highest quality natural honey you can get. (If you can buy it directly from the beekeeper, do so.) I most often pour or spread the honey onto the bread.

---

according to your own tradition.

10   Helpful hint: Beeswax can be bleached naturally by laying it out in the sun. It can then be colored with natural colorings as necessary.

11   See Addendum C.

12   Suggested by Brother Moloch.

13   See Addendum A for incense recipes. There is also, in the Solomonic tradition, a consecration ritual for incense. See the *Key of Solomon*, Book II, Chapter 10. Otherwise bless the incense according to your own tradition.

## MILK

I usually use whole milk — though cream (even half and half) works wonderfully. The triad of milk, bread, and honey represent all that is wonderful in life, and therefore can be offered to absolutely any spirit under any circumstance.[14]

## ALCOHOL/LIQUOR

Spirits love to drink, and alcoholic beverages (such as wine) have been used in religious ceremonies around the world. Try to seek out a drink that is in sympathy with the spirit. For example, entities of Venus would prefer a sweet wine. Jupiter spirits prefer something fruity or woody. Martian spirits want something hard like whiskey or rum, or at least red wines. Earth spirits want something dark and earthy (like a dark beer), while aerial spirits prefer something light and airy.

Along with these, I have had further suggestions for offerings that most any spirit will find acceptable: Olive Oil (usually poured over bread), Dates, Figs,[15] and *Mola Salsa*.[16]

In most cases, I include most or all of the above seven items in each and every offering I make. Even for more elaborate feasts, I start with these and add several items more specific to the nature of the entity:

# OFFERINGS SACRED TO THE STARS AND ELEMENTS

Besides the standard offerings suitable for any spirit, there are also items that are in sympathy with specific occult forces. Or, to put it another way, there are items that are sacred to specific entities. To know what is proper to offer to a given spirit, as well as what might offend or drive it away, you need to consider which force(s) the offering itself embodies. (For example, foods fructified in the Sun for solar spirits, plants that grow in lakes for lunar spirits, cultivated crops for Jupiter spirits, etc.)

---

14    Brother Moloch, in his essay *Ancestor Offerings*, suggests milk should be reserved for higher spiritual beings (angels, saints, etc.) and must only be used when your magick has pure and good intentions.

15    For more on olive oil, dates and figs, see Frater Ashen Chassan's *Whispers from a Skull*.

16    "Mola Salsa" was a popular standard offering throughout ancient Rome. See Nick Farrell's *Offerings in Roman Deity Magic*.

Following are some foods, liquors, plants, animals, metals, and stones[17] that have specific occult — mainly astrological — correspondences. *This list is not exhaustive nor immutable!* With time and experience, your intuition (and the spirits) will guide you to further options.[18]

## Saturn Offerings

Poisons (henbane, hemlock, etc.). Thorns and nettles. Bitter foods (black coffee, unsweetened chocolate). Dark beers and liquors. Black roses and flowers. Lead objects. Onyx or obsidian. Sacred animals: Lapwing, cuttlefish, and mole.

## Jupiter Offerings

Fruits, vegetables, grains, breads, cereals, etc. (Anything that grows on a farm or that you would picture coming out of a cornucopia — harvest foods.) Fruity or woody wines, and mead. Blue roses and flowers. Tin objects. Lapis lazuli or blue sapphire. Sacred animals: Eagle, dolphin, and hart.

## Mars Offerings

Hot (spicy) foods. Red Peppers. Red meat (well done, no blood!). Cigars. Red wine or hard liquor. Iron/Steel objects — especially weapons, nails, railroad spikes, etc. Carnelian or red coral. Sacred animals: Vulture, the northern pike, and wolf.

## Sol Offerings

Citrus fruits. Sun-dried foods and fruits (raisins, dates, etc.). Yellow peppers. Pomegranates. Angelica. Red meat or rooster meat (well done, no blood!). Yellow roses and flowers (especially sunflowers). Golden objects. Sunstone or yellow sapphire. Sacred animals: Hawk, rooster or swan, sea-calf[19] and lion or cow.

---

17    Metal and stone can be offered to a spirit just as food can. However, in most cases, offerings made of these materials will be in the form of gift offerings. More on this later.

18    Again, see Zadkiel's *The Elements of Making Offerings* for important details on spirit-divination.

19    Sea-calf is given by Agrippa in his *Three Books of Occult Philosophy*, Book II, Ch. 10 — where he gives a bird, fish and animal for each planet. What we call a sea-calf today is not a fish, though it is a sea animal nonetheless. (Note that the dolphin is sacred to Jupiter, and it is not a fish either.) I suspect a better term here might be sea-lion, and it may gain its solar correspondence by sharing a name with the land creature sacred to the Sun. Of course, if we are going by name alone, why not the sunfish (opas or molidae)?

## VENUS OFFERINGS

Honey. Passion Fruit. Sweet Chocolate. Candy. (Things you would give to a lady on a date.) Fresh flowers — especially roses (red or green) and green flowers. Brass or copper objects. Emerald. Sacred animals: Dove, thymallus, and goat.

## MERCURY OFFERINGS

Pomegranates. Honey. Strawberries. Cinnamon/Cassia. Saffron and Saffron Flowers. Annual Mercury (an herb). Beef, Mutton/Lamb, or Pork (no blood!). Sweet and fruity or dry white wines. Honey mead. Orange or multicolored roses and flowers. Mercury or any metal alloy (such as pewter). Tiger's eye or citrine. Sacred animals: Ibis or stork, mullet, and baboon or ape.

## LUNA OFFERINGS

Corn or other seasonal produce. White wine. Water. Fish. Sweet potatoes. Milk. Honey. Lotus Flowers. Jasmine, Lavender, White Roses. Any water plant (such as lilies). Silver objects. Moonstone or pearl. Sacred animals: Owl, sea-cat[20] and cat.

## ELEMENTAL AND ZODIACAL OFFERINGS

Elementals (Salamanders, Undines, Sylphs, and Gnomes) as well as other daemons of the elements can be offered the same things as certain planets:

- **Fire** spirits: Mars offerings.
- **Water** spirits: Luna offerings.
- **Air** spirits: Mercury offerings.
- **Earth** spirits: Saturn offerings.
- **Zodiac** spirits can be offered items according to their elemental triplicity, or according to the planet that rules them, or both. Thus, for example, if you wish to make offerings to a spirit of Leo, you could make a Fire offering and/or you might offer foods sacred to Sol. If you wish to offer to a spirit of Taurus, you could make an Earth offering and/or foods sacred to Venus. Etc.

---

20   It is unclear what Agrippa (ibid.) meant by "sea-cat." I have seen suggestions that it should mean "sea-lion," but I find this unlikely due to the sea-calf (or sea-lion) that is sacred to the Sun. There is, however, a species of sea catfish called the ariiead or arrid catfish. Like the sea-lion, I suspect this one gets its correspondence though sharing a name with the land animal sacred to Luna. Again, if we are going by name alone, why not the moonyfish (monodactylidae)?

| Sign | Element | Ruling Planet |
|------|---------|---------------|
| Aries | Fire | Mars |
| Libra | Air | Venus |
| Taurus | Earth | Venus |
| Scorpius | Water | Mars |
| Gemini | Air | Mercury |
| Sagittarius | Fire | Jupiter |
| Cancer | Water | Luna |
| Capricornus | Earth | Saturn |
| Leo | Fire | Sol |
| Aquarius | Air | Saturn |
| Virgo | Earth | Mercury |
| Pisces | Water | Jupiter |

# ANCESTOR OFFERINGS

It is not the purpose of this manual to teach the art of working with ancestors or the dead.[21] This can be a tricky and even dangerous practice if attempted without training — especially if you intend to enter any graveyards! However, if you are working a *proper* ancestor altar:

- Always keep fresh water on the altar. It is traditional to have nine glasses of water, though I have seen instances of seven. You will have to regularly clean and refill them.

- Keep a white seven-day candle, and/or several tea-lights, lit on the altar at all times.[22]

- Ancestors should be offered things they owned[23] or enjoyed in life. If they smoked, give them cigarettes. If they drank coffee, give them

---

21   For more on this topic, see Brother Moloch's essay *Ancestors & Offerings*. Nick Farrell also discusses the subject in his *Offerings in Roman Deity Magic*.
22   Unless, of course, it is unsafe to do so in your circumstances.
23   Jewelry that was worn by the deceased is very popular, as are medals, rosaries and other religious items. You will of course need to stick with smaller objects. Gift offerings will be further discussed later.

warm cups of coffee. Cook their favorite meals. Offer them their favorite flowers. Etc., etc., etc.[24]

# Burnt Offerings

Many offerings can be given to spirits by reducing them to ash in a fire. This is usually best done when working outside with a bonfire into which offerings can be cast.

In some cases, especially holy days and celebration feasts, you may be preparing a meal that includes grilling or open-fire cooking — and in such cases you will be using the sacred fire to cook the offerings rather than reducing them to ash.

In either scenario, it is helpful to build the fire with wood that is in sympathy with the spirit. Plus, of course, the wood itself becomes part of the burnt offering. The *Key of Solomon the King*, Book II, Ch. 23, gives us the following list of woods and their planetary correspondences:[25]

**Saturn**: Juniper, Pine, or brambles
**Jupiter**: Box, Oak, or Cedar
**Mars**: Cherry-wood or Bay Tree
**Sol**: Laurel or Palm
**Venus**: Myrtle or Hazelnut
**Mercury**: Hazel
**Luna**: Willow

If you cannot obtain the proper wood, you can instead use normal firewood (or wood charcoal) and sprinkle generous portions of the proper incense and related herbs into the fire. In fact, this is acceptable to do even if you are burning the proper wood.

---

24   In his essay, *Ancestors & Offerings*, Brother Moloch stresses that foods containing garlic or onions are not to be given as offerings to ancestors.
25   I have created this list from different manuscripts of the *Key of Solomon*, plus some of my own studies.

# BLOOD OFFERINGS, SACRIFICE, AND MEAT OFFERINGS

**A Warning About Blood:** For the purpose of this manual, I will suggest that you *NEVER* offer blood to a spirit.

This is not a condemnation of the practice, nor of ritual sacrifice as practiced in religions such as *Lukumi* and *Voodoo*. However, such traditions that employ sacrifice also have strict protocols and procedures for doing it, along with dire warnings about breaking those protocols.[26] They also come with a fully established system of community support. If you perform a sacrifice there, it will be only after you have been educated, and your godparent will be present to guide your first ceremonies.[27] This is entirely different from a solo practitioner feeding blood to whatever random spirit(s) he or she wishes to summon.

As I learned from my exposure to *Palo Mayombe*, blood is absolutely the most primal substance you can offer to a spirit. As such, it engages the most primal aspects of the spirit itself. (Consider how giving honey to a spirit will sweeten its disposition toward you. What effect, then, do you suppose blood would have?) What may have once been an intelligent and civilized familiar can, if given blood, quickly become a ravenous beast. It can become aggressive and demand more and more, finally attempting to take it from you or others by force.

I've encountered this same lore in several traditions — some refer to the spirit becoming a "cougar" and some say a "leopard." I've even encountered a reference to "vampire." Most of these have come from conversations with practitioners of various ATR or ATR-influenced systems. What all of these have in common is the imagery of a primal predator that seeks blood.

The protocols and procedures I mentioned above exist to ensure the safety of the practitioners. The sacrifices take place in a specific religious context, utilizing meticulous rituals performed by initiated priests and priestesses, so the spirits involved do not descend into their primal and ravenous aspects. And so they don't decide the person making the offering is also edible!

---

26  This is covered somewhat in Gilberto Strapazon's essay *Offerings in Ceremonial Magick and ATRs (Risks and Influences)*.
27  This is discussed in Denise Alvarado's *Ritual Offerings in New Orleans Voudou*.

This short manual is hardly the place to teach these important protocols. Therefore, unless you are an initiate of such a tradition, I would personally avoid the entire blood issue. I choose not to use it in my rituals — not even to anoint talismans. I'm aware that many of my readers may utilize such techniques, but it is not something that should be covered here.

## BLOOD SUBSTITUTES

The use of blood substitutes for sacrifice is an ancient practice, not merely a modern refuge for the squeamish. The excessive force associated with blood is rarely called for in any typical situation, and most cultures that practice sacrifice have developed alternatives.[28] For example, the ancient Greeks used red wine — reasoning that the wine was the "blood" of the grape. There is also an Egyptian myth wherein beer was colored red and fed to a bloodthirsty goddess to calm her.

In the Lucumi faith there is a substance made from water and sacred herbs, called *Omiero*, that is considered as powerful as blood. The mysteries of its creation are closely guarded, but the general concept of herbal-infused waters has become standard in folk traditions like Hoodoo. If you wish to create a powerful herbal blood substitute, here is a method:

- It is first necessary to consecrate salted water, such as instructed in the *Key of Solomon*,[29] or according to your own tradition. The salt is important, as saline is a basic blood component.

- Next, take a generous portion of herbs, plants, and/or flowers sacred to the spirit[30] and tear or chop them into small pieces (tearing is best). While you do this, recite Psalms or other invocations to the magickal force embodied by the sacred herbs.

- Then place the herbs into a pot of fresh spring or rain water[31] (*not* the holy water!) and bring them to a gentle boil. As soon as the water boils,

---

28   See Jason Miller's *Severed Head Cakes and Clouds of Dancing Girls* for more about blood and sacrifice substitutes.
29   See the *Key of Solomon the King*, Book II, Ch. 11: "Of the Water, and of the Hyssop."
30   A great source for plants and herbs organized by their occult correspondences is Scott Cunningham's *Encyclopedia of Magical Herbs*.
31   See the section on Standard Offerings for different waters that can be used for different types of spirits.

reduce the heat and allow them to steep until the water is dark — like a tea. Strain out the plant material.

- Finally, add some of the salted holy water to the "tea," trying not to significantly lighten the color of the liquid.

This herbal holy water can then be offered in a bowl upon the spirit's altar, poured out as a libation, and even used to wash any object that will be placed upon the altar as well as the altar itself.

## MEAT OFFERINGS

Animal flesh can be safely offered to the spirits, so long as it is thoroughly cooked. That means *well done, with absolutely no pink in the center*! This is, again, to avoid the blood issue.

- See the section on planetary offerings for meats sacred to each.

- Also see the previous section on burnt offerings for woods sacred to each planet. If you can cook the meat over a fire burning the proper wood, it is all the better. If not, use natural wood charcoal and add incense and/or herbs sacred to the spirit to the fire.

- You might obtain your meat from a local Kosher or Halal butcher. Even better if they are a small business that obtains its meat from local sources. This will, at least, increase the probability that the animal was raised humanly and slaughtered to proper ritual standards.

Season, grill, and serve the meat just as you would for a dinner. (You can also season it with the spirit's incense.) I will generally cut it into the proper number of pieces.[32] Make sure to bring it to the altar while it is still fresh and warm, so the pleasant smell fills the area.

---

32  See Addendum D for the numbers sacred to different spirits.

# Gift Offerings

Gift offerings are of a different sort than food offerings, as they are not intended to give energy to the spirits. However, they are no less important and play a vital role in the process.

For the most part, gift offerings will be made to your patron/house gods and familiars — entities who will have an established altar in or near your home. In some cases, you can leave gifts for spirits out in nature, so long as they are not harmful to the local environment. Gift offerings are, as you may suspect, items given as gifts to the spirits — either offered in gratitude and devotion, or specific tools that enable the spirit to do its job most efficiently.

In the former case — that of devotional gifts — you will be placing objects upon the altar that your spirit finds pleasing, such as:

- Images of the spirit itself: statues, icons, drawings, photos, etc.

- Figures of animals or objects that are sacred to the spirit.[33] These are best when cast in a metal that corresponds to the spirit's nature (see the list of Planetary offerings), or carved from a stone or jewel in sympathy with the spirit. Pictures and photos of these objects are also acceptable, along with Tarot cards and other graphical representations of corresponding spiritual forces.

- Stones or jewels sacred to the spirit.[34]

- Toys and candy, if the spirit in question is a child or child-like — or just wants them.

- Fresh flowers in sympathy with the spirit (see the list of Planetary offerings).

---

33   In our home we have an altar to Bast, the Egyptian Cat Goddess. The central figure on the altar is a large Bast statue, and surrounding it we have put several smaller figures of cats. We include one for each of our house cats, and consider the figures to be "Bast's kittens." Our daughter *loves* to play with these small figures at the altar (she even feeds them cat food and water), and Bast thoroughly enjoys the playtime.

34   See Zadkiel's *The Elements of Making Offerings* for great information on offering semi-precious stones.

- Anything you find in your travels that further expands or beautifies the altar (or which the spirit directly asks for) — new altar cloths, censers, candle holders, libation bowls, offering plates, unguent jars, etc., etc.

- Where possible, try to find objects of the proper color(s) for the spirit,[35] as well as the proper materials.

- In the case of ancestral spirits, give them objects they owned and loved in life — jewelry they wore, their favorite books, religious trinkets (rosaries, crosses, medals), keepsakes and knick-knacks, etc.

- Photos of your passed relatives are also important — so long as you remember to include *no photos with living people in them!* You do not want to place the living on an altar to the dead.

Such gift offerings are what will cause your spirit's altar to grow — in both size and beauty — over the years. Your spirit's altar may begin rather sparse, with only the bare necessities, but it should expand according to your growing relationship with the entity. Just make sure you offer these gifts in payment for work done, rather than simply heaping gifts upon the altar that the spirit has not earned.

You may also make gift offerings of tools for the spirit to use in its own realm. For example, I once attended a sacrificial ritual done by a *Palero* to feed a familiar spirit (called a *Prenda* or *Nganga* spirit). After the chicken was sacrificed and the blood offered, the *Palero* proceeded to divide the chicken into parts. The head was given to the familiar so that it could see in the spirit world. The wings were given to it so it could fly. The chicken's feet were given to the spirit so it could use the claws when protecting the home.

We can likewise give the spirits inanimate objects that are sacred to them and tools that will make their jobs easier.[36] For example, an altar to a God of Language and Writing can include a pen and paper, or a stylus and papyrus. An altar for a spirit that will protect the home can be given weapons — swords, knives, guns, etc. An altar for a healing angel can hold medicines or medical

---

35  See Addendum C.
36  For an example, see *Ritual Offerings in New Orleans Voudou*, where Denise Alvarado discusses specific weapons given to the spirit Black Hawk, which he needs in order to properly work for you.

instruments. We can give them model vehicles to drive, airplanes to fly in, and more — the possibilities here are endless.

The same can be done for tools that you intend to use yourself, but which you want the entity to own and/or bless. Oils, incenses, and magickal tools are great examples. But, also, a police officer can leave his badge and gun on the altar of the spirit who protects him on the job. A doctor can leave his medical bag on or beneath the altar of a healing entity. A skilled laborer can leave his tools on his patron's altar. A writer can leave the pen he writes with. Again the possibilities are endless, depending on your own profession and spiritual needs. Just leave the items on the altar when you are not using them.

# MAGICKAL TIMING

You will want to make your offerings during a time that is sacred to the spirit in question, and when his star is fortunately aspected on a zodiacal chart. This does *not* mean your magick will fail if you perform it at any other time, but it is a significant help to the process if you work with the natural astral tides. As the grimoires tell us, a spirit does not rule *only* during his time, but he does rule *especially* during that time. By choosing the best time to make the offering, we increase the energy available to the spirit and thereby increase the likelihood of success in our goals.

- The best time to work is at dawn on the day that is sacred to the spirit. Hence, Solar entities receive offerings on Sunday, Lunar entities on Monday, Martial entities on Tuesday, Mercurial entities on Wednesday, Jupiterian entities on Thursday, Venusian entities on Friday, and Saturnine entities on Saturday. Dawn is always the most powerful portion of the day; as the Sun rises, the darkness flees and the world begins to awaken.[37]

- If you are working with one of the four elements, you can work on Tuesday for Fire, Monday for Water, Wednesday for Air, and Saturday for Earth. Also, the magickal hours for the Elements are dawn for Air, noon for Fire, dusk for Water, and midnight for Earth.

---

37  See Addendum B for a chart of planetary hours and how to calculate magickal hours.

- Also remember that some spiritual beings — such as saints and several archangels in Orthodox and Catholic traditions — have established feast days. We know of feast days for a number of pagan deities as well. If you find such feast days in your study of the entity, use them.

- If none of the above applies directly to your spirit, you might consider using established holidays (holy days) based upon your magickal goal. For example, offerings to martial spirits and soldier ancestors can be made on Memorial Day. Offerings for love spells can be made on Valentine's Day. Offerings for prosperity can be made on Thanksgiving. Offerings to the dead and chthonic spirits can be made on Halloween. Etc.

- Finally, if you are experienced with electional astrology, you may certainly employ that in the magickal timing of your offerings as well.

- Offerings to your ancestors, should you have a proper ancestor altar, should be made on the Sabbath day. Which day this is will depend on your most recent ancestors — if they were Christian (even if you are not), then Sunday will be the Sabbath for them. If they were of Jewish descent, then Saturday. Etc.

## IMPORTANT PROTOCOLS — READ CAREFULLY!

- Once again, *never* offer blood to a spirit unless you are doing so within an established tradition and have guidance from an experienced teacher.

  - The same guidelines apply to any bodily fluids — semen, vaginal fluids, saliva, sweat, urine, excrement, etc. — and items such as your hair, nail clippings, etc. Also be careful with personal items such as clothing, toothbrush, hairbrush, etc. Remember that anything placed upon the altar during an offering becomes the *property* of the spirit. And that includes you!

- As stated previously, remember to never overfeed your spirits — either by feeding them too often or feeding them too much at once. Animal flesh should only be offered when *a lot* of energy is needed.

- In most cases, you should share the food offerings with your spirits. This is a matter of respect. You would not invite a beloved friend to dinner and then sit there and watch him eat alone. Join in the feast! Raise a toast to the spirit! Take a bite or a sip from every item on the altar, inhale the sweet perfumes, and feel the warmth of the candles. This is much like a Eucharist — you are ingesting the blessed energies of your spell and making them a part of you, just as the spirit is doing in his realm. This is extremely powerful.

  Also, if you are making an offering as part of a larger holiday feast (such as Thanksgiving), it is important to offer the spirit the first and best portions of every dish. The rest of the participants will eat from their own plates, *not* those belonging to the spirit.

  o **Important Exceptions:** *Never* eat from offerings left to the dead or to chthonic or infernal spirits! You do not want to ingest death. If you wish to have such spirits — like ancestors — share in a feast with you, give them their own portions on their own plates and do not eat from those plates.[38]

- When making an offering, avoid kneeling on both knees. One knee can show respect, but you never kneel on both knees before (the representatives of) Fate. In the same light, never bow or rest your head toward any spirit less than your own head-spirit (Patron God, Holy Guardian Angel, etc.) — *especially* never toward the dead or chthonic spirits.

- In a similar light, remember you must *never* show the slightest hint of weakness or fear to any spiritual entity. This also includes irresolution: If you say something, mean it. If you promise or threaten something, follow through. Otherwise the spirits will lack respect for you.

---

38  Apparently this is a tradition-specific protocol, which I picked up from *Palo Mayombe* and *Lucumi* (Santeria). Other traditions may lack this restriction. See *Ancestors & Offerings* by Brother Moloch, which discusses sharing the offerings made to one's ancestors.

- Find out what might offend and drive away your spirit! For example, if you are working with Faery or Jinn, you cannot wear or offer iron or steel. According to their lore, iron represents mankind's rape of the earth and subsequent descent into warfare and environmental destruction. Therefore the metal offends them, and can be used to drive them away. This is why it is important to know the established traditions regarding your spirit, or to divine directly from the spirit what it prefers and what offends it.

- If you need to work any magick at a cemetery,[39] you *must* announce yourself and pay a toll at the gate before you enter. A traditional method is to knock three times, announce your intentions to the guardian spirit(s) of the cemetery, and then drop some change on the ground just outside the gate. (Nine pennies is the traditional toll. Some use only three, and others simply drop whatever pocket change they have on them.)[40]

  o If you have come to the cemetery to make an offering to remove a curse or "crossed" (unlucky) condition, remember to leave the graveyard and return home without looking back. Some practitioners also choose to take a different route home than the one they came by.

  o When you get home from the cemetery — no matter what reason you went — take a cleansing ritual bath.

- There is similar lore involved with entering a forest (or woods or *any* natural place) for magickal purposes.[41] Announce your intentions to the guardian spirits of the land and drop a few coins by the entrance. Seven or three pennies would suffice, or just some random change.

- To offer a cigar (or cigarette), light it and draw smoke into your mouth. (Do not inhale it.) Immediately blow the smoke onto the altar, statue, icon, etc. Do this at least three times, or the number of times sacred to

---

39  *Especially* if you intend to remove anything — such as grave dirt.
40  In the practice of *Palo-Mayombe*, it is also taught to enter the graveyard backward — apparently so any nearby spirits (who may be hungry) will think you are *leaving*.
41  Again, this is *especially* true if you intend to remove anything from that place. See Zadkiel's *The Elements of Making Offerings* for more on this subject.

the spirit. Then place the still-lit cigar/ette on the altar in an ashtray and let it burn out naturally.

o   Another method of offering a cigar is to light it, turn it backwards, *carefully* place the lit end into your mouth, and gently blow. The smoke will "shotgun" out the other end.

o   If you cannot smoke for any reason, it is acceptable to offer the cigar/ette without lighting it. Simply unwrap the package and place it on the altar. Explain to the spirits why you cannot light it.

•   If any offerings are contained in sealed jars or bottles (such as alcohol), don't forget to open them.

•   When offering alcohol, it is traditional in the ATRs to take a swig of the drink and "spray" it over the altar and/or other offerings. Then, whether you do that or not, leave the opened bottle on the altar.

o   If you are working outside and wish to pour out the remaining alcohol as a libation, make sure to lay the empty bottle on its side. (Never leave an empty bottle standing there.) If you do not wish to leave the bottle behind, it can be picked up after it has been laid briefly on the ground.

•   Finally, I remind you once more to treat the spirits with respect, but to *always* stay in charge of the deal! You must be willing to give the spirit what it requires, but establish your limits and stick to them. If a spirit demands too much, or requests something unreasonable or harmful, dismiss it and find a more amicable spirit.

# MAKING YOUR OFFERINGS

From the *Key of Solomon the King*, Book II, Chapter 23, "Concerning Sacrifices to the Spirits, and How They Should be Made":

> "But when we make sacrifices of food and drink, everything necessary should be prepared outside of the circle, (the table

previously washed or new,) and the meats should be covered with some fine clean cloth, and have also a clean white cloth spread beneath them; with fresh bread, and precious wine, but in all things those which refer to the nature of the planet. Animals, such as fowls or pigeons, should be roasted. Especially shouldst thou have a vessel of clear and pure fountain water, and before thou enterest into the circle, thou shalt summon the spirits by their proper names, or at least those chief among them, saying:

> *In whatsoever place ye may be, ye spirits, who are invited to this feast, [NNN][42] come ye and be ready to receive our offerings, presents, and sacrifices, and ye shall have hereafter yet more agreeable oblations.*

"Perfume the viands with sweet incense, and sprinkle them with exorcised water; then commence to conjure the spirits until they shall come. This is the manner of making sacrifices in all arts and operations wherein it is necessary, and acting thus, the spirits will be prompt to serve thee."

You may notice in the above several echoes of the instructions I have given elsewhere in this manual. The procedure I am about to outline is also very similar to what the *Key* instructs,[43] though I will go into much more detail here.

If you are making the offering in your home, you will want to set up an altar. If you have established shrines for your house gods and familiars, use them. Otherwise, a temporary altar can be erected.

If you are working outside, you have the option of building an altar from stones. Try to find larger stones — natural ones, rather than bricks. Use the number of stones (or a multiple thereof) that is sacred to the entity.[44]

As it happens, I make most of my offerings indoors in my private temple. Each of my spirits has its own shrine either in the temple itself or elsewhere

---

42    I have added this [NNN] to indicate where the spirits who are being called to the offering should be named.

43    I should also note that these procedures are also very similar to what you will find in the ancient Arabic *Picatrix*, which is the likely source for this kind of offering magick in the Solomonic tradition.

44    See Addendum C.

in my house, but due to space restrictions I usually bring them to my larger working altar for their offerings.

## Preparation

- Try to work on the magickal day and hour during which your chosen spirit is most powerful.[45] If you cannot work on the proper day, then you can at least work on a proper hour. It will also be helpful if the spirit's planet is currently in an astrological sign that it rules and is fortunately aspected. (Also try to work when the planet is above the horizon.) The moon should be in increase (waxing).

- Before the chosen time, you will prepare for the offering ritual in whatever manner is common in your tradition. In the Solomonic system, this involves purification (a ritual bath), seclusion, fasting, and prayer. You may do this for seven days beforehand for important rituals, but three days is good enough for standard working, and twelve hours will do in an emergency.

- I generally prepare two invocations to use in my offering rituals. The first is to the Highest, wherein I give praise and ask that the angel be sent to enjoy the feast. The second invocation is to the angel itself, wherein I offer further praise and make an invitation for the entity to come and partake of the food, smell the incense, etc. I also choose several Psalms — as many as the spirit's sacred number — that have some bearing on my goal. (Even if it is just thanksgiving to the entity.) You may, of course, utilize sacred scripture from your own tradition.

- I also often include a written petition to the angel I am working with, asking for help with a situation or general blessings. I write the petition on consecrated paper with a consecrated pen. This petition can be read aloud during the invocation ritual, but it is not required.[46]

---

45  See Addendum B.
46  In some cases I allow others to write their own petitions to include on the altar. Since these petitions may be private, it is never required for them to be read aloud, either. In such cases I never even see them at all.

• Make sure to have plenty of holy water and a proper incense[47] on hand — both consecrated.[48]

• At some point during your period of purification, use the holy water and incense to consecrate the working space, the altar, and every item that will go on the altar. Sprinkle each object with the water and cense with the incense, while reciting a prayer of exorcism and/or blessing.[49]

## ESTABLISHING THE ALTAR

• In most cases, I orient my altar facing eastward. This can change, however, if the spirit you are working with is traditionally associated with another direction. If you are not sure, then face it east.

• Cover the altar with a properly colored cloth. (Remember, if the spirit does not have a known sacred color, you can use white for celestial entities and black for lower and chthonic spirits.)

• If you have one, place a consecrated statue, icon, or other image of the entity on the altar.[50] It should be situated on the side of the altar furthest from you and facing you. (Thus if the altar faces east the image should be eastward on the altar top facing west.) This is the focal point of the ritual, a place for the entity to stand and consume the offerings.

• If you are using a talisman with the entity's signature (sigil) on it, place it in the very center of the altar. (If you intend to offer the spirit a single candle — see next section — the candle will be placed directly on top of the talisman.) This serves the same purpose as the icon or image, giving the entity a focal point. You may use both an image and a talisman if you wish; I often do just that.

---

47  See Addendum A.
48  Solomonic consecrations for Holy Water and Incense can be found in the *Key of Solomon*, Book II, Chapters 10 and 11. Otherwise bless these items according to your own tradition.
49  I will often consecrate all of the objects, along with the altar itself and the temple room, at the same time using holy water, consecrated incense and the lengthy dedication prayer of Solomon's Temple in 1 Kings 8:22–53.
50  I do not hesitate to search for suitable images online and print them out for the occasion.

- If you have penned a petition to the angel, fold the paper *toward yourself* the number of times sacred to the entity. (Or a number that will evenly divide it — so, for example, a petition for an angel of Mercury could be folded four times instead of eight. A petition to Lunar entities can be folded three times instead of nine.) The petition is then laid at the feet of the statue or icon on the altar — or directly beneath the entity's talisman or offering candle.

- The rest of the altar space will be used to lay out the offerings.

## LAYING OUT THE OFFERINGS

- Remember that items placed on the altar should, wherever possible, be of the color sacred to the spirit. This includes the dishes used to make the offering. Likewise, offerings should be given in the proper number, or a multiple (or division) of that number.[51]

- First place candles of the proper color onto the altar. It is best to use the proper number of candles, but failing that you can use a single candle placed in the center of the altar (directly on top of the entity's talisman if you have one). I generally use paraffin seven-day jar candles for this purpose,[52] though candles made from beeswax are even better. Remember to exorcise and/or bless all candles before they are used.[53]

- Next place a glass of fresh water (*not* salted holy water!) next to each candle. Once the candles are lit, you will quickly feel the energy that is generated by this fire/water combination on the altar. Also see the "Standard Offerings" section for different types of water that can be offered to different spirits.

- Prepare the feast just as you would for your own table. Make sure the plates, cups, and bowls are freshly washed. Cold dishes can be prepared

---

51   See Addendum C for numbers and colors for the spiritual forces.

52   Years ago, "seven-day candles" really burned for seven days. Today, you're lucky to get five days out of them.

53   See the *Key of Solomon*, Book II, Chapter 12. Otherwise bless the candles according to your own tradition.

beforehand and placed in a refrigerator, but you will want to cook meats and anything else that will be warm *immediately* before the ritual. The warm items, especially, must be carried to the altar while they are still fresh from the fire, so their pleasant aroma will fill the area.

- Any food placed on the altar before the ritual begins should be covered with a clean cloth — white is traditional, though the color of the spirit could be used here as well.

- Once your offering feast has been laid out upon the altar, light the incense. In the *Key of Solomon*, the following exorcism and blessing of the fire is recited as the coal is lit:

  > *I exorcise thee, O creature of fire, by him through whom all things have been made, so that every kind of phantasm may retire from thee, and be unable to harm or deceive in any way, through the invocation of the most high creator of all. Amen.*

  > *Bless, O Lord all powerful, and all merciful, this creature of fire, so that being blessed by thee, it may be for the honour and glory of thy most holy name, so that it may work no hindrance or evil unto those who use it. Through thee, O eternal and almighty Lord, and through thy most holy name. Amen.*

  > [*The Key of Solomon the King, Book II,* Chapter 10, "Concerning Incense . . ."]

  Otherwise bless the coal according to your own tradition. Then use the holy water and incense to consecrate the items on the altar. You may recite a simple prayer of blessing as you cense and sprinkle everything.

- Finish with a brief prayer to the spirit(s) you are feeding, telling them you have prepared a feast for them and (if it applies) that successful completion of your goal will bring further offerings. (The short prayer quoted from the *Key of Solomon* at the head of this section — "*In whatsoever place ye may be . . .*" — is appropriate.) Recite the prayer in each of the four quarters of the working area — moving from east to south then to west and finally to the north.[54]

Following are some pictures taken of offering altars I have erected in the past:[55]

*Offering Altar for Archangel Iophiel (Jupiter)*

---

54  In the Solomonic system there is a consecrated trumpet, or bell, that can be sounded in each of the four quarters before reciting the prayer. See the *Key of Solomon*, Book II, Chapter 7.
55  You can find all of these photos (and more) in full color on my blog. They include full write-ups of how I made the offerings, and the invocation rituals I used with them. See http://aaronleitch.wordpress.com

*Offering Altar for Archangel Michael (Sol)*

*Offering Altar for Archangel Sachiel (Jupiter)*

*Offering Altar for Archangel Samael (Mars)*

*Holiday Offering to Iophiel, Thanksgiving Day.*

## THE OFFERING RITUAL

Note that the following is intended as a stand-alone ritual. It has many uses, from honoring and empowering your guardians and house spirits to initiating contact with new entities to direct spell work with your familiars. However, it is entirely possible to make your offerings — as described thus far — within the context of other rituals, regardless of your tradition.

- Just before the chosen magickal hour, I prepare the meal, take a ritual bath, and don my robes. The offering is then spread out upon the altar as described in the previous section, along with the call to the spirits in the four quarters, alerting them a feast is about to be offered.

- When the proper magickal hour arrives — I usually work at dawn on the angel's day — I open a window to let the morning sunlight hit the altar[56] and add more incense to the censer. Then I remove any cloths covering the food and light all candles. In the *Key of Solomon*, the following exorcism of the fire is recited while lighting the candles:

  > *I exorcise thee, O creature of fire, in the name of the sovereign and eternal Lord, by his ineffable name, which is YOD, HE, VAU, HE; by the name IAH; and by the name of power EL; that thou mayest enlighten the heart of all the spirits which we shall call unto this circle, so that they may appear before us without fraud and deceit through him who hath created all things.*
  > *[The Key of Solomon the King, Book II, Chapter 12, "Of the Light and of the Fire"]*

Otherwise bless the flames according to your own tradition.

- I next recite the invocation to the Highest I prepared beforehand and then the chosen Psalms. Then, I recite the invitation to the angel himself *as many times as his sacred number*. I may finish by reading the petition I have prepared, though that is optional.

---

56   If you can't work at dawn, you may choose an hour assigned to the planet that rules the spirit. See Addendum B.

- When all of this has been done, I share the feast with the angel by taking a bite or sip of every food item — *if appropriate*.[57]

At this point, I spend some time communing with the presence of the angel. I also ask the entity to deliver any necessary information to me either immediately or within its sacred number of days. (The same amount of time the offerings will sit on the altar. See the next section.) This may include any answers or instructions concerning your petition, as well as anything special it wants you to do with the offering leftovers. It is possible the spirit will want you to dispose of them in a specific place and/or a specific manner.

It is also possible the spirit will instruct you to make further offerings — either just as you have already done or to go to a specific place and make a specific offering in a specific manner. (More on this in the "Other Manners of Offering" section.)

- Finally, I add fresh incense to the censer and leave the room. Because I am fortunate enough to have a dedicated temple room, I leave the candles burning and shut the door behind me. The altar will not be disturbed again until the offerings are removed.

# How Long Should the Offerings Stay on the Altar?

In most cases, I will leave the offerings on the altar for the spirit's sacred number of days. If you are working with an entity with a large sacred number (such as Mercury — 8, or Luna — 9) you may use a number that will evenly divide the sacred number. So four days could be used for Mercury, or three days for Luna, etc.

You can also watch the altar for signs that the spirit is done with the food. If a candle burns out completely, liquid evaporates leaving empty glasses, bread and fruit dry out and/or shrivel, these are signs the spirit has finished with them. These items can be removed from the altar and set aside in a sealed container for later disposal (see the next section). Also, if a food item shows *any* sign of decay, it means the spirit is either done with it or (most likely) has rejected it. In that case you *must* remove it from the altar *immediately*!

---

57    Again, remember *never* to share food offered to chthonic entities or the dead!

If you are making your offerings in some outside location, it is unlikely you will return to pick up the leftovers at all. Instead they will be taken care of by nature and the elements. Just make sure to leave only biodegradable material in such offerings — everything else should be disposed of properly.

## What About Rotting Food, Pets, and Bugs?

This is a question I am often asked, as soon as I suggest leaving offerings on an altar for a number of days. Once again, this applies mainly to offerings made in your home, and not to offerings you intend to leave out in nature.

First, I have found (and others have confirmed via their own practices) that food offered to a spirit rarely rots or draws bugs. It is more common to see the foods and drink simply dry out, evaporate, etc. I believe this is because the spirit is consuming the life force of the food, which slows down its natural process of decay.

A notable exception is milk, which will usually separate and solidify as you would expect milk to do within a day or two. When this happens, I remove the milk from the altar.

Only in a few cases have I seen a food item begin to rot or draw flies while still on the altar. (I have sometimes seen foods remain semi-fresh for days, then suddenly degrade into a mess overnight.) As stated previously, this is a certain sign the spirit is done with that food — or, if it begins to rot right away, the spirit has rejected it for some reason — and I take it immediately off the altar.

As for pets, it is best if you make your offerings in a place your pets cannot reach. However, if they do get to the offerings and eat some of them, do not fear. They are natural creatures, which makes them eligible to eat of the offerings just as if you'd left them out in the woods. I would strongly suggest keeping them away from offerings left to chthonic spirits or the dead — though I have had pets eat from these offerings, too, without any noticeable ill effect.

For these reasons, as well as any candles you leave burning on it, the altar must *never* be forgotten during the days of rest. Check on it every day to make sure the flames are lit and the food is in good condition. Once you remove all of the offerings, you can give thanks to the spirit and break down the altar.

# Disposing of the
# Leftovers — Completing the Spell

After the allotted time of rest, and if I have made the offerings on an altar at home, I gather all of the biodegradable foodstuff and take it to a local river. Standing on the bank, I offer further prayers of thanksgiving to the angel I have fed, then I toss in the food leftovers. The river takes them away for the creatures of nature to consume, and the energy is carried out into the greater universe where my magickal spell can take root.[58]

If you lack a nearby river, you can leave the offerings at a crossroads instead. This place will have the same effect of carrying the energy of your spell out into the universe where the spirits can begin making your desires manifest.

There is, however, an issue with leaving offerings at crossroads. If you know of an isolated little dirt crossroad somewhere in the country, there is little harm in leaving infrequent offerings there, to be cleaned up by the elements and nature's creatures. However, if your best option is a major intersection in your city, the last thing anyone wants is garbage left on the side of the road rotting in the sun. In the Santerian community, this problem is solved by simply finding a dumpster nearby the intersection, and disposing of the leftovers there.

Another option is to burn the leftovers to ash in a fire, then the ashes can be taken to a river or crossroads and sprinkled there.

I have been asked if the biodegradable leftovers could be placed in a compost heap. While this is not a horrible idea, I worry that a compost heap will have the effect of containing energy rather than releasing it into the greater world. If a compost heap is all you have, by all means, use it. But I would personally rather use a river or crossroads for the obvious symbolism of mobility and expansiveness.[59]

The least-desirable option is to simply throw them in the garbage at home. I see this as having the same basic problem as the compost heap, so it should only be used if you simply can't get to a river or crossroads. Some

---

58    See Gilberto Strapazon's *Offerings in Ceremonial Magick and ATRs (Risks and Influences)*, where the importance of disposing of the offering leftovers is discussed — including how doing it wrong can even be used for harmful magick.
59    To be fair, some spirits will request you bury their offering leftovers — which would be symbolically similar to putting them into a compost heap.

practitioners who resort to this will first offer a prayer to whatever entity is associated with garbage in their tradition (often a trickster), and make the leftovers an offering to him.[60]

Finally, there is the possibility that the spirit may instruct you to dispose of the leftovers in a specific place or a specific manner. It may give you a new ritual to perform, or invocations to recite, while doing this. In any case, follow the spirit's instructions completely, so long as they are within reason.

# Other Manners of Offering

Also remember that you are not restricted to making your offerings on an altar in your home. There may be some cases where you will need to make offerings to spirits in magickally significant places. For example:

- Offerings to celestial entities are traditionally made in high places — such as the tops of mountains or large hills, rooftops, etc.

- Offerings to chthonic or infernal spirits (as well as Gnomes) can be buried in holes, or left in ditches or caves. (Putting them underground is the key here.)

- Offerings to Undines can be left at the seashore, or tossed directly into the sea.

- Offerings to Salamanders can be consumed in a fire.

- Offerings to Sylphs can be left in high places or sprinkled directly into the air during your invocations.

- If you are working with spirits of Saturn or the dead, you can leave them offerings in regular cemeteries.

- If you are working with the spirits of Mars or dead soldiers, you can leave them offerings at war memorials or military cemeteries.

---

60   See Nick Farrell's *Offerings in Roman Deity Magic* for information about the Goddess Caca and her association with sewers and waste.

- If you are working with spirits of Venus or magick for sex, leave offerings at a stripper club or brothel.

- If you are working healing magick, leave offerings at a local hospital.

- If you are working magick for marriage, leave offerings at the local wedding chapel.

- If you need help with the courts, leave offerings at the courthouse.

- If you need help with the Church, leave offerings at the church house.

- If you need help or protection from police, leave offerings at the police station.

- This applies to any place or organization that you need to deal with in your life. Go to that place and make offerings to the spirits who control that land, in order to make those spirits friendly toward you. Just be very careful not to break any laws while making offerings in public places!

The above are just a few examples of places you can leave offerings for specific spells, or places in which a spirit might tell you to make an offering to achieve your goal. In the latter case, remember to follow the spirit's instructions on how to make the offering — including any invocations or rituals that should go along with them. (It is very unlikely you would be required to go back and retrieve the leftovers, so don't leave anything behind that you would rather not lose.)

# CONCLUSION

The methods of magick outlined in this manual are very ancient and very powerful. They will doubtlessly "supercharge" your magick, but always remember this applies to the good you do as well as the harm you can bring to yourself or others. It is not within the scope of this text to warn you of all the dangers that can come with direct spirit work of this type. I have done my best to give you some good common-sense warnings along the way and present the techniques in a manner that will be safe and effective.

However, always remember that spirits are as divers in their personalities as humans, and therefore you must always proceed with utmost caution. If a lesser spirit *can* get the better of you, it mostly likely will try. There are also warnings that could be given about dealing with other practitioners who are using the same methods.[61] All of these, however, could make an entire book of their own. This manual is aimed merely at providing a reference for the practice itself.

Use divination to speak with your patrons and helpers, and clear with them any new spirit you wish to work with. And, as I have stressed often here, know yourself and what you find acceptable. Your greatest defense, besides your existing guardian spirits, is knowledge and experience, and a willingness to dismiss a spirit when it proves unwilling to work fairly with you.

# ADDENDUM A: INCENSE RECIPES

Following are recipes for Planetary (and Elemental) incenses.

In a best case scenario, you would want each incense to include the planet's sacred number of ingredients. Thus, Saturn incense should include three ingredients, Jupiter incense should contain four, etc. The downside to this is when you reach the higher-numbered planets: six ingredients for Sol and seven for Venus isn't so much, but by the time you reach Luna's nine ingredients the recipes begin to get unwieldy. Another option is to have all the recipes include the same sacred number of ingredients. Three and seven are always "standard" sacred numbers for nearly any purpose.

I generally choose three ingredients for mine — representing each of the three worlds described by Agrippa (physical, mental, and spiritual) or the three shamanic worlds (celestial, terrestrial, and the underworld). I have found that simpler is better when it comes to mixing aromatic powders together. Quite often, substances that you think would smell wonderful when burned together, instead create acrid and unpleasant burning smells. Whatever number you choose, it will take some trial and error before you find the exact mixture that works best for your spirits.

---

61 See Gilberto Strapazon's essay, *Offerings in Ceremonial Magick and ATRs (Risks and Influences)*, for more information on this downside of offering magick.

## Incense of Saturn/Saturday:
1 part Myrrh
1 part Asafoetida
1/4 part Sulphur

## Incense of Jupiter/Thursday:
1 part cedar
1/4 part clove
1/8 part apple pectin
A few drops of pine oil

**Note**: This is a rare case where I use more than three ingredients, and four is sacred to Jupiter. I find that apple pectin tends to have an acrid burning smell — so I add very little and then offset it with the pine oil.

## Incense of Mars/Tuesday:
1 part Pipe Tobacco (or, my favorite, "Black and Mild")
1/2 part Cinnamon
1/8 part Crushed Red Pepper

**WARNING!** Martian incense is one of the most dangerous substances I've worked with! It is, quite simply, tear gas. If you make this, do not add too much red pepper. And when you burn it, do it in small quantities. Never, for any reason, lean over the censer and inhale or draw in breath! Too much pepper or direct inhalation can burn your throat and lungs.

## Incense of Sol/Sunday:
1 part Frankincense
1 part Copal
1/2 part Benzoin.

**Note**: You may also use standard "Church" incense, which can be found in most botanicas or christian supply stores.

## Incense of Venus/Friday:
1 part Sanalwood
1 part Benzoin
1/2 part Red Rose Petals

## Incense of Mercury/Wednesday:
1 part Benzoin
1/4 part Frankencense
1/8 part Lavender Blossoms

## Incense of Luna/Monday:
1 part Calamus
1/2 part Juniper Berries
1/4 part Gardenia Flower

**Note**: I generally find that the various flowers used in the above incenses tend to produce a burnt smell when placed on hot coals. A good solution is to replace the flowers with a drop or two of essential oil instead. Just be careful, as too much flower essence will quickly overpower the other ingredients in the recipe.

You should, of course, test these recipes and tweak them according to your tastes and intuition. Or, if you feel inspired to do so, try making scents with the planetary number of ingredients. A wonderful resource for this work is Scott Cunningham's *Incenses Oils and Brews*.

Also, you can use these for Elemental incenses as well:
- **Fire**: Martian Incense
- **Water**: Lunar Incense
- **Air**: Mercury Incense
- **Earth**: Saturn incense[62]

---

62   Personally, I find Saturn incense too noxious for Earth. My favorite Earthy scent is Patchouli.

# Addendum B: Magickal Hours

## Daytime Hours

|  | Sunday | Monday | Tuesday | Wednesday | Thursday | Friday | Saturday |
|---|---|---|---|---|---|---|---|
| Dawn | Sol | Luna | Mars | Mercury | Jupiter | Venus | Saturn |
| 2 | Venus | Saturn | Sol | Luna | Mars | Mercury | Jupiter |
| 3 | Mercury | Jupiter | Venus | Saturn | Sol | Luna | Mars |
| 4 | Luna | Mars | Mercury | Jupiter | Venus | Saturn | Sol |
| 5 | Saturn | Sol | Luna | Mars | Mercury | Jupiter | Venus |
| 6 | Jupiter | Venus | Saturn | Sol | Luna | Mars | Mercury |
| 7 | Mars | Mercury | Jupiter | Venus | Saturn | Sol | Luna |
| 8 | Sol | Luna | Mars | Mercury | Jupiter | Venus | Saturn |
| 9 | Venus | Saturn | Sol | Luna | Mars | Mercury | Jupiter |
| 10 | Mercury | Jupiter | Venus | Saturn | Sol | Luna | Mars |
| 11 | Luna | Mars | Mercury | Jupiter | Venus | Saturn | Sol |
| 12 | Saturn | Sol | Luna | Mars | Mercury | Jupiter | Venus |

## Nighttime Hours

|  | Sunday | Monday | Tuesday | Wednesday | Thursday | Friday | Saturday |
|---|---|---|---|---|---|---|---|
| Dusk | Jupiter | Venus | Saturn | Sol | Luna | Mars | Mercury |
| 2 | Mars | Mercury | Jupiter | Venus | Saturn | Sol | Luna |
| 3 | Sol | Luna | Mars | Mercury | Jupiter | Venus | Saturn |
| 4 | Venus | Saturn | Sol | Luna | Mars | Mercury | Jupiter |
| 5 | Mercury | Jupiter | Venus | Saturn | Sol | Luna | Mars |
| 6 | Luna | Mars | Mercury | Jupiter | Venus | Saturn | Sol |
| 7 | Saturn | Sol | Luna | Mars | Mercury | Jupiter | Venus |
| 8 | Jupiter | Venus | Saturn | Sol | Luna | Mars | Mercury |
| 9 | Mars | Mercury | Jupiter | Venus | Saturn | Sol | Luna |
| 10 | Sol | Luna | Mars | Mercury | Jupiter | Venus | Saturn |
| 11 | Venus | Saturn | Sol | Luna | Mars | Mercury | Jupiter |
| 12 | Mercury | Jupiter | Venus | Saturn | Sol | Luna | Mars |

The length of the day and night changes over the course of the year, so they will not always match the 60 minutes of clock time. To calculate proper magickal hour length for the daytime, you'll need to know the times of sunrise and sunset. Using those times, determine how many *minutes* there are in the entire day, then divide that number by 12. The result will be the approximate length — in minutes — of each hour for that day.

The length of the hours for the nighttime will not match the daytime hours (except on the equinoxes). So to calculate nighttime hours you'll need the times of sunset for that day and sunrise for the *next* day. Then once again determine how many minutes there are in the entire night and divide that number by 12.

Or avoid all of this hassle and simply perform your work at dawn, as it will *always* be the hour of the planet of the day.

## Sacred Times of the Elements

If you are working with elemental correspondences instead, you can follow this timing:

> **Air**: Dawn
> **Fire**: Noon
> **Water**: Dusk
> **Earth**: Midnight

# Addendum C: Numbers and Colors of Magickal Forces

The magickal forces are associated with specific colors and numbers, both of which should be utilized in your offering rituals. The numbers are as follows:

| | | | |
|---|---|---|---|
| **Saturn**: | 3 | **Mars**: | 5 |
| **Venus**: | 7 | **Luna**: | 9 |
| **Jupiter**: | 4 | **Sol**: | 6 |
| **Mercury**: | 8 | | |

- If you are working with any of the Elements, four can be used as their sacred number.

- If you are working with any of the zodiac signs, use the number of its ruling planet. (For a list of the signs and which planets rule them, see the section entitled "Offerings Sacred to the Stars and Elements.")

The colors of the magickal forces are as follows:

**Celestial Spirits**: White          **Lower Spirits**: Black[63]

**Saturn**: Black                    **Venus**: Green
**Jupiter**: Blue or Purple          **Mercury**: Multicolored[64] or Orange
**Mars**: Red                        **Luna**: Purple, Silver, or White
**Sol**: Yellow or Gold

**Fire**: Red                        **Air**: Yellow
**Water**: Blue                      **Earth**: Black

**Aries**: Red                       **Libra**: Green
**Taurus**: Red-Orange               **Scorpius**: Blue-Green
**Gemini**: Orange                   **Sagittarius**: Blue
**Cancer**: Yellow-Orange            **Capricornus**: Blue-Violet
**Leo**: Yellow                      **Aquarius**: Violet
**Virgo**: Yellow-Green              **Pisces**: Red-Violet

---

63    Notice that these first two colors — white and black — cover broad categories of spirits: Celestials (those who embody the planets or stars) and "lower spirits" which includes nature entities, chthonic spirits and the dead. Use these colors if you do not know the specific force or color to use for a given spirit.
64    This is often called "pied" — meaning a mixing of many colors.

# Bibliography

Abramelin:
> *Book of Abramelin: A New Translation, The.* trans. Steven Guth. ed.
> Georg Dehn. Nicolas Hays, Inc, 2006 ISBN: 089254127X
> *Book of the Sacred Magic of Abramelin the Mage, The.* trans. Samuel
> Mathers. Dover Publicatoins, 1975. ISBN: 0486232115

Agrippa, Henry Cornelius. *Three Books of Occult Philosophy.* ed. Donald
> Tyson. Llewellyn Publications, 1992. ISBN: 0875428320

Betz, Hans Dieter. *Greek Magical Papyri in Translation, The.* University of
> Chicago Press, 1997. ISBN: 0226044475

Cunningham, Scott. *Encyclopedia of Magical Herbs.* Llewellyn
> Publications, 1985. ISBN: 0875421229

*Key of Solomon the King, The.* trans. Samuel Mathers. Weiser Books (2000).
> ISBN: 087728931X

Leitch, Aaron. *Secrets of the Magickal Grimoires.* Llewellyn Publications,
> 2005. ISBN: 0738703036

*Ananael (The Secrets of Wisdom) Blog.* http://aaronleitch.wordpress.com

*Picatrix, The Complete.* trans. John Michael Greer, Christopher Warnock.
> Lulu.com, 2011. ISBN: 1257767852

Werness, Hope B. *Continuum Encyclopedia of Animal Symbolism in Art,
> The.* Continuum International Publishing Group, 2007. ISBN:
> 0826419135
> Also found at Google Books:
> http://books.google.com/books?isbn=0826419135

# THE ELEMENTS OF
# MAKING OFFERINGS
## THE OFFERING AS SACRIFICE

*Zadkiel*

**Note:** *Although I have practiced Solomonic magic in the past, I am also an initiated babalawo. I have taken care to write this without reference to any Osha or Ifa-specific information. While I am forbidden from discussing certain magical and religious processes with those who are not initiated, I have attempted to provide generic information to at least give people an idea of how to work with spirits. Anyone wishing to receive the appropriate initiations and learn the processes and procedures of Lukumi Orisha practice or Ifa would find themselves richly rewarded, but hopefully this at least gives the beginner a place to start without requiring a lifetime commitment.*

et's start with a statement sure to make people uncomfortable: *All magic is based in sacrifice.*

The idea of sacrifice is an unpopular one in modern Western culture. The word "sacrifice" causes many people to think immediately of bloody altars, dead animals, and Hollywood claptrap. While animal sacrifice is certainly one traditional form of sacrifice, sacrifice comes in many other forms (all more accessible to the Western magician). Magicians sacrifice time and energy in making tools, consecrating spaces, burning rare spices, spending money on supplies, daily practice, and a thousand other ways. Making ritual offerings is yet another form of sacrifice and will be the focus of this short guide.

The core concept of sacrifice is balance. Balance is simple; the sacrifice must match the reward. If the offerings are insufficient, the desired result will only manifest partially or not at all. If the offerings are too extravagant, the working will "flare" and produce either extreme results (the classic "too much of a good thing" immortalized in Disney's *Sorcerer's Apprentice*) or unwanted side effects.

The most common straightforward method of sacrifice is to make offerings. Such offerings may be made to a spirit either 1) in thanks for a successful outcome or 2) to pay for its services to accomplish a goal. To list every possible type of offering is flatly impossible; there are an almost infinite list of things that could be included.[65] Despite this open-ended nature, there are a number of restrictions that will quickly guide the magician to a list of possible ingredients, such as 1) the chosen system of work, 2) the nature of the spirit, and 3) divination.

---

65    Readers of my *Liber Donariorum* would do well to keep that in mind! -ed.

The last is most important; divination will be the difference between happy spirits producing successful workings and unhappy spirits with unpleasant or no results.

# DIVINATION —
# THE ESSENTIAL INGREDIENT

I cannot stress enough the importance of having a functional system of divination. Without the ability to speak with spirits directly, magical practice is reduced to a sort of puppet show, trying to indicate what is desired through a pantomime with maximum confusion in both worlds. Traditional magical systems emphasize this point over and over; divination can bring a great deal of clarity to the practitioner's life in general as well as their relationship with spirits.

Every aspiring magician is urged to find a simple divination system and learn it by heart. Some good examples:

- Pendulum dowsing
- Sortilege (dice/sticks/coins)
- Geomancy[66]

These are not the only useful systems of divination by any means, but what is important for purposes of summoning spirits is that the system 1) is fairly simple, 2) gives a clear, unambiguous yes/no answer, and 3) is portable, able to be done quickly in any location. More complex divinatory systems such as astrology and tarot, while useful in their own right, tend to be too complicated and ambiguous in meaning for working with spirits on these types of questions.

Once a form of divination has been selected, it should be practiced frequently. Choose a divination device and cleanse it both physically and ritually. After it is clean, keep it safe and use it only for personal divination. Don't place too much reliance on the answers you get at first; allow yourself time to learn

---

66    I suspect that Geomancy is the West's system of spirit-divination *par excellence* — comparable to the *Obi* system of divination in the ATRs. It can be used without the astrology to obtain simple yes/no answers, or astrology (another native Western system of divination) can be included to obtain more elaborate answers. -ed.

the system and the specific tool (not all tools work the same, not even all tools of the same type such as pendulums). Once you have established what means yes and what means no, ask for answers to short, straightforward questions that you don't currently know but that will be revealed in a short time period:

- Will I speak to a woman/man first today?
- Will I find money on the street?
- Will I see someone else stumble today?

And so forth. The specific questions don't matter; what matters is that the questions be clear and the answers difficult to predict. Simple questions of this nature can be tracked and the accuracy of the results tested, improved, and eventually proven. Constant divination practice will also serve to increase the accuracy of the results. Space considerations don't allow a thorough treatment of divination practice, but there are many good guides for beginning simple divination like pendulum dowsing. (A quick word of advice based on experience: When you have a new divination tool such as a pendulum, ask the device to show you "yes," and then to show you "no." Not all pendulums use the same signals.)

Once the practitioner has mastered simple divination, an entire new world of practice unfolds. Using divination, the magician can now ask directly: Is this spirit willing and able to assist me in my goal? Is this an effective way to accomplish my goal? Is X ingredient preferable to Y ingredient for this working? And so forth. Such divination is also very useful in identifying the preferred offerings for spirits and any additional, non-standard offerings that should be made.

Divination, even a simple yes/no divination, like pendulum dowsing, is as shallow or deep as you make it. Experienced practitioners have standard questions that they ask to focus in quickly and efficiently on the answers needed to move forward. As noted by many practitioners, devising a simple ritual for use when divining is an excellent step. Take care, however, not to make the ritual so complicated that it cannot be done in other locations, or in a short period of time — divination is most useful when it is easily accessible. While you may not want to whip out the pendulum in the produce section of a grocery store, having a brief ritual that can be done in a short period of time in reasonable privacy like a hotel room or quiet park will greatly assist in getting timely, useful answers.

Appropriate offerings for divination practice include white candles, cool water, and sweet perfumes. Non-emergency divination should be done in a space that is physically clean and has been at least quickly blessed and purified. If working with a particular spirit for divination, any offering the spirit is accustomed to receiving at short divination sessions (keep it simple). It may also be beneficial to occasionally "feed" the divination tool itself, placing it in a container of water, gin, perfume, or whatever else might be recommended by divination. Note: **DO NOT** offer the tool meat or animal products other than milk, as it can render the tool unfit for divination.

# Practical Offerings — Theory and Practice

Every system that makes use of offerings will present guidance on how to make them. Procedures differ, just like regional languages and cultures. Additionally, different spirits have different preferences, and in many traditions generations of magicians before you have faithfully catalogued those preferences. This will generally provide a short list of ingredients to divine from, but there are certain general categories of item that can be good to consider when building an ingredient list.

A word of advice: Before taking anything from nature, whether dirt, stones, plants, or other items, it is important to leave at least a token payment for what is being taken. Bread, coins, fresh water, and small food items have all been used historically to indicate appreciation for the resources. As modern magicians, we should *not* leave anything that does not break down in nature, such as plastic or wrapped items; any positive benefit from paying for the items being removed is far offset by the damage caused by pollution.

Let's examine the various types of offering ingredients on a general level.

## Stones

One of the universal categories of potential offerings is the stone. Since the earliest times, stones (especially semi-precious stones) have been recognized to possess their own specific vibrations and energies which can strengthen and empower workings which are in harmony with their natures. Numerous catalogues of the effects of precious and semi-precious stones exist, both modern and historic. Divination can be used to confirm that the spirit desires or will accept specific types of stone before they are acquired.

Another way in which stones may be used is less about their internal structure and more about their source location. Stones from a crossroads can be used to represent the fast changing, fast moving energy of the crossroads. Stones from a cemetery can be used to represent the energy of death and the dead. Stones from the ocean, river, or forest can be used to represent those energies as well. Dirt from these places is also an acceptable substitute. As always, confirm your choices with divination either before collecting the items or before making the offering to ensure that they are acceptable.

Finally, individual stones can just resonate with a particular spirit. Divination can indicate that a spirit wants one specific stone to be part of the offering, and such requests should always be honored if at all possible (although difficult requests can usually be negotiated — nobody expects to give up the diamond from their engagement ring just because a spirit wants something shiny!).[67]

## Plants

Plants have been a part of magical practice since the beginning. Living plants can be kept as constant "memorial offerings" if not actual vegetable familiars.[68] Living plant leaves, stems, and flowers can be infused into teas, washes, and baths. Dried plants can be powdered for inclusion in other workings or burned as incense. Paracelsus, Agrippa, and many other medieval writers categorized the parts of the plant, ascribing different uses, powers, and natures to flowers, stems, roots, leaves, and fruits. All traditional systems of practice are rooted (pardon the pun) in a basis of practical herbalism, with extensive lists of types of plants and how to use them.

## Animals

Animal sacrifice is a complicated subject, worthy of treatment at a length which space considerations do not permit. Therefore, I will sum it up like this — unless you are the holder of proper initiations in a tradition which permits animal sacrifice, and have **also** received the necessary training in how, why, and when to do it, **don't do it**. Animal sacrifice is very rarely required, even in systems (such as the Afro-Caribbean religions) that utilize it. While

---

67    Another good example of *staying in charge of the deal*. See the introduction of this book for more. -ed.

68    I discuss working with plant spirits in Ch. 3 of my *Secrets of the Magickal Grimoires*. -ed.

space considerations do not permit a deep dive into why this is so, there is a famous teaching story in Lukumi tradition where the supreme god Olofin proclaims *addimu* (bloodless offerings of objects or cooked food) the most powerful sacrifice which can be made. Too much sensational attention is paid to animal sacrifice; other offerings usually work just as effectively and don't call for the life of a living being. If such an offering must be made (usually in extreme cases of physical health) it **must** be made by a properly initiated, properly trained priest in order to be effective and not cause even bigger problems for the recipient of the working.[69]

That having been said, there are a myriad of ways in which both living and dead animals can contribute their energies to offerings and other magical workings. Living animals may be kept as familiars, providing a symbolic "home" or link to familiar spirits. Another common shamanic practice is to use pieces of animals which are ritually appropriate to lend their energies to all types of magical works (feathers, claws, teeth, bones, etc.). Knowing someone who works at a zoo can provide even more exotic materials — along with the knowledge that the items that you are using were gathered humanely.

One final note: Know the laws in your area! Do not just run out and buy or collect pieces from dead animals without knowing what you are legally allowed to own, transfer, or use. Spirits advise based on energy, not on local, state, and Federal law; that part is up to the magician.

## CRAFTED ITEMS

One often-overlooked type of offering is things made by humans. This ranges from cooked food to crafts to coins and other products of modern civilization. Divination will reveal if the spirit has particular favorites among foods; prepare them and serve them to the spirit however it instructs you to do so. There are literally an infinite number of items that can be included here. Preferences are as varied as the number of spirits. The list of possible preferences is as infinite as the potential types of offering, but some initial points of attention:

- **Material**: Ask the spirit if they prefer a particular type of metal, wood, clay, or other material. Provide offerings made of that substance.

- **Color**: Ask if the spirit prefers things of a particular color or combination of colors. Perhaps the spirit prefers green and blue together,

---

69   See my essay *Liber Donariorum* for more information on the dangers of blood offerings. -ed.

or red and yellow. This type of preference is good to determine early, because it will naturally lead to ideas as far as preferred offerings. For example, if the spirit indicates a love for yellow items, then bananas, grapefruits, squash, yellow cloth, etc., all immediately present themselves as possibilities.

- **Physical structure**: Some spirits prefer items which have an organic, rounded appearance; others prefer clean lines and angles. Some prefer short, squat shapes, and others would rather have things which are elongated and thin. Divination can guide you as to which would be the best offering.

- **Number**: Many spirits have a preferred number; work this in either as a total of offering items, a total of items of one type, or a number of times the same offering is presented in the same way. Repeated identical offerings are an excellent way to increase the connection with the spirit and provide energy for large or ongoing tasks.

# PRESENTATION

After the items to be offered are determined, the next thing to consider is presentation. Offerings to spirits should always be presented in a way that is balanced, harmonious, and pleasant to the eye. Never just throw everything in a pile; present the offering as you would present a meal to an honored guest. If, as sometimes happens, the offering is composed of oddly shaped items, place them in such a way as to create a pleasant visual effect. Not everyone has the necessary skills to design elaborate constructs and presentation pieces, but at least make the effort to show the spirit that you value their assistance.

Many spirits will prefer to have a particular location and/or dish used to accept their offerings. (I use the term "dish" loosely; such a dish could be a plate, a bowl, a piece of stone, a tile, or anything else that provides a flat surface on which offerings can be placed.)

Ideally, each spirit should have their own dish; at the minimum, a set of reserved dishes should be used for offerings and nothing else. Do not make offerings to spirits on the dishes that you use for yourself or guests, as this can lead to all sorts of unpleasantness and misunderstandings. Use a set of dishes for offerings that are very visually distinct from the daily dishes; make the offering dishes all white if your daily dishes are colored, or something similar, for ease of identification. If the system in which you are working uses sigils for spirits, paint or inscribe the sigil of the spirit on the dish in question as permanently as possible; this will eliminate confusion on the human side, and mark the dish as belonging to the spirit so that it knows without a doubt that anything placed on that dish is an offering. Never place items which are offensive to the spirit on that dish, because offering a spirit something that it finds offensive is a good way to drive it away.

Spirits will occasionally instruct you to leave offerings in locations which are not the "usual" location. Some offerings may go to a specific place related to the work in question (the building where you work, for example). Others will be a place of a specific nature (the ocean, the woods, a busy road, etc.). While offerings should be placed attractively where possible, do not stop in a busy intersection to lay out an elaborate offering unless you live somewhere like Brazil where such things are accepted! Placing the offering items in a brown paper bag and setting it discretely to one side in a busy location is just as acceptable. Avoid littering. Place biodegradable offerings wherever instructed, but please try wherever possible to avoid leaving plastics, metal items, and the like in nature. Spirits don't always consider the ramifications of what they ask for on this plane — leaving non-degradable items in the woods, the seashore, and so forth result in problems for all of us down the road.

When making offerings in the home, do not be surprised to see unusual things occur. Fruits set out may stay perfectly fresh for weeks, then decay over-night. Cooked food may go bad immediately, growing enormous quantities of mold or fungus within a day; it may also appear untouched for days or weeks. Animals may avoid the food completely, even if they would normally love to eat it (the opposite may also occur, so beware of pets eating inappropriate foods). Don't be unduly surprised by any of it — this is all part of working with spirits. When making offerings in nature, wild animals will often appear and consume the food in front of you; all such manifestations tend to be good signs. Treat them as positive omens and carry on.

Always take care to ask through divination how long a particular offer-ing is to be left, and how to dispose of it when it is taken up. Some spirits are emphatic that their offerings are to be disposed of in nature, or under the sky; others are completely indifferent to how they are disposed of, so long as they are gone. It is up to you to determine in conjunction with your spirits. Once the process is established, the "usual method" will quickly be revealed for any given spirit and then you will only need to ask if the offering for a given working needs special treatment.[70]

# GENERAL GUIDANCE AND WARNINGS

In my experience, problems with working with spirits generally come from one of a few common misconceptions. The following will help you avoid some pitfalls:

## 1. Follow the directions.

This could also be summarized bluntly as "You are not smarter than every other magician who has ever worked with this spirit." If your chosen system provides a list of preferences for a given spirit, use it. If it wants something that is not on the list, it will eventually tell you; there is no need to begin asking if the spirit would like random items if you already have a list of predefined acceptable offerings. For example, if all the preferences noted are for cool, white, smooth offerings, do not ask about items which are steaming hot, red, and spicy. Likewise, if a spirit is listed as only being available under certain circumstances (e.g., only summon at night, only summon when Moon is waxing, etc.), follow that guidance — don't try to call it at an off time, alter the summoning ritual, or use any other shortcuts until you are familiar with the spirit and have confirmed through divination that it will accept the modification. Systems are designed the way they are for solid reasons; until you know those reasons, your own safety may suffer from disregarding them. At the very least, your workings won't be as effective . . . and at the end of the day, that's reason enough to follow the directions.[71]

## 2. Do not make offerings "just because."

Random offerings are at best wasted offerings. At worst, they attract the attention of trickster spirits who will promise all manner of elaborate results and then fail to deliver. This is the same as setting a banquet table out in the middle of Times Square; anyone and everyone could be eating, and there is

---

70 The angels I work with have largely shown indifference to how their offerings are disposed. I usually just default to taking them to the river. See *Liber Donariorum* for more on disposal of offering leftovers. -ed.
71 Please re-read this paragraph. Then come back tomorrow and read it again. -ed.

no guarantee that the spirits that show up to consume the offering have any interest (or ability) to help the magician with anything. This is related to another common issue . . .

## 3. Don't make open-ended offerings (i.e., "spirits of this place")

This is for the same reasons stated in guideline 2 above; there is no way to know which spirits are specifically being addressed, and anything and everything around could be cadging a free meal with no guarantee of return for the magician who made the offering. Spirits can be just as unappreciative as humans.

## 4. Don't reward poor behavior.

Although this may seem intuitive, many people seem to miss this point. If you promise a spirit to make an offering in exchange for work, and the spirit does not deliver, **do not make the offering**. Why would you? Would you pay a mechanic for work that he or she had failed to do? The same is true for spirits that cause disturbances in the home or other environments; rewarding bad behavior gets the magician more of the same. If at all possible, call the spirit again and explain specifically why the offering is not being made. If circumstances permit, give the spirit a second chance to hold up its end of the bargain the first time there is a problem, but never pay for work that was not received.

## 5. Use clear language.

When dealing with spirits, just like dealing with humans, always make sure that everyone understands what their specific tasks are in any agreement. If the spirit is expected to do something, make sure that you explain exactly what is required in straightforward terms. Likewise, if you are expected to make an offering or perform other services, make sure that the exact tasks to be performed and offerings to be made are clearly defined. Many people seem to feel that summoning spirits is a good time for elaborate, flowery pseudo-biblical language, or even speaking in a foreign language . . . the exact opposite is true. Be as clear, unambiguous, and direct as possible; avoid all metaphors, similes, and other expressive language, just as you would when communicating with a small child or someone who does not speak the language well.

# Conclusion

Working with spirits is a rewarding practice. It teaches you more about yourself, and about the world around you, than any other activity I could name. If I had to summarize my entire twenty-year practice into one bit of advice for the new practitioner, it would be this:

*Be polite.*

This is very simple advice to give, and very hard advice to follow. Nevertheless, treating spirits as you would treat other humans that you very much want to be friends with is the best way to start (and continue) the successful practice of spirit magic. Spirits have individual preferences just like humans; they have likes and dislikes, and they don't always get along with each other (or everyone who calls them). Eventually you will have a few spirits that you work with all the time who are like friends or roommates. Making the offerings that they like will come to seem like second nature, and the time you spend talking to them will be as rewarding as time spent talking to any other good friend. Enjoy the journey.

# *Whispers from a Skull:*
## Lessons in Spiritual Offerings from a Conjured Familiar

### Bryan Garner
### (Frater Ashen Chassan)

# The Spirit Familiar or Ally

can easily recall the first time I learned about spirit familiars, servitors, and supernatural assistants as I was instantly intrigued by the idea. For the longest time, however, such notions were simply remote magical intrigue. A spiritual assistant was something definitely within the realm of possibility but one still foreign in practicality and experience.

For many years prior to the writing of this essay, I had been successful with a number of traditional ceremonial evocations, so I knew existence of spirit familiars or allies was plausible but had no direct example of what that would entail. I had never constructed a fulltime ancestor altar that many pagan and ancient religion practitioners use, nor had I practiced any form of African Tribal Art[72] involving spirit or ancestral worship. Nothing I had encountered up to that point would be what I considered an ever-present, disembodied spirit, a being I could speak with, see, and hear continuously with little to no preparation, timing, or lengthy invocations.

Yet the prospect of having a powerful spirit readily on hand, and one that was sympathetic toward my magical endeavors, was too enticing to ignore for long. It did not take long before I began researching just how a modern magician might go about securing a spirit ally or classic familiar. Often the first step in uncovering the relevant pieces of historic text concerning supernatural events is the comparison to recorded history with lasting traditions of spiritual interaction.

Historic references to familiar spirits, assistants, or allies appear frequently in both western mythology and European folklore in one form or another. Such tales of supernatural helpers and guides are not to be excluded even

---

72   "African Tribal Art" refers to the same traditions I have called "African Traditional Religions" (ATRs) elsewhere in this book. - ed.

from modern-day media. Medieval European folklore as well as accusations of witchcraft contain a multitude of references to spirits assisting witches and cunning folk in their practice of magic. Most historic records of alleged spirit familiars you find are in the forms of animals such as cats, dogs, birds, and other small animals. Much of what is recorded is obvious superstition, typically with intent to persecute those who were suspected of being witches. Anyone who happened to have a pet or domestic animal could be considered in possession of a spirit "familiar," and this often assisted in sealing the fate of an accused witch.

According to Emma Wilby in *Cunning Folk and Familiar Spirits: Shamanistic Visionary Traditions in Early Modern British Witchcraft and Magic*, familiar spirits could also appear in anthropomorphic, "clearly defined, three-dimensional forms, vivid with color and animated with movement and sound."

Depending upon whom they served, the spirit familiar could either be benevolent or evil, inflicting any amount of mischief or disaster on whomever the witch decided to sick their familiar upon. Those who were considered "cunning folk" apparently had a gentler reputation than the predisposed "witches" of the medieval era, although the distinctions between the two were often blurred. According to the findings of Wilby, the familiars of witches were often categorized as demons, while others were more commonly thought of and described as fairies.

The role of a familiar spirit was to inform and protect its master and assist them in any manner of their "craft." Accounts of animal familiar spirits are found where they are sent off to retrieve information, spy, or travel a distance where their master is unable to do so. These accounts match heavily with those of the shaman of other cultures where their animal spirits are sent to retrieve information or soul pieces to heal others.

Many times we find that familiar spirits and allies were not merely servants but highly respected guides and close confidants. For tribal shamans, helper spirits appeared during times of extreme illness or near death which is often the initiatory rite the shaman undergoes when introduced to the spirit world. There are also accounts of magicians forming intimate relationships with their familiar spirit and in some cases wedding themselves to their spirits for life.

Historically the manner in which witches or cunning folk acquired familiar spirits vary. In some instances it is recorded that the familiar spirit simply appeared to the person during routine chores or other mundane activates, seemingly out of the blue. In a few accounts some familiars seem to be bequeathed from another sorcerer (usually a parent or elder family member) who is nearing death as a sort of heirloom to pass on. In a few other accounts the familiar was said to arrive during times of great crises, tragedy, or trial in life just as with many shamanic initiations. Emma Wilby states that, "their (witches and cunning folk) problems [. . .] were primarily rooted in the struggle for physical survival — the lack of food or money, bereavement, sickness, loss of livelihood and so on." The spirit seemed to arrive just in time to offer a way to overcome their difficulties and trials. In some cases, the magical practitioner then made an agreement or entered a pact with their familiar spirit.

The length of time that the witch or cunning person worked with their familiar spirit varied between a few weeks through to a number of decades. In most cases, the magical practitioner would conjure their familiar spirit when they needed their assistance, although there are many different ways that they did this: The Essex witch Joan Cunny claimed, in 1589, that she had to kneel down within a circle and pray to Satan for her familiar to appear, while the Wiltshire cunning woman Anne Bodenham described, in 1653, that she conjured her familiars by reading books. In some rarer cases there were accounts where the familiars would appear at times when they were unwanted and not called upon; for instance, the Huntingdonshire witch Elizabeth Chandler noted, in 1646, that she could not control when her two familiars, named Beelzebub and Trullibub, appeared to her, and had prayed for a god to "deliver her therefrom." James Sharpe, in *The Encyclopedia of Witchcraft: the Western Tradition*, states: "Folklorists began their investigations in the 19th Century and found that familiars figured prominently in ideas about witchcraft."

Deeper studies into the subject of spirit familiars sparked further intrigue when I came upon a passage from a book titled *Communing with Spirits: The Magical Practice of Necromancy* by Martin Coleman. The author of this book theorized that the Witch of Endor (Hebrew: רוד ויעמ בואה תלעב) sometimes called the Medium of Endor, had most likely called upon the aid of a familiar spirit within a vessel to summon forth another ghost or spirit. In the First Book of Samuel, versus 28:3–25, the Endor Witch or necromancer summons the prophet Samuel's spirit, at the command of King Saul. The woman or necromancer is described as "a woman with an *ob*" (בוא), which has been translated to mean a talisman or wineskin (spirit container — a bottle made from animal skin used by a necromancer). There are a few works which go into detail about "spirit pots/vessels," and authors Aaron Leitch, Frater Rufus Opus, and Jake Stratton-Kent have written about this subject a few times in great detail.

Upon further research I also discovered that a particular spirit container was sometimes a human skull. Archeologists have unearthed skulls containing various spells and incantations written in Aramaic which were found in ancient Jewish communities in Babylonia. Many classical images of wizards or alchemists contain at least one human skull pictured on a table or tucked in some dusty bookcase. Illustrations of scholarly men writing intently away are often depicted with a skull on one corner of the desk. Have you ever wondered as to the nature and use such articles were put to? Though undoubtedly originating from multiple cultures in various parts of early history, my particular findings stemmed from sources in ancient Hebrew folk magic.

From what I've researched, there have been over two thousand spell skulls found with Ancient Hebrew or Aramaic writing scrawled in complex patterns within bowls, pots, and skulls alike. In the case of the "Witch of Endor," the skull spirit is what the author Martin Coleman alludes to as possibly being the assistant which summoned the shade of the prophet Samuel. The idea of a "fetch" or spiritual informant resource seemed highly beneficial to anyone involved in the occult or spiritual world who dealt with disembodied intelligences. I definitely could not pass up the opportunity to secure an assistant who could retrieve other spirits to communicate with me, or garner information that was only obtainable in the spirit world.

In the popular occult *Dresden Files* novels by Jim Butcher, the wizard Harry has a skull named Bob that is basically a magical encyclopedia and storehouse of occult knowledge. This idea further sparked my interest in being able to create a real version of this helpful spirit. "Bob" helps Harry solve a plethora of occult mysteries and riddles with his vast occult knowledge that makes up the entire purpose of the spirit. Basically, the skull is a spirit pot which is thus used as an oracle or astral information source.

Besides the macabre and "cool" classical image a skull represents, I wondered what was the appeal of a human skull for housing a spirit. The answer to this question somewhat eluded me until I became successful drawing a spirit within one, and I asked my spirit this question myself. The spirit replied matter-of-factly saying, "It's suitable because human beings recognize the head and face, even that of a bone one, as a suitable image to hold a conversation with." In other words, the skull is a close proximate to a human head, and something we hold conversations with more than anything else. That seemed a reasonable enough answer for me.

The process for acquiring a skull and formulating the ritual to bind a spirit within it was several years in the making. Only small pieces of the ritual seemed to come together at auspicious times and the entire operation was to be a group effort of myself, my scryer, the Archangel Cassiel, and the spirit itself. When I was finally able to acquire a skull, I inscribed the most potent binding litany I could fathom along with appropriate sigils and symbols within grimoiric and ancient Hebraic folk magic. The complete method and circumstance of how I was able to succeed in conjuring the spirit within a physical container (which happened to be a real human skull) will be revealed in a future work.

*Familiar Spirit at home in his skull.*

What is shared below are the answers I received since the completion of that operation and the discoveries I've made about working with and feeding a spirit. The information provided below stems primarily from my times speaking with the spirit on a daily basis and what the spirit itself said regarding the use and preparation of its offerings. Included is further knowledge about what my spirit dictated to me concerning how it and other spirits use the offerings for nourishment which wasn't readily apparent when I first began giving offerings. I hope you find the following information as useful and intriguing as I have.

The benefits of having a veritable spiritual ally is quite beyond anything I ever imagined. Being able to experience having another intelligent entity point out important points which were missed during an evocation, supply information that I had no other way of accessing, and offer sound advice for the best courses of action to take in my magical development has been life changing.

From my own experience, and reading of those who have also successfully obtained spirit familiars or spirit helpers, I have learned they are willing participants and residents. As with anything, you really do get out what you put into it, and having a spirit familiar would be like adopting a child or having a pet that required daily and constant care. *Relationship* is the key word here as both you and it will form stronger and clear ways to communicate and work together. Care of a spirit was an aspect I was previously unfamiliar with — thinking a spirit required nothing, was self-sustaining, and if it could be conjured and bound to a direct place or thing, it would be there for my use whenever I desired it. As I've learned several other times in magic, something does not come from nothing.

Working with a spiritual being is a relationship and commitment, as it is with any other being or endeavor. It requires your time, your attention, and your willful participation to achieve anything of worth from the interaction. There are several cultural and ethnic practices which involve forming relationships with ancestral spirits or other benevolent incorporeal beings. To the occultist wishing to form a bond with a spirit that is helpful in their magical pursuits, you may want to consider the type of spirit or entity you wish to come in contact with. From there you can decide how you can best house and nourish your spirit familiar.

For instance, the well-established traditions dealing with ancestor veneration are an excellent place to start if you are new to "spiritual interaction." There are several ways to contact a spirit helper, guide, familiar, ancestor, or whatever the case or terminology might be, and form a relationship with them. The number of methods and types of spirits are as numerous as the traditions to contact them, if not more. For an occultist, you may want to consider if an ancestral spirit would be your primary source of information and assistance in esoteric endeavors. Contacting your ancestors or having an ancestral altar may be highly beneficial in establishing links to the otherworld and healing bloodlines but may not be your best source of esoteric insight. There are elementals, genius loci, other spirits of the dead, and so forth.

There is an interesting formula for necromancy found in *The Sefer Ha-razim* (The Book of Secrets), a Jewish mystical text which was allegedly given to Noah by the angel Raziel and eventually passed down to King Solomon himself. In this text there is found a ritual where one can contact, converse, and apparently control a spirit of the dead. It is presented as thus:

> If you wish to question a ghost; stand facing a tomb and repeat the names of all sixty-two angels of the fifth encampment while holding in your hand a new flask containing virgin olive oil mixed with honey and also a branch of myrtle wood. [After this, there is a recitation of sixty-two angelic names, which I will not include here.] After this you are to say:
>
> > *I adjure you O spirit of the ram bearer (Hermes) who dwells among the graves upon the bones of the dead, that you will accept from my hand this offering and do my will and bring me the spirit of _____ son of _____ who is dead. Raise him up so that he will speak to me without fear and tell me true the things without concealment. Let me not be afraid of him and let him tell me for my question, the answer I need from him.*
>
> He [the spirit] should appear immediately. But if he does not, repeat the adjuration a second time and up to three times if necessary. When the spirit appears, set the flask before him and after this speak your words while holding the branch of myrtle wood in your hand. When you wish to release the spirit, strike the spirit three times with the myrtle branch and pour out the oil and honey, and break the cup, and throw the myrtle from your hand, and return home by a different route. If you wish to speak with the spirits, go out to "The place of the killed." And call out there in a singsong whimpering way:

*I adjure you in the name of the angels who serve in the fifth encampment, and in the name of the overseer who is over them, who is 'SYMWR, that you will hear me at this time and send me the spirit of HGRGYRWT. She shall go accordingly to my will for whatever I send her and shall obey me in everything until such a time as I release her.*

If you see opposite you a column of smoke, speak your words and send her for whatever purpose you wish.

My purpose here, besides sharing a recipe for contacting spirits of the dead, is to bring the reader's attention to the food offerings, notably the flask containing virgin olive oil mixed with honey. I found this particularly interesting since these were two ingredients my own spirit familiar requested to be placed on bread for his offerings.

After reading this, I questioned my spirit as to the significance of this combination. It said that honey and olive oil were both highly prized in his day and that both would last longer than any other consumables and made an excellent source of lasting nourishment. According to my spirit, the combination was a delicacy on bread and kept the flavor and preserved the bread longer.

The honey and olive oil combination seems to appeal to spirits who were once human and is an excellent offering for ancestors and ghosts/spirits alike. Food offerings for spirits is a theme you find from the far east to the far western cultures, and many ancient civilizations would not be without ways to provide food offerings to relatives long after they had passed on. The above ritual should give the western occultist plenty to consider if conjuring a spirit of the deceased is desirable.

# Feeding the Spirits

It could be argued that spiritual traditions which developed out of the desire to commune with supernatural or spiritual beings predate the formalization of any of the major religions. Few other spiritual and religious customs have endured through the centuries as have communication and offerings to spirits and ancestors. Most burial sites archeologists have uncovered from ancient cultures show important figures buried with the same effects they treasured or required in life. Weapons, armor, valuables, and food offering all accompanied the body of the deceased on their journey to the otherworld.

The notion that spirits desire and/or require food is one which can also be traced back to several ancient cultures and the associated practices of remembering ancestors and loved ones that have passed on. Such was the belief in the assistance and continued care of disembodied relatives that to not acknowledge them was thought to bring unforeseen calamity and ill fortune. Lore of "hungry ghosts" can be traced back to source some of the most notorious "monsters" in mythic lore such as the vampire. Legends of vengeful and frightening spirits practically eclipse the lore of the helpful ones.

So prevalent were belief in harmful spirits, cultures across the globe had a plethora of names and titles given to these types of hungry spirits. More familiar to the western person are the vampires, ghouls, revenants, and wraiths which have become notorious archetypes in popular fiction and television. Earlier examples of these predatory spirits were the *Lamiae*, forerunners to the vampires and succubi that usually seduced young men and then fed on their blood. In the Philippines were the *Ekek*, flesh-eating, winged humanoids that would attack travelers.

Chinese folklore relates similar beings called the *Egui* (*èguǐ*) who are driven by intense emotional needs and cravings. An ancient festival was thought to appease hungry ancestors, so the ghosts of their ancestors would return to their houses at a certain time of the year, hungry and ready to eat. A festival called the Hungry Ghost Festival (*Yúlánpén*) is still held in some areas to honor the hungry ancestor ghosts, and food and drink is put out to satisfy their needs. According to transcribed oral tradition, some Chinese villagers believe that spirits may be granted permission to return to the world of the living and to take what they can from there if these spirits had not been given sufficient offerings by their living relatives.

You find similar concepts in the celebration of *Samhain* for the Celts where feasts were had, and which the souls of dead kin were beckoned to attend and a place set at the table for them. *Mumming* and guising were part of the festival and involved people going door-to-door in costume (or in disguise), often reciting verses in exchange for food. Such traditions evolved into what we now celebrate as Halloween.

Much of the lore stemming from vengeful or "hungry spirits" arose from those who die without resolution from intense suffering, still clinging to fears, addictions, and pain. Spirits that refuse to pass on or retreat from the physical habitations of men. These spirits roam the earth as hungry ghosts, looking for something to satisfy their cravings or express their fears. The wandering dead belonged to families, many are loved and missed, but they themselves are tormented and not ready to heal or move on.

Much of this folklore should serve as a warning to anyone attempting to contact and present offerings to spirits haphazardly. Although highly advantageous to the magician or *cunning person* called to establish such relationships, blindly offering foods or other substances to unknown entities could prove to be disastrous to both people and environment.

If you decide to invoke your ancestors during ritual work, be mindful that you are not inviting the wandering dead. Many if not most of the aforementioned lore of the spiritual monsters are these hungry ghosts who cling to a person or place attempting to live vicariously through them. Unfortunately for the conjurer who is caught unaware, sudden mood shifts and energy levels can fluctuate due to a spirit attaching itself to them. They will start having difficulty discerning the ghost's pain from their own and can fall into confusing emotional states of torment themselves, as they process the ghost's anger, fear, grief, etc., through their own bodies and minds.

Wandering spirits are able to recognize people who are gifted and open, and they hover around them, hoping to be seen, heard, or attach themselves to the receptive individual. Children are generally very sensitive and are often seen talking to ancestors or other spirits. Another very vulnerable population is that of addicts and alcoholics. By becoming inebriated or sedated by drugs, one vacates their body, leaving it open to any passing hungry ghost. Ghosts, who were addicts in life, will tend to prod susceptible hosts to pick up the same addictions. Ancestors may not automatically have our best interests at heart. Many were not necessarily wonderful and helpful people while they were alive and may not be so in spirit. Some of us have ancestors which were monsters while they were alive. Many such specters are those ancestors and dead relatives which are still trying to cause havoc in the afterlife. Still, the good will typically outweigh the bad as most family lineages have stronger bonds of love and care than they do spite.

Many cultures have established religions and traditions specifically for honoring ancestors and other spirits. In the Japanese religion of *Shinto* there are little house altars which are placed in a high central point of most traditional homes, businesses, and martial arts *dojos*. The *kamidana* or "god-shelf" is a miniature household altar provided to enshrine a *kami* or *ofuda* (charm or object dedicated to a spirit). The kamidana shelf typically contains a wide variety of items related to Shinto-style ceremonies, the most prominent of which is the *shintai*, an object meant to house a chosen *kami*, thus giving it a physical form to allow worship.

The form the majority of Kamidana shintai take are small circular mirrors, though they can also be stones — yin and yang shaped smooth stones called *magatama*, jewels, or some other object with largely symbolic value. The kami within the shintai is often the deity of the local shrine or one particular to the house owner's profession. A part of the kami (*bunrei*) was obtained specifically for that purpose from a shrine through a process called *kanjō*.

Worship at the kamidana typically consists of the offering of simple prayers and food in the form of rice, fruit, water, and flowers. These food offerings to the Kami are called *Shinsen*. Generally shinsen consists of rice (*kome*), rice wine (*sake/O-miki*), water (*Omizu*), and salt (*Oshio*). The interesting inclusion of salt in this case is noteworthy as in most other traditions; salt is considered to be a deterrent to all spirits and would seem rather offensive.[73] After further consideration, I wondered if the spirits of the Japanese kamidana vacated the shrine for a time when salt was offered as a means to "clean" the space before returning. This, however, is just a personal hypothesis.

After "*kensen*" food offering, a prayer is usually extended toward the kamidana in the form of gratitude for any blessings received and also a place to state an oath of personal intention. Two formal bows follow the conclusion of the prayer along with two claps and a final bow. Shinto ritual is highly involved and one that has a long history of ancestor and other spirit "kami" veneration. Much of my initial exposure to "domestic spirit communication" stemmed from my studies of Shinto. Between the various cultural traditions dealing with spirit worship, there are striking similarities between how offerings are prepared and delivered. An established tradition and practice should be integrated if not followed strictly from an established ceremony to honor and strengthen your spirit.

In Voodoo traditions you will find striking similarities to other spirit worshiping religions in which the ancestors are venerated and beseeched for assistance. From my understanding, anyone becoming initiated into Voodoo practice should first build a strong working relationship with their ancestors.

---

73   See Nick Farrell's *Offerings in Roman Deity Magic* for another example of salt used in offerings. -ed.

Once this relationship is built one will be able to commune with other spirits or *loa* and ask for assistance in almost any aspect of their lives.

Classical magic and western folklore of spirit relationships do not have as many clear records but undoubtedly shared many of the traits listed in the above traditions. The western word for familiar spirit is rooted in the Latin *familiaris*, which means a "household servant," and is intended to express the idea that magicians, cunning folk, witches, sorcerers, etc., had spirits as their servants or assistants which could provide a number of services. Those attempting to contact the dead, even to this day, usually have some sort of spirit guide who acts as an intermediary. These are familiar spirits.

My first introduction to offering foodstuffs and other items to ancestors was through the Celtic *Samhain* festival which I mentioned above. In the ritual I participated in, plates of food and photos of deceased relatives and ancestors were left out on Halloween. Besides the two aforementioned examples in spiritual relations and offerings, I did not have experience in a daily practice where I dealt with a spiritual entity on an everyday basis. That was before I succeeded in bringing a spirit to a vessel (skull) which was to become one of my most essential allies and teachers on the esoteric. The process took a tremendous amount of planning and effort, but once I was able to see and hear the spirit on a regular basis, experiences began to unfold at an amazing rate.

In an earlier magical experiment, I conducted a ritual intent on conjuring and conversing with the elemental king of Earth, Ghob. The elemental being appeared as a giant humanoid form which came out of a stone wall. One of my questions for Ghob was if he would grant me any elemental familiars to protect my household and belongings. The king of the gnomes said he would grant this request but that the spirits would need to be fed at least once a week from a "stone bowl" for them to provide the service. The elemental king explained the offering as a simple part of the "give and take." I consented to this agreement which was over a year ago from this writing and have not regretted the decision.

Regardless of the type of entity the magician or spirit liaison chooses to work with, I have found there is typically an exchange which is required for long term assistance. Forming a relationship with a spirit is not the same as being able to see, hear, and interact with one. If you are starting out in a practice where you've had no previous encounters or experiences in talking with a nonphysical being, you may have some groundwork to do first. The entire process is one in which many elements are needed for the relationship to be beneficial to both parties.

First thing I recommend is to learn as much as you can about your own lineage as possible. Get to know your ancestors on an intellectual level first, which starts to form the necessary mental bonds with them. Find out about their history, their likes and dislikes, their hobbies and passions. This will help you to know not only what possible offerings they would like but also which ones to stay away from or keep from influencing your person and space. By learning a bit about their personalities, you'll be able to provide them with the things they enjoyed most while they were alive and form links to their residual identity. As you formulate connections with your ancestors you can also research various spirits which may be accessible in your area. I recommend choosing a tradition if you are able to and one which adheres to your personal tastes and background.

# Types of Offerings

## Food Offerings

Before my spirit was even conjured and invited into the skull receptacle which was to become its physical link and habitation, the Archangel Cassiel made it clear that the spirit is to be fed and attended to every day. To be clear, the spirit itself offered what sorts of offerings it appreciated and how they could be delivered. I am careful in my preparation and selection of food offerings to spirits whether they ask for something directly or not.

For instance, I try to avoid giving spirits food containing high amounts of salt as it is a known to deplete etheric energies in many traditions. I also try to avoid giving spirits any sort of artificial type foods or candies besides the *Fae*, which seem to enjoy candies, chocolates, and other foods which are in no way naturally processed. Through dealing with my personal spirit, who claimed to be a live human at one point, I notice that it preferred foods that were known to exist and be found in the area it claimed to be from. A spirit requesting familiar substances would make sense and create thus another bridge to the physical world.

When I asked the spirit directly what it would like for offerings, it listed off several fruits and ingredients which I found interesting. Upon further research the corresponding energetic and traditional values became even more substantial. The foods my spirit listed as being preferable offerings are listed below:

## Honey

When my spirit listed honey as one of its preferred offerings, I thought back to what I knew of its mystical correspondences. Honey, in some forms of Hoodoo and folk magic, is used to sweeten someone's disposition towards you.

In a popular magical application honey is poured into a jar or saucer on top of a slip of paper containing the person's name, a photo, or possibly any article or physical link. A candle is placed in the saucer, and burned until it goes out on its own. In another version of the spell, the candle itself is dressed with honey.

Some ancient cultures used honey for embalming rituals. It is one of the rare natural "foods" which practically lasts forever without going bad. It is also purported that honey is an appropriate offering to leave at grave-sites. As listed in the necromantic ritual above, *The Sefer Ha-razim* uses a mixture of honey and olive oil to summon forth a spirit.

In addition, the folklore of a number of societies indicates that a blend of honey and milk is a traditional offering for many god forms. Triple offerings of milk, honey, and water or alcohol are common offerings found in the ancient world, from Greece to Ireland. Honey was also said to be sacred to the goddess of love and beauty, Aphrodite. In Hindu texts, honey is described as one of the five sacred elixirs of immortality. The Buddhist faith celebrates *Madhu Purnima*, which honors the day that Buddha made peace among his disciples — and honey is given as a gift to monks in his honor.

Honey, because of its sticky properties, can also be used in magic to hold two things together. Some magical traditions use honey to bind people or events that have a shaky relationship. If you want to do a honey binding on a couple — or even on two friends who are struggling with their friendship — you can use dolls or poppets with a layer of honey between them, and then wrapped with a cord.

## Dates

My spirit claims to be the shade of a person who lived around the same time as such monumental biblical figures as King David and King Solomon. Dates are the fruits of a kind of palm tree that has been cultivated in Africa for over

7,000 years and were most certainly traded and exported to parts of the Middle East at that time. Dates were considered sacred in Babylon and Greece, and the Hebrews made syrup from them as an offering to God. The fruits were also used by ancient Persians to celebrate the death and resurrection of Zoroaster, a Christ figure who dates back to 500 BC.

Dried dates are considered fruits of the spiritual realm and are symbolic of the eternal resurrection of the soul. My familiar spirit seems to enjoy dried dates as well as fresh ones without much comment on its preference between the two. Dried dates and food offerings seem to last a bit longer as well and are excellent if you are unable to give food offerings each and every day. I will often leave a few dates in my spirit's offering bowl while replacing the other more perishable fruits. The scent of them is pleasing and is actually one of the ingredients included in the mixture to fume Solomon's secret seal and vessel.

## Figs

Another fruit my spirit mentioned it prefers were figs. It actually went into a rather long speech about how fig trees and the fruit were such a monumental source of food, trade, and product in its day. Figs are one of the most ancient foods and had an important role in the Mediterranean diet for millennia. There are some writings which claimed Egyptian priests would bite into a ripe fig at the conclusion of certain consecration ceremonies. The Greeks considered them the ideal food, and figs were never harvested until a priest declared them ripe. In Asia, the Banyan fig tree is sacred to Buddha and is said to have its roots in heaven. In eastern cultures the fig was said to symbolize the rewards of meditation.

The fruits are actually flower cases that contain both the male and the female flowers during fertilization, a striking Mercurial correspondence. After fertilization, the flower cases swell with seeds and ooze sweet nectar. The word "fig" actually comes from the Arabian word for testicles, though esoterically, they are thought to embody only the highest powers of fertility and love. Growing a fig plant (such as *Ficus carica* or *Ficus benjamina*) indoors is purported to bring good luck and abundance to the room in which it is placed. Further mystical folk tradition states that if you have someone bite into a fig while you are holding it makes them instantly infatuated with you.

## Cinnamon

Besides its passionate aphrodisiac associations with the Greek goddess Aphrodite, cinnamon is also commonly used in folk magic for "heating things up." It is commonly associated with the sun and fire element — whether they be for love, money, success, or protection.

To "heat up" a spell means to make it happen more quickly or more strongly. Cinnamon is found in the ancient holy anointing oil recipe from the Bible and in ancient Egyptian incense recipes from a complex kyphi to a simple blend of cinnamon, frankincense, and myrrh. In root-work cinnamon is an ingredient in the popular "fiery wall of protection" blend, as well as other cleansing and protective incenses, but is most commonly used to bring good fortune and prosperity to a business. Burn cinnamon at your business and/or make a tea of it and pour it on your front step to bring in customers and their money. Burning cinnamon mixed with frankincense and myrrh is used to purify people, objects, or rid a place of evil influences and attached spirits.

## Bread and Olive Oil

The significance of these items was covered earlier in this essay.

My spirit informed me that besides their preference and resonance with what is offered, the types of offerings have the ability to strengthen the intentions and persuasions of the magician. The offerings do this through their symbolic meaning along the similar lines of correspondences the offerings represent. That is to say that if the offering has ties to money, movement, love, destruction, harm, or some other action, the offering should mirror the intention and considerations of the one making the offering.

First and foremost should the preferences and consideration of the spirit be referred to. If the spirit does not request something specifically, it should be asked if such an offering would be welcomed or suitable. This is an important factor since some food or substances may be disagreeable to the "tastes" and nature of the spirit itself. Such offerings would only agitate or dilute your intended purpose.

Despite the above list I have offered my spirit a variety of other fruits and breads and drinks but have selected carefully what they might like. I'm also informed when the spirit needs the previous offerings removed and new ones brought forth, but most of the time, I do this without having to be asked. I'm not overboard with altars and offerings, and the two rituals I attend to the closest are the ones my skull spirit requests and the ones I leave weekly for the Earth spirits to protect my home and belongings.

For those wishing to refer to a classical work of magic concerning offerings, refer to *The Key of Solomon*, Book 2, Chapter XXIII, Concerning Sacrifices to the Spirits and How They Should be Made.[74]

## Liquid Offerings

Along with food offerings, most spirit veneration traditions include offerings of a liquid sort to their honored spirits:

### Water

Before any solid food is actually given I will present a small vessel of water to a newly contacted spirit assuming it is not an angel, demon, godform, elemental, or fae. Water is the most common liquid given and quite fitting due to its inherent nature. In the mystical sense, the element of water is closely linked to deep emotions, dreams, psychic visions, healing, rest, cleansing, dissolution, astral travel, death/rebirth, and the otherworld.

Within *The Key of Solomon,* in the chapter dealing with sacrifices for the spirits, there is a section which covers food and liquid offerings and it states that "especially shouldst thou have a vessel of clear and pure fountain water." Spirits are said to draw energy from water, and Martin Coleman in his *Communing with Spirits: The Magical Practice of Necromancy* suggests offering a glass of water to spirits that successfully carry out your tasks and requests. I recommend one always have a source of water nearby for your spirit as the essence of water and the spirit realm seem to go hand in hand.

### Milk

This is also a traditional offering and historically was offered to many gods and potent spirits.

### Beer, Whiskey, Wine

Beer, whiskey, wine, and other alcoholic beverages are also known to be offerings and used widely in Voodoo and African tribal religions. The more "intense" or alcoholic the beverage, the more it is said to spur the spirits into action. Care should be taken, however, when offering alcohol to ancestor spirits; be sure none of them were alcoholics or reacted violently with alcohol in life.

---

74    This chapter of the *Key of Solomon* is explored in my essay *Liber Donariorum*. -ed.

## Blood

Blood and other bodily fluids have also been used as offering but are not widely used. Some of the more chaotic beings and especially darker demons may request blood and other bodily fluids.

I personally do not engage in this sort of offering for a number of reasons. For one, blood and the procuring of it is more of a sacrifice than it is an offering. Most traditions who offer blood to their spirits or gods often drain it from the body of a sacrificial animal. If not from an animal, the blood can be a direct link back to the person it was drawn from and thus become a liability to them and possibly to the magician even if it was not their own. However, for those seeing historical methods for offering such substances, I again refer you to the *Key of Solomon*, Chapter XXIII, Concerning Sacrifices to the Spirits and How They Should be Made, which states:

> In many operations it is necessary to make some sort of sacrifice unto the demons, and in various ways. Sometimes white animals are sacrificed to the good spirits and black to the evil. Such sacrifices consist of the blood and sometimes of the flesh. They who sacrifice animals, of whatsoever kind they be, should select those which are virgin, as being more agreeable unto the spirits, and rendering them more obedient. When blood is to be sacrificed it should be drawn also from virgin quadrupeds or birds, but before offering the oblation, say:
>
> > May this sacrifice which we find it proper to offer unto ye, noble and lofty beings, be agreeable and pleasing unto your desires; be ye ready to obey us, and ye shall receive greater ones.
>
> Then perfume and sprinkle it according to the rules of art.

The text then goes on to list a number of woods, each sacred to a planet, that can be used to kindle the fire upon which such sacrifices will be cooked.[75] Each one is intended to further correspond to the type of planetary spirit you are sacrificing to as well as the nature of the spirit and intention of the sacrifice.

---

75    See my essay, *Liber Donariorum*, the section on Burnt Offerings, for a complete list of these planetary woods. -ed.

I'll state again that I have no experience or desire to participate in the sacrifice of animals or anything for that matter, as the other offerings listed seem more than adequate to illicit the response of the spirits.

Again, care should be taken when preparing, pouring, and offering a liquid to your spirits. The most common way liquid offerings are presented to spirits is just like they would be to a live and physical recipient, within a glass or cup. The substance of the liquid receptacle can be just as important as the contents. Certain spirits will have a certain draw or disdain for certain material, especially metals. Be sure your spirit is agreeable with not only the contents but the type of container. Glass, copper, metal, silver, wood, horn, and clay are all fairly common substances made into drinking vessels. The nature of your tradition, spirit, and purpose will help determine the most appropriate vessel to choose, but the most reliable will be the direct advice from your spirit itself.

One other method for presenting a liquid offering to your spirit is simply to pour it out in front of them upon the ground, or all around and possibly on their altar. This is an offering of libation, a pouring out of liquid offering to your spirit familiar or ancestors. This act of offering or pouring out will of course depend upon the location and presentable restrictions for your spirit.

## Disposing of the Food and Liquid Offerings

In some traditions it is acceptable to eat the food offerings once they are ready to be replaced with new ones. Caution should be used, however, as food left out for any reason will begin to decay and collect bacteria rapidly. Another possible deterrent for consuming food which has already been given as offerings is the complete absence of etheric nurturance, as it would have already been consumed by the spirit(s). Theoretically ingesting the spiritually drained food would not conceivably be as nourishing.

I was relieved when my own spirit instructed me to dispose of its offerings outside when they were removed and not to leave them out anywhere else within the house. Obviously this should be done with care and not in a manner where it would attract rodents, insects, or cause a foul stench in your backyard. If you do not live in an area where such offerings could be disposed of outside, I would create compost pile or perhaps a waste receptacle specifically for collecting old offerings which could be disposed of elsewhere at a later time.[76]

This may be particular to my spirit, however, and I could also theorize that if you partook of a spirit's food, it would further bond the two of you together on an energetic level. This, however, is just speculation as I have never attempted this before.

Early into our communications, I asked my familiar how it and other spirits actually "eat" food offerings. He advised me to move closer and asked if I could smell the fruit offerings I had placed in a bowl for him. I responded that I could. He said as soon as the food or liquid offerings come into being, they start to decay and parts of them begin to drift up into the air till they become "of the air" or ethereal which we can easily detect as smell or scent. The particles of food which dissolve into air, he described, are the actual nourishing properties of the offerings as they undergo the "natural transformation from substance to spirit" via the process of decay and oxidation, the very occurrence of which is a release of energy which spirits can consume.

In other words the "energy" or natural release from the decaying process is what the spirits actually eat. Incenses, smoke, and vapor also offer a nourishment of a different variety. I thought this lesson from my spirit was fascinating and pondered if other environmental factors in the area also contributed to a spirit's nourishment. Perhaps the purported "cold spots" and rapid temperature fluctuations which are attributed to paranormal activity have commonalities with this phenomenon.

In the realization of the above concept, I advise against leaving prepared foodstuff out in the open or lying around. The same goes for glasses of water or other consumable liquids if you don't want uninvited guests hanging around expecting free meals. The risks or potential hazards of this were already explained above in the section dealing with "hungry ghosts." Besides the possibility of attracting ravenous specters, spiritual parasites and other "feeders" will infest the places which are not kept physically and spiritually "swept" and clean by the practitioner.

Tending to a spirit familiar and its offerings is an ongoing discipline of mindfulness and attention to detail. When going on trips or if you plan

---

76    How you dispose of the offerings is an important part of the process. See *Liber Donariorum* for further instructions. Also see Gilberto Strapazon's *Offerings in Ceremonial Magick and ATRs (Risks and Influences)* for important warnings against improper disposal of offering leftovers. -ed.

on being away, it's imperative to inform your spirit and have perhaps larger offerings for your spirit while you're away. In my house, my wife helps tend to the offerings and speak with my spirit when I am away, which she finds enjoyable. My wife's first experience being able to see, hear, and converse with a spirit was with my familiar spirit, and she became quite fond of him as an honored guest of the house. I cannot fully express the enjoyment having my familiar around has been for the entire family. I have a personal esoteric teacher, assistant and confidant, and one who also takes it upon itself to be considerate of the family's overall safety and wellbeing.

## INCENSE OFFERINGS

The offering of scented spices, herbs, and resins to spirits is nearly as old as food offerings. The fragrant perfume released in the smoke of burning incense continues to be a prevalent element in most major religions around the world and has only increased through the millennia. Use of incense in ritual is popular in many cultures and may have their roots in the practical and aesthetic appeal of the aroma.

One common motif is incense as a form of sacrificial offering to a deity. Such use was common in Judaic worship and remains in use, for example, in the Catholic, Orthodox, and Anglican churches, Taoist and Buddhist Chinese *jingxiang* (敬香 "offer incense [to ancestors/gods]"), etc. In magical and spirit workings it is used frequently if not ubiquitously during ritual and has even been purported to supply a spirit with a more physical form in which to appear to the magician.

I find that mixing and blending specific incenses will strengthen rituals, especially those where the mixtures have a long history within a certain esoteric tradition. Likewise, if your spirit comes from a specific tradition or you evoked it through a known cultural, religious, or historic tradition, I would utilize incense mixtures known to that tradition. For instance, *Ketoret* was the incense offered in the Temple in Jerusalem and is stated in the Book of Exodus as a mixture of stacte, onycha, galbanum, and frankincense.

The forms and methods used for burning incense differ between cultures and have evolved with advances in technology and increasing diversity as well as the reasons for burning it. There is strong evidence that the ancient Egyptians used incense in a variety of ways, both mundane and magical. Its frequency was such that it was thought to be used as a simple luxury to cause places to have a more pleasing aroma and to mask other malodors, but also implemented as an offering to the many gods and spirits of their culture.

In excavations of prehistoric tombs in El Mahasna, various incense resin balls were discovered. The Temple of Deir-el-Bahari in Egypt contains a series of carvings that depict an expedition for incense. The Babylonian mystics and priests utilized prayer while presenting incense offerings in order to receive oracles. The use of incense in such divinatory and religious practices are found throughout much of the ancient world, spreading from ancient Babylon to Greece and Rome, and from India to China.

At around 2000 BC, ancient China began the use of incense in the religious sense, namely for worship. Incense was used by Chinese cultures from Neolithic times and became more widespread in the *Xia, Shang,* and *Zhou* dynasties. Incense usage reached its peak during the *Song* Dynasty where structures were built specifically to hold incense ceremonies. In the 15th and 16th century, appreciation of incense became a true art form in Japan called *Kōdō* and it steadily spread to the upper and middle classes of Japanese society. In Taoist traditions, incense is associated with "yin" energies of the dead, temples, shrines, and ghosts. The Taoist Chinese would not burn undedicated and unattended incense in the home, believing that it would draw the attention of dangerous hungry ghosts that would consume the smoke and cause ruin in the home.

I encourage the reader to experiment where they can but to be mindful that not all scents mesh well together. For starters, I would select from traditional incense components dating back several hundred years that have been tried and tested and integrated into many spiritual traditions. For a list of the most prevalent incense ingredients, refer to the following list:

Makko powder (*Machilus thunbergii*), Borneol camphor (*Dryobalanops aromatica*), Sumatra Benzoin (*Styrax benzoin*), Omani frankincense (*Boswellia sacra*), Guggul (*Commiphora wightii*), Golden Frankincense (*Boswellia papyrifera*), the new world Tolu balsam (*Myroxylon toluifera*) from South America, Somali myrrh (*Commiphora myrrha*), Labdanum (*Cistus villosus*), Opoponax (*Commiphora opoponax*), and white Indian sandalwood powder (*Santalum album*).

In Chapter 10 of the Key of Solomon, "Concerning Incense, Suffumigations, Perfumes, Odours and Similar Things Which are Used in Magical Arts," the grimoire states that "there are many kinds of incense, suffumigations, and perfumes, which are made for and offered unto the spirits; those which are of sweet odour are for the good, those which are of evil savour are for the evil. For perfumes of good odour, take thou incense, aloes, nutmeg, gum benjamin, musk, and other fragrant spices."[77]

I've experimented with all of the above combinations with equally comparable results and I find the mixtures an excellent source of offerings for stronger spirits of the angelic or sublunary realms. It's best if you can gather the ingredients or mixtures from a reputable supplier and one familiar with magical workings such as www.alchemyworks.com.

The Key of Solomon next instructs you to consecrate the incense before its use. These are steps I would not overlook and are an excellent addition to further consecrating the incense to your spirit alone rather than for general use.

THE EXORCISM OF INCENSE from the *Key of Solomon*:

*O God of Abraham, God of Isaac, God of Jacob, deign to bless these odoriferous spices so that they may receive strength, virtue, and power to attract the good spirits, and to banish and cause to retire all hostile phantoms. Through thee, O most holy ADONAI, who livest and reignest unto the ages of the ages. Amen.*

*I exorcise thee, O spirit impure and unclean, thou who art a hostile phantom, in the name of God, that thou quit this perfume, thou and all thy deceits, that it may be consecrated and sanctified in the name of God almighty. May the Holy Spirit of God grant protection and virtue unto those who use these perfumes; and may the hostile and evil spirit and phantom never be able to enter therein, through the ineffable name of God almighty. Amen.*

*O Lord, deign to bless and to sanctify this creature of perfume so that it may be a remedy unto mankind for the health of body and of soul, through the invocation of thy holy name. May all creatures who receive the odour of this incense and of these spices*

---

77    Other manuscripts read "frankincense, aloe, myrrh, galbanum, and similar spices"; or "frankincense, wood of aloes, myrrh, and any other things that have a sweet smell."

*receive health of body and of soul, through him who hath formed the ages. Amen.*

Following the prayer above, the *Key of Solomon* instructs you to "sprinkle the various spices with the water of the art, and place them aside in a piece of silk or in a box destined for the purpose, so that thou mayest have them ready prepared for use when necessary." Finally the grimoire instructs you in the proper way of burning the incense on charcoals which should be in "earthen vessels newly glazed within and without."

There is a consecration for the charcoals you place the incense on as well.[78]

## CANDLE AND LIGHT OFFERINGS

You will be hard pressed to ever find an area dedicated to a spirit or spirits, whether religious or otherwise, that do not have at least one candle on or near it. Candles and lamp flames are as prevalent in spiritual worship as any other form of offering. They light up the area casting a warm and inviting glow which attracts both spiritual and physical entities alike. Most are familiar with the small votive candles seen in churches and cathedrals and upon the altars of other religions. They can be seen flickering in numerous quantities in front of icons of Jesus, the Mother Mary, the saints, and so forth. Votive candles are typically white or yellow and made from purified beeswax or a careful mixture of both paraffin and beeswax.

The use of votive candles is an ongoing tradition utilized as burnt votive offerings in religious ceremony. In the Catholic and other Christian traditions votive candles are lit while saying prayers for themselves or others. To "light a candle for someone" indicates an intention to say a prayer for another person, and the candle is an active symbol of that prayer. Burning a votive candle as a prayer for someone or some situation is practiced in many traditions and faiths all over the world. In India, people can be found offering votive candles to float down the river Ganges. In the Buddhist tradition the candlelight votives are offerings which serve as a symbol of illuminating wisdom and a reminder for his disciples to follow the teachings rather than the teacher himself.

Making your own candles can be a delight and done rather easily in this day and age since all the supplies can be easily purchased at a hobby or craft store. There are several types of candles to choose from and the materials

---

78 See *Liber Donariorum*, section "Making Your Offerings — Laying Out the Offerings" for the Solomonic exorcism of fire to recite over the coals. -ed.

used can either assist or detour the interaction with you and your spirit. As with all offerings, the participant should make all initial efforts to discover the preference their spirit has for candles if any. Natural Beeswax candles are ideal for most traditional workings and burn with a wonderful glow and subtle sweet scent. Pillar candles are large cylinders of wax often with multiple wicks and can be several feet in length. You can buy paraffin candles of any color or shape, unscented, or with any fragrance you can imagine.

My familiar spirit seems to appreciate richly scented candles or natural olive oil lamps best. It actually requested more than once that I speak with it by light of candle or lamp flame rather than the electric lighting of my magical working room. It said that the light was more conducive for communication and the imparting of visions.

As an added offering to your spirit, droplets of fragrant essential oils can be added to your olive oil lamps or "dressed" on your candles for a double offering effect.

The number of candles is left up to the tradition and preference of the practitioner. A candle for each spirit or venerated ancestor can be arranged in a space specific for this purpose. For my spirit familiar I light two candles on either side of his altar behind his skull vessel. Large candles can be inscribed with your spirit's sigil or seal if you have one or simply have its name written on it. Find oils and scents it prefers and "dress" or rub the candle down with the oils and herbs. Simply having a couple of white candles on either side to represent purity in your space designated for the spirit would be perfectly adequate to start. The tall seven-day type votive candles in the glass containers are very affordable and convenient.

The light(s) are consistent reminders for you and it that you are keeping your relationship strong, focused, and active. Some traditions keep such altar candles burning indefinitely. For many, this is risky and not always practical for those away from the home often. For me, lighting the candles initiates the beginning of my conversation with my spirit for that time, sparking the conversation into reality, along with my other offerings and words of intention. For the traditional mage looking to fashion candles in line with the historic grimoires, I again refer the reader to *The Key of Solomon* which states,

> It hath been ever the custom among all nations to use fire and light in sacred things. For this reason the master of the art should also employ them in sacred rites, and besides those for reading the

conjurations by, and for the incense, in all operations lights are necessary in the circle. For this reason he should make candles of virgin wax (which is to say the wax never be for being used for any other reason) in the day and hour of Mercury; the wicks should have been made by a young girl; and the candles should be made when the moon is in her increase, of the weight of half a pound each, and on them thou shalt engrave these characters with the iron pen (stylus) of the art.

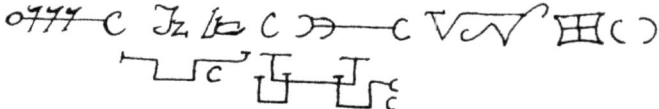

After you engrave the sigil on the candle, the *Key* instructs you to pray the following Psalms over it:

> [Ps150=KJV150] *Laudate Dominum in sanctis eius* (Praise the Lord in his sanctuary)
> [Ps102=KJV103] *Benedic anima mea Domino* (Bless the Lord, O my soul, and all that is within me)
> [Ps116=KJV117] *Laudate Dominum omnes gentes* (Praise the Lord, all nations)

and finally seal the candle with these prayers:

> *O Lord God, who governest all things by thine almighty power, give unto me, a poor sinner, understanding and knowledge to do only that which is agreeable unto thee; grant unto me to fear, adore, love, praise, and give thanks unto thee with true and sincere faith and perfect charity. Grant, O Lord, before I die, and descend into the realms beneath, and before the fiery flame shall devour me, that thy grace may not leave me, O Lord of my soul. Amen.*
>
> *I exorcise thee, O creature of wax, by him who alone hath created all things by his Word, and by the virtue of him who is pure truth, that thou cast out from thee every phantasm, perversion, and deceit of the enemy, and may the virtue and power of God*

*enter into thee, so that thou mayest give us light, and chase far from us all fear or terror.*

After these prayers the magician should sprinkle the wax candle with holy water using the aspergillum. The *Key* continues:

> Then thou shalt take a square lantern, with panes of crystal glass, and thou shalt fit therein the candle lighted, to read by, to form the circle, or any other purpose for which thou shalt require it. After this thou shalt sprinkle them with the water of the art, and incense them with the usual perfumes.

When you are ready to use the candle, the *Key* includes an exorcism of the fire to be recited as the candle is lit.[79]

## Word and Conversation Offerings

Since conversation and interaction with your familiar spirit is a primary medium of the relationship, it should go without saying that speaking with your spirit should be among the top priorities. This is quite different than simply talking at your spirit. Two way communications is the only viable way to get the benefits of a separate intelligence and understand what is really going on between you and the spirit.

For those who have yet to achieve audible and veritable communication with a spirit, this may seem like a difficult obstacle to overcome. Indeed few in the esoteric community seem to have been able to hear the voices of spirits distinctly and claim they have what has been termed clairaudience. Regardless of your current state on the matter, two-way communications should be the goal if it is something which is not present during the intentional onset of securing a spirit familiar.

Establishing links and communication with your ancestors, opening up your senses, and simply keeping a continual mindful openness to the avenues of commutation will be your best initiator if you are starting from little to no experience. There's nothing more frustrating trying to do guesswork on what your spirit is attempting to tell you, all the while trying to provide it with offerings you are unsure if it really wants or enjoys and you have no idea

---

79   See *Liber Donariorum*, section "Making Your Offerings — The Offering Ritual," for the Solomonic exorcism of fire to recite over the candle flames. -ed.

how it can assist you with your magical workings. I don't desire nor enjoy ambiguous spiritual communications, and I prefer to know exactly who and what I'm dealing with and what intentions and information the spirit has for me specifically. As an occultist, the words, prayers, and questions you share with your spirit will make all the difference. They will either lead you to delightful insight or confusing rambling, to benefits and blessings or insubstantial banter. Like any relationship, attentive care must be given to create the most harmonious exchange.

I asked my spirit familiar exactly how he was able to speak so clearly to me, and it replied that it had the ability to tap directly into my particular pattern of thought, as if it were a radio wave with a certain signature, and match its own methods of communication directly to mine, allowing me to hear him clearly and also receive images as if I were tuned into his particular frequency as well. It went on to explain how it was able to do this with any person it came in contact with and was able to get a sense of where they were, what they were thinking and feeling, and what their general state was without having to be in close "physical" proximity to them. I found this fascinating and also very informative in the ways spirits interact with conscious beings on the physical level. My spirit said that it had been at practice for this for many, many years and become quite adept at it which was why I and others were able to hear him so easily.

Communication in and of itself is a complicated subject. Beyond languages, cultures, customs, expressions, and nonverbal communication, intelligent beings express themselves in a multitude of ways. The way ideas and messages are exchanged are so numerous it would be beyond the scope of this work to go into them all. What is important for our work here is to get a full understanding of how you as the practitioner communicate and comprehend and how your spirit chooses to communicate as well.

Initially, trying to speak clearly with your spirit familiar can be like learning a new language or custom. Don't expect your spirit to communicate in a way you are used to or expect. This may be a considerable hurdle or frustration until you are able to quiet your mind enough to be open to your spirit's particular form or frequency of communication. We must inevitably quiet the voices in our own minds in order to perceive, "hear," and comprehend what our spirit is trying to tell us.

I suggest speaking to or at least greeting your spirit familiar at the beginning of each and every day. The daily act of a sincere morning greeting and acknowledgment is a good way to begin building the relationship with your spirit. You should also speak with your spirit some time before going to bed each night. Prayers, song, blessings, conversation with the intent to build relationship and communion are all appropriate.

My spirit familiar instructed me on the best way to conjure it, which involved a tracing of its sigil while speaking its names three times and asking it to arrive in a certain manner. The repetitious and constant effort of this seemed to assure a clear level of communication each and every time. I've also gotten into the habit of thanking and blessing my spirit after speaking with each time. Be mindful of your mood and mental disposition; before speaking, take a moment to clear your thoughts and open your heart. Speak intentionally and with meaning as you would to a respected friend or teacher. Words, especially words to your spirit, should always be meaningful and with direction.

## Other Offerings

### Artwork and Pictorial Representations

Images of spirits are richly represented in the texts of classical magic. From illustrations in medieval manuscripts to block style prints, spirits are depicted in a plethora of mediums and scenarios. The notorious Book of Spirits, or *Liber Spiritumm*, is an excellent example of this concept where the magician is able to bind the essence of the spirit into its illustrated depiction.

Further inquiry to my spirit informed me that some spirits appreciate this also, as it gives them one more "hold" and "form" in the physical world. However, not all spirits desire this as it will also give them a more substantial link on which to be bound, manipulated, or controlled. Drawing their image, as you've seen it/them, and including any other symbols or sigils will strengthen the spiritual link to that piece of artwork. Unsurprisingly, simply reprinting pictures or copying from other works does not seem to have the same effect. The whole effort of the magician creating an image through their memory and own hand seems to contain enigmatic elements for the picture to "come alive."

Everything from the material used to draw the spirit on, to the implement used to draw the spirit with should be considered and possibly consecrated just to this purpose. Historically, a Book of Spirits should be made of white vellum or (virgin) white paper. If you are unable to create or buy a book of vellum parchment, I suggest using a blank journal of the highest quality, acid free, unused paper you are able to afford.

In essence, the Liber Spitumm is a journal of important prayers, invocations, seals, hours, and sigils of the spirits whose places and spheres are known. A record of all the answers received from the spirits you've questioned should also be included as well as any images or symbols that were revealed to you. The Book of Spirits could also contain records of new or unknown spirits to be contacted for future working, all for the sake of calling up with ease at other times.

In my first publication on angelic evocation, I shared how powerful the correct creation of a Book of Spirits was, even when I was not intentionally trying to use it. The spirits would let me know they were quite close just by gazing at images I drew. After my first operations, I drew the spirit's image on the selected page of my book and placed my parchment lamen within as well. I became fascinated with my drawing and would flip to it while entering further information of successive evocations. When I absently gazed at the picture, I got a swift headache and a pulling sensation in my abdomen. The feelings were quite sudden and uncomfortable. It took two more instances of forgetting not to do this until I became convinced of the book's potency and that of the energetic link between the spirit and its drawn image. I then made conscious steps to avoid this occurrence in the future. I was amazed by how much of a direct contact the book is to the spirits. When a veritable Book of Spirits is considered, the spirit really is accessed where its image and sigil is.

The *Fourth Book of Occult Philosophy* also warns us that our Liber Spirituum may lose its potency if handled carelessly or left open and unsecured:

> Which book being so written, and well bound, is to be adorned, garnished, and kept secure, with Registers and Seals, lest it should happen after the consecration to open in some place not indented and endanger the operator. Furthermore, this book ought to be kept as reverently as may be: for irreverence of mind causes it to lose its virtue, with pollution and profanation.

The above should remind one to put care and constant attentiveness toward any drawn images of your spirit and treat them as a sacred and consecrated objects, imbued with the essence of your spirit helper. I leave it up to the reader who decides to illustrate his or her spirit whether they leave the artwork open and revealed or cover it after working with them. This may be a preference on privacy and the possibility of others touching or becoming associated with the drawing in ways you would rather not have them do. Regardless, any images of spirits should be kept in a place of reverence, and as a key link to your spirit, it should always be present when attempting to contact it. Care should be taken to keep the artwork free from becoming blemished, worn, or damaged in anyway, and should it become so, a new piece of artwork should take its place.

# Spirit Altars

By now the reader will have realized the need for a suitable amount of space in which to present offerings to spirit familiars. An altar is the most general and appropriate term for a space designated and reserved for offerings and articles belonging to your spirit or spirits. A safe place to arrange your spirit's vessel, offerings, artwork, and an area where you can go and speak to your spirit in its habitat is ideal if not essential for this practice.

As mentioned in the paragraphs above, many religions and traditions have their own version of the spirit altar; from the various shrines of ancient tribes and Voodoo to the kamidana of the Japanese Shinto faith, each has its own unique setup and observations. Making and tending to your altar should be no small affair. It does not need to be extravagant or elaborate but should be well thought out, arranged, and designed to fit yours and your spirits needs.

If you have or plan on making an ancestral alter I would suggest you keep it separate from that of your spirit familiar's altar. Ancestral altars are intended to create energetic links between you and your ancestors beyond the veil. The tradition of Voodoo has spiritual practices steeped in the veneration of ancestors and the *Lwa* themselves are often seen as ancestral spirits.

Just as *The Key of Solomon* instructs for the food offerings, you should attempt to make your altar on a new or clean small table or flat surface and cover it with a pure white cloth. Again, make sure that this space is dedicated only to your spirit and never use it for any other purpose.

Next you can place your spirit's vessel, pot, or physical link in a centralized location on the altar. Following this, I would add a large dish or two for your food offerings. I use two cup-sized silver containers on either side of my spirit's skull vessel where I place the food offerings.

Nearby should also be placed a vessel for water and other liquid offerings. Preferably these should be made out of one of the materials listed above in the "Liquid Offerings" section, or one selected directly by your spirit. The water can be changed daily and, at the very least, a minimum of once a week. Never let it get stagnant and certainly not cloudy or dirty. Arrange a candle or candles on either side, preferably behind or to the side of the spirit's vessel. The more you spend time at your altar, the more the energy will build in that area and communication with your spirit strengthen.

As mentioned previously, before you approach your altar and begin speaking with your spirit, take some time to clear your mind and focus on what you are doing. The clearer your thoughts and mood, the clearer and more productive the exchange with your spirit will be. Intentionality and continual mindfulness will make a world of difference with this practice. It will cause you to step out of your daily routine, shifting moods and happenings of your day-to-day life to really be present with the intelligent being you are connecting with. The entire altar should be cleaned and items replaced if they become worn or damaged over time. Re-consecrate everything with the same dedication you did the first time and listen to the guidance of your spirit as the relationship evolves.

*Central Angelic Temple Altar*

*Altar for Celtic Deity Lugh*

*Altar for Archangel Michael*

# Conclusion

The relationship formed between magician, shaman, necromancer (or whatever title is used), and spirit is a deep and intimate connection. The practices are by far among some of the oldest on the earth. Deep reservoirs of knowledge, assistance, and insight can be taped into by this interaction, but as I have previously mentioned, something does not come from nothing. The relationship between person and spirit is one of attentiveness and responsibility. The benefits will come with practice and work and will increase the senses of the mage with continued interaction.

One of the questions put to my familiar skull spirit was, "What would happen if you stopped receiving offerings, and interaction of any kind?" I was curious what would happen although I didn't plan on ever stopping my relationship with him, but wondered what would happen if somehow I were unable to provide offerings and speak with him. If I were suddenly disabled mentally or restrained, or even after I passed on, I wonder what would happen if his skull, his vessel would be left unattended, perhaps left in a storage box somewhere. The binding enchantment I engraved onto the skull was to be everlasting, so I wanted to make sure he was somehow taken care of. His reply was, "If I were to be left alone and received no more offerings and no one was around who could see or hear me, I would simply withdraw until my connection to the physical world became dormant, still residing within the skull, but dormant. Should the skull be broken or lost, I would simply return to my place of origin within the deep ethereal." It seems the attention, care, and effort which goes into the offerings makes the difference rather than the amount or expense of them. The interaction and attentiveness keeps the relationship strong, vibrant, and relevant for the practitioner.

If one looks closely, the Hermetic elements of Air, Fire, Water, and Earth are all present within the full range of offerings given to spirits. The breath and words of the devotee, shaman, magician, cunning person are as the Air and winds of intention put into vibration to reach and collaborate with your spirit. For this reason I often speak aloud to my spirit even when it isn't necessary and I could just as well commune through thought alone. Putting thoughts into spoken word is the arcane step of initial manifestation and decree. The offerings of "word and conversation" should be the first, last, and most frequently utilized offering between you and your spirit as ideas, words, and images will be the most abundant exchange and manifestation you will behold, etc.

The fire of your devotional candles and lamps will serve as the beacon and continual communion with your spirit as an active heat and energy, brightening and revealing the further mystery of creation as the relationship between you and your spirit unfolds.

Your liquid offerings and hospitality will nourish your spirit through the very element of the psychic depths of the unconscious. The very presence of water will establish a symbolic doorway to the astral worlds, bridging the understanding and communication between you and your spirit. Allow the effects of this libation to assist you with deeper understanding and feelings that words alone could not hope to convey.

Finally, your offerings of food will give your spirit familiar, ancestor, or servitor the physical link it requires to have any effect on the world of matter. The substance of your offerings will nourish and strengthen the ties, understandings, and efforts your spirits put forth to fulfill your desires and requests. Painting its image, seal, sigil, or name will give it further links to the world of form.

If we look to the fifth element of spiritual essence through each of the offerings and union, it will only be as strong as the combined intentionality, ability, focus, and will of you and your spirit as you travel this road of union and mutually beneficial assistance. Recognize the ebb and flow of your connection and successful working with the spirit as a matter of course. Stay constant and true in your practice and marvel in the mystery that is a magical companion nourished by effort.

# Sources

I. *Cunning Folk and Familiar Spirits: Shamanistic Visionary Traditions in Early Modern British Witchcraft and Magic* by Emma Wilby

II. *Communing with Spirits: The Magical Practice of Necromancy* by Martin Coleman

III. *The Sefer Ha-razim* (The Book of Secrets).

IV. *Le Comte de Gabalis by Abbe' Nicholas de montfaucon de Villarsand the Irreconcilable Gnomes* by Antoine Androl

V. *Incense: Rituals, Mystery, Lore* by Gina Hyams, Susie Cushner (2004).

VI. *Cunningham's Encyclopedia of Magical Herbs.* Llewellyn Worldwide. 2000

*The Key of Solomon* (Clavicula Salomonis) Edited by S. Liddell MacGregor Mathers Revised by Joseph H. Peterson, Copyright © 1999, 2004, 2005. All rights reserved.

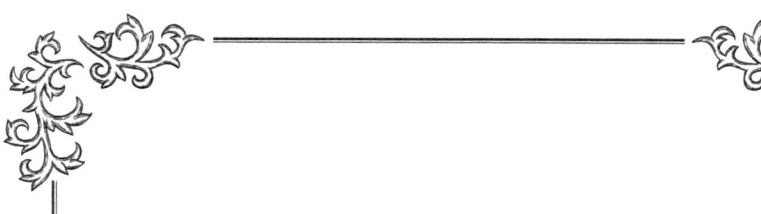

# Ancestors & Offerings

*Brother Moloch*

From time immemorial, sorcerers have worked with a wide variety of non-physical entities (hereafter referred to as NPE's) from cthonic spirits to celestial personages and many in between. However, in the distant past, the distinction between the classes of NPE's was not always as clear cut as they've been in the last hundred or so years. For many sorcerers, the first NPE's to work with have been their very own ancestors.

Unfortunately today, when one uses the term "ancestors," often there is a bit of misunderstanding going on since there are two levels of ancestors:

1. Family: These are the folks who are directly connected to you by blood or DNA and who comprise your personal family relationships. Often grandparents, great-grandparents, and so forth are found in this category.

2. Generational: These are all of the ancient dead who have walked the earth before any of us were thought of. They may not be directly linked to your DNA or bloodline, but they're human like you and they helped shaped modern humanity in their own indomitable manner.

There is a third group that few people get to experience in their life and those are adoptive ancestors. For instance, when you are adopted into someone's tribe or family, their own ancestral lineage takes you on as one of their very own. This is an honor and very few modern adults ever consider how truly wonderful this is.

Today with many children put up for adoption, growing up in adoptive families becomes far more common than most folks realize, which presents an opportunity to learn about the adoptive family's ancestral line. I've counseled a number of metaphysical folk who lamented that they were adopted and knew not who their birth lineage was all due to adoption records being sealed shut by court order.

I explain to these folks that they have a wonderful opportunity to have not just one set of family ancestors but two to call upon. They have their very own through their bloodline as well as their adoptive ancestors. (How awesome is that?) Often the first lamentation I hear is, "But I don't know who my real parents are so how will my real ancestors know me?" and I have to explain to them that their ancestors are spirits who share their blood and DNA. Their ancestors *know* who you are even if you don't know who they are.

# ANCESTORS & SHRINES

Ancestors are spirits who are to be courted much like many who court the Gods and familiar spirits. By this I mean far too many people mix up the use of altar and shrine. An altar is where you do your spiritual work and a shrine is where you interact with your spirits.

A shrine is a place of reverence and devotion where you interact with the divine and spirits. Typically here is where you talk to them, ask them for help, tell them what's going on in your life, and so on. You also give your offerings here at your shrine rather than your working altar, because you may have something immediate that comes up that requires you to fire up your altar, and if it is occupied with offerings for spirits, you will be unable to use it.

Shrines vary from culture, class, and economics. I've seen some very elaborate shrines that cost a small fortune to build out of rare woods and precious metals like gold and silver. I've also seen many shrines that were little more than a cardboard box with a cloth draped over it. Utility is the key here because you have to be the one to utilize it. What good is a $1,000+ handmade shrine if you never use it?

My late grandfather had a good rule of thumb: "Start out small and build from there." Always the pragmatist, Gramps saw that it was best to try your hand at the easiest aspect first then move to the harder things as you gain experience. If you're full of piss n' vinegar, ready to tackle a major job, then by all means there are a lot of elaborate types of shrines that one can build.

In the African Religious Systems (ARS)[80] there is precedent for using stair stringers and wooden two-by-sixes to construct what essentially are stair steps but are used as a Three Step Shrine.

Many like the idea of the Three Step Shrine as it is an ideal number representing the three types of spirit: the Dead, the Saints, and God. The only downfall to using the Three Steps Shrine is that it takes up quite a bit of floor space. Thus if you are space conscious, this type of shrine may not work well for you. I have this problem so I went for a wall shrine.

Wall shrines typically are shelves hung on the wall. That's it. Plain and simple. I got the rails, supports, shelves, and hardware from a do-it-yourself store, and with an electric drill, a tape measure, and a level, hanging the shelves was no difficult thing to do.

The drawback to having wall shrines is that you are limited by how deep the shelves are and how sturdy they are. Thus setting lots of heavy weight on them is a big no-no. You'll need to watch for the studs in the walls, and if you're in an old house where the studs are not every so many inches on center, you may need one of those anchoring kits to hold the screws in the lath or drywall.

Most of you will want to start off with something right away to get you going, which is a great idea, because the idea is to begin to work with your ancestors rather than just read about them.

Find a spot other than your bedroom to interact with spirits. This is because spirits, even good ones, may get ornery and begin to haunt your dreams or cause you hassles at night with making noise while you're trying to rest. Yes, I know some of you are going to say, "But I have nowhere else!" Then you will need to create a partition of some kind that separates you from your shrine. Even just hanging a sheet or blanket between your shrine and your bed will help. Or get one of those old dressing room dividers sometimes called a Three Fold.

## PREPARING THE SHRINE

Regardless of whether you opt to use a corner of your dressing room table, a chest of drawers, a corner in your kitchen counter, or even a wall shelf as a shrine, you first need to prepare it properly. Why? You don't invite a guest into a dirty home, do you?

---

80    These are the same traditions that I have referred to elsewhere in this book as "African Traditional Religions," or ATRs. - ed.

Simple soap and water is ideal for this stage of the work. Nothing more needs to be added because all you are doing is cleaning off the filth and dirt which is primarily dust. A dampened sponge with some warm water and a little bit of household soap will work fine. By household I mean something simple like Spic and Span. No harsh detergents needed unless the area is really filthy like, say, next to a bird cage or something that could get grime all over it quickly. If such *is* the case, then perhaps you need to rethink where you plan on placing the shrine.

Once the area is clean, then wipe down whatever it is you will be using as your shrine with the same soap, water, and sponge/rag. When the shrine itself is cleaned, wipe off excess moisture with fresh paper towels. Then pour a bottle of Florida Water and a bottle of Kananga Water together into a bowl. Pray over it and ask the spirits to bless it. Pour this into a spray bottle — the sort that has a spritzer head on it which you can get for about a dollar at any discount store. Use this to lightly spritz your shrine and then wipe it down with a paper towel.

The smell of the Kananga and Florida Waters are pleasing to the spirits and ancestors, and you can use this once in a while to lightly spritz your tools and wipe them down as well. The citrus flavoring in the waters tends to break up psychic vibrations and gives sort of a cleansing effect.

Use the water mixture mentioned in the previous paragraph to wipe the candle holder and outside of the glass you will use to fill with water for your spirits. Once this is done, you will set your shrine and shrine tools in the middle of the floor, where you will stand to the west of them while facing east, holding a lit tea-light candle without wearing any clothes.

Say, *"Spirits of my ancestors, father's side, mother's side, I come humbly to you naked as I was born into this world asking you to bless my shrine and all that I will be using on my shrine. Please help me make good decisions. Thank you."* Bend your knees slightly without bending forward and then come straight back up.[81]

Walk clockwise around the shrine until you are on the east side and facing west. Say, *"Spirits of my ancestors, father's side, mother's side, I come humbly to you naked as I was born into this world asking you to bless my shrine and all that I will be using on my shrine. Please help me make good decisions.*

---

81   You will note, in *Liber Donariorum*, I warned that the head should never be inclined toward the dead or chthonic spirits. - ed.

*Thank you."* Bend your knees slightly without bending forward and then come straight back up.

Now turn left and walk counter-clockwise until you reach the south and are facing north. Say, *"Spirits of my ancestors, father's side, mother's side, I come humbly to you naked as I was born into this world asking you to bless my shrine and all that I will be using on my shrine. Please help me make good decisions. Thank you."* Bend your knees slightly without bending forward and then come straight back up.

Finally, turn right and walk clockwise until you reach the north and face the south. Say, *"Spirits of my ancestors, father's side, mother's side, I come humbly to you naked as I was born into this world asking you to bless my shrine and all that I will be using on my shrine. Please help me make good decisions. Thank you."* Bend your knees slightly without bending forward and then come straight back up.

# OFFERINGS

## FIRE

Much has been written all over the Internet about offerings to Spirits. The first rule of thumb is that you need to give Them fire and water. Fire in the form of a candle is ideal. A plain, unscented, small white candle is ideal. Typically I use the unscented white tea-light candles for this and they work well. They burn about two hours before going out and the Spirits appreciate them.

You can use the Shabbat candles which are the Jewish religious candles that come in white and are much like the white household candles you can get at the store. Those tend to need a special-sized candle holder to be safe. I looked online and found two brass candle holders for the Shabbat candles which work quite well for the household-sized candles as well.

Another candle size that works are the votive-sized candles. Small and easily obtained from many stores, these are available in a wide variety of colors as well. Typically though you will want WHITE because you are dealing with the ancestors and that is one of their colors. Further, white encompasses all colors because it has all but black in its spectrum so using white for any project is acceptable.

I have not experimented with the chime-sized candles because it is difficult to find a safe candle holder for them. Thin metals and plastics just are not fire safe in my opinion, and the cost you save on the candles is offset by the hassle of using more than one. Chime candles do not burn long, roughly about an hour, and you really should have a little more than that burning. Thus, you either burn one right after the other, which is acceptable, or you break down and use one of the other candle sizes mentioned.

Can you go bigger? Certainly you can! For years I would obtain cases of white seven-day jar-encased candles which typically sell for $4–5 each nowadays. Back when I could get them for $1.25 each, I bought them by the case, but today they are too cost prohibitive both to purchase and to ship. Thus I prefer to use the smaller candles which are less expensive and easier to obtain.

# LIQUID OFFERINGS

## Water

The next thing you will need to give to your ancestors is water. This substance is the universal drink for all spirits bar none, especially the ancestors. They love it and it refreshes them.

The ideal water is rain water, but you have to have a system of collecting it, and in some states here in the US that practice is now illegal, so what to do? Okay, you can buy spring water to give to the spirits. This works well, and it is easily obtained from most anywhere from convenience to grocery stores. A gallon goes quite a ways, because it is not necessary to pour an entire glass of water for the spirits; just a quarter or a third of the glass is all that's needed.

Why not tap water? Most tap water has chlorine in it, and chlorine has been found to kill magic. At least it has in my experience. Thus, if you do not wish to nullify your magic, then do not use tap water. The way around this is simple: Fill a container with tap water and allow the chlorine to evaporate for twenty-four hours. That's it. Once the chlorine has evaporated, the water is safe to use in magic. I often fill a gallon jug and use a loose-fitting lid and let the lid sit loosely. Once it has sat for a full twenty-four hours, the chlorine smell is gone and it is safe to use.

You should use a glass made from real glass. Why? For some reason, the spirits like real glass as opposed to metal or plastic glasses. Oh, to get started if all you have is plastic cups, by all means use one. Just make certain you get either a glass or a ceramic cup later on. Yes, I realize that a large majority of you reading this have metal chalices used on your altar for libations and what not, but while that's acceptable to you, that does not mean it is acceptable to use with the spirits. Typically I use a small ceramic cup for my water offerings to my spirits, but I have used glass tumblers as well.

## White Wine

An acceptable alternative to water for spirits is white wine. It can be used as an incentive for the ancestors to work harder as a reward for helping you attain some desired goal. Female spirits tend to like this more so than male spirits do.

Are you a recovering alcoholic? Well, they do sell non-alcoholic white wine which is acceptable to the spirits. Your ancestors will not hold you guilty over this just because you have a cross to bear and are doing your best dealing with it. Buy the non-alcoholic brands and use them with confidence.

Barring that, you can use sparkling white grape juice as well, which is also an acceptable substitute for those who are recovering alcoholics.

## Coffee

Universally, coffee is a drink that many praise, sing, and shout to the heavens. It is a bitter drink that some put sugar and milk into, while others like it harsh, bitter, and strong. As the old Toyota commercial goes, "your mileage may vary" where this drink is concerned. However, when it comes to your ancestors, keep it simple and keep it black.

Must it be brewed? No, but you can. Can you use instant? Yes, you can. The ancestors and all spirits, as a matter of fact, love coffee. I've offered this drink to ancestors, deceased relatives, grimoire spirits, and so on. It's a universal drink and one that many prefer to have to wake themselves up.

Must it be top-shelf coffee? No. Taste and quality do not seem to be an issue for the ancestors where coffee is concerned. Now this does not mean, however, that if you have a deceased relative who had a fetish for a premium imported Columbian brand that you just not give them that. *Au contraire.* However, you make them *earn it.* Offer whoever your ancestor is that loved that imported premium Columbian coffee a steaming cup and remind them how good it was. Tell them that more is to come when they help you resolve _____. Always make your spirits earn special rewards and gifts. Never just give them these things else you will create a sense of entitlement in them, and woe unto you if you allow that to happen!

I purchased a set of Espresso cups from Amazon.com that I use for my temple room. Each cup holds only a small amount of coffee, and it makes making, handling, and pouring coffee so much easier than trying to mess around with full-sized cups. Further, the smaller sized Espresso cups take up much less room on each spirit's shrine, thus maximizing space.

Each cup also came with its own color-coded saucer to match the cup's color. This can be handy because spirits are territorial where Their things are concerned. You do not want to give your Head Spirit's cup to some other spirit by mistake. By using colored coffee cups, you eliminate any such risk.

So when should you give coffee? I typically give my spirits coffee when I feel they deserve it. My Head Spirit gets it more often than the rest, but if one of my others gets it, the rest get it. I prefer things to be simple and easy. Coffee can be reserved for when you need something to come through and you want your ancestors to step up their game and get a move on. Promise them some coffee if they do X and help with _____. Then when X gets done, give them some coffee. When _____ gets finished, offer them some coffee, maybe this time with a shot of liquor in it!

Oh, and realize that the Dead are crazy about coffee. Thus, if you ever have to work with a spirit of the dead who is being a bit uncooperative, promise it coffee and see if that won't help settle it down a little. In Haitian Vodu, it is a drink loved by the Guinea nation.

## Red Wine

Red wine is for hot spirits or rather making spirits hot. Thus, if you have a desire to get your ancestors moving fast on a request, you promise them a shot glass with some red wine with your demand under it.

Now just as in the white wine situation, if you happen to be a recovering alcoholic, I understand that and that's okay. You can buy the non-alcoholic red wine as well, OR, if you'd rather, get yourself some delicious red grape juice. It is an acceptable substitute and the ancestors are down with it. They understand and will NOT be offended regardless of what anyone tells you.

## Milk

Milk is reserved for the holy ones. It is for those who think they are pure and exalted; thus, you reserve giving milk to those who are like this. Only use this if you have pure or clean intentions in your demand. Thus, you would never give a negative demand to a spirit using milk.

## FOOD OFFERINGS

Now we come to the fun part, food! Spirits love to eat. Well, okay, they partake of the essence of food, or as my Vodu teacher likes to say, "They love to be reminded of what good food was like when they lived!" Thus, everything from ribs to chicken to pulled pork to steamed vegetables is up for grabs where food is concerned.

Now, before you start worrying what sorts of foods are appropriate to serve your ancestors, realize that what you do not want to give are things with onions and garlic in them. Why? I do not know. They just don't like it is all. I thought this was downright silly, so I set out to prove my teacher wrong by giving my spirits food made with onions and garlic.

When you leave food sit on a shrine for twenty-four hours, it usually has a certain look to it. The look is as if the food has been preserved somehow as if all of the essence of the food itself has been drawn away. But when I put food on their shrine that contained garlic and onions, it looked like any food you just left set out on your table. Yuck! So lesson learned. Give the spirits what they ask for and all will be well.

Do you cook the food? You can, but it is not necessary as you can go to the grocery store or to a restaurant and buy pre-cooked foods for Spirits. Just order it made without any garlic and onions, and you should be fine. Once in a great while I will give one of my Thralls (i.e., a minor, created Spirit) a hamburger from a fast food restaurant. I ask for it to be made plain: no condiments, no pickles, and no onions. Just a burger patty and bun. That is acceptable to the spirit.

You can offer other meats, fish, grains, nuts, vegetables, and so on for a meal just as you would the person in life. Realize that most spirits like meals served to them. It's presumed that this gives them the energy they will need to do the tasks the practitioner needs to be done.

The key is to present the meal to the four corners, i.e., east, west, north, and south, on a plain white dinner plate. The dinner plate should be ceramic, not plastic. Sit a small shot glass of liquor next to the food on the dinner plate, stand facing east, and say:

> *"Spirits of my ancestors, father's side, mother's side, I offer this food for you to eat and enjoy! May you use it to help me grow and prosper in all ways."* Now, as before, slightly bend your knees without bending forward then come straight back up. Turn right

to face west. Repeat. When finished in the west, remember to turn left (counter-clockwise) to the north and repeat. Then turn right to face the south and repeat.

When you are finished, place the white dinner plate with the food and drink on the ancestor's shrine. Now, using your index finger, take a tiny portion of the food and eat it. Say, *"Spirits of my ancestors, father's side, mother's side, I eat with you!"* Then take a tiny sip of the liquor and say, *"Spirits of my ancestors, father's side, mother's side, I drink with you!"* Then you are finished.

The eating and drinking is important and should always be done here so that your ancestors know that the food you provide is wholesome and something you yourself would eat. Believe it or not, there are fools out there who think they could get by giving their ancestors food from garbage cans. That will get you into trouble with your ancestors quickly.

## OTHER OFFERINGS

Of all the spirits out there, none are so easily satisfied as are the ancestors. They ask so little and are willing to give so much. Things that can make them feel very fond of you are hunting for and locating precious mementos that belonged to them while they were alive.

In some families, attics, basements, garages, sheds, and storage units are places where such mementos can be located and acquired. If you are able to acquire a favored lighter of a great uncle or penknife that your cousin loved or perhaps a recipe box your grandmother treasured or some such, you can acquire these and give them to your ancestors for their shrine.

You can give cigarettes, pipes, cigars, and such without having to light them up. Just open the pack of cigarettes and place them on the shrine. Open the cigar from its packaging and put it on the shrine. Tamp a pipe full of grandpa's favorite tobacco and set it on the ancestor shrine for him. No need to add fire. They'll understand, especially if you live where you can't smoke or you have allergies to it.

Another thing you need to give your ancestors are flowers. You do not need to buy a whole dozen either as one flower is plenty. Ancestors tend to like white flowers, so stop at a floral shop and buy them a white flower. Female spirits tend to like flowers more, but the male spirits will be thankful as well.

Colognes, after shaves, razors, hand mirrors, hair brush, combs, and make up kits are all things ancestors like as gifts. Again, do *not* simply give these gifts to your ancestors, but rather make your ancestors earn these or any gifts. They will appreciate them more and work harder for you.

Have an ancestor who liked games of chance? Put a deck of playing cards and/or a pair of dice for them to play with on the shrine. Maybe one liked comic books? Buy one of his favorites and put it on there after he has earned it.

Ancestors prefer to earn their gifts as they like to prove they can do things to win, succeed, and overcome for the sorcerer. Use their willingness and cooperative attitude. Now, realize you don't offer a gift to the ancestors every time you want them to do something for you. No! That'd get expensive and your shrine would be overly cluttered.

Typically your ancestors will work for three things: food, liquor, and money. Yes, they like money as well, and not that fake Hell Money that the Chinese Spirits like but real money like one dollar bills.

Just get a small wicker basket and set it next to your shrine. When you ask your ancestors to do something routine or not so special, put a one dollar bill into the wicker basket which pays for their help. If they feel that more payment is due for the amount of work needed, they will come to you and let you know in no uncertain terms, usually in your dreams.

Every time you ask your ancestors for help, give them the fire of the candle, the glass of water or some other liquid as discussed, and a one dollar bill. Then expect them to work for you. Not work miracles, mind you, but to work and help you succeed, overcome, and make your way through tough situations.

# Simple Workings with the Ancestors

Before I begin to explain how to work with your ancestors, it is first prudent to discover if you even need to do anything. You will need to begin to sleep with a glass of water and a white candle at your bedside table. This is so that you can ask for passage from your ancestors.

Stand and face east. Hold a small white candle safely in a candle holder with one hand and a small glass or ceramic cup of water in the other hand. Say, *"Spirits of my ancestors, father's side, mother's side, I come to you and ask passage for help with (explain what it is you need help with here). Feel free to speak clearly to me in my dreams."* Now, slightly bend your knees without bending forward and come straight back up. Turn right and face west. Repeat. Then turn left and face north. Repeat. Then turn and face south. Repeat. Sit the candle on your nightstand. You can snuff the candle out if you wish. Go to sleep.

Pay attention to your dreams. Realize that your ancestors may show up as deceased relatives or even folks who are living today. You can tell when you ask them to tell you their name. I've had some masquerading as a living relative. It's nothing to be frightened of nor any sort of bad omen at all. Instead, it is just a way of the ancestor to use imagery so as not to confuse nor scare us.

## GENERAL WORKINGS

Let it be said that the ancestors are both the first and last line of defense for the practitioner; thus, it behooves one to create a solid relationship with them. Unlike other spiritual avenues, this is not a get-rich-quick sort of route. By that I mean unlike some of the grimoire spirits who promise great wealth, it is not wise to form a bond with the ancestors on Saturday and then immediately on Sunday begin to pester one's ancestors for fast cash.

This is not to say that your ancestors do not care about you or won't intervene; however, they look upon your life as any authority/parent/relative would who is alive. Often the ones alive will listen to your problems and more often will chide you for making dumb decisions that got you there in the first place. Ancestral spirits, however, rarely speak back so boldly if you need to be told.

For me, they often visit me in my dreams as the dream world is far easier for a spirit to enter and communicate from than it is to materialize here. Thus, I have had to learn to pay more attention to my dreams and in particular *who* is in my dreams. There have been times my late grandparents have shown up, a few times my father, and once in a while other relatives I haven't spoken to in a long while.

## CONFESSION

One of the things I like to do is confess things I've done or said wrong to my ancestors. I use a formula that seems to work well and it goes something like this:

Using your forefinger, draw an equal-armed cross in the air over your shrine and say, *"Spirits of my ancestors, father's side, mother's side, I ask the Guardian of the Gates to open the way for me so that I may enter and speak with the spirits."*

Now say, *"Spirits of my ancestors, father's side, mother's side, by the right and the power of the governing spirits who watch over this place, I ask that you take heed and listen to me. I call out to (insert names of known deceased relatives here) to bear witness to what I will say. (Speak what weighs heavy in your heart)."*

When finished simply thank the ancestors for listening and ask them to continue to watch carefully over you as you pass back into the realms of man. Draw the cross in the air again over their shrine while you say, *"Guardian of the Gates, I salute and thank you for allowing me to enter and speak with my ancestors about these grave matters. Much honor to you."* Done.

## GENERAL ASSISTANCE

As I previously stated, the ancestors are not ones you merely conjure up for quick-fix situations; however, their role in your life is akin to walking in front of you and trying to smooth out the rough spots or point out the pitfalls so that you steer clear of them.

Do not get the idea that you are never to have *any* troubles, because what sort of life would that be? Boring! Troubles and problems create opportunities for us to utilize our skills, gifts, and talents as well as give us goals to work towards. That in themselves are mighty and worthy goals, are they not?

Here is my very own invocation, albeit choppy to allow you plenty of room to add names of ancestors as well as things you want or need in your life. This invocation should be said every morning when you get up so that your ancestors know what you need.

It's been my experience in working with spirits from a wide variety of sources since 1989 that often I have to repeat my requests to the spirit(s). Why? I do not know. My theory is that, wherever they are, they are working on things that interest them, and my requests, while highly important to me, are petty to them. Thus, repeated requests seem to work well for getting what it is I want.

*"By the spirits of my ancestors, father's side, mother's side, and by the power of the Guardian of the Gates, by the power of the Master of the Crossroads and by the power of Lord of the Cemetery, I call upon my personal ancestors (here insert deceased ancestors names) to come and partake of this water and fire and listen to my requests. First I would like to thank you for (here you list several things you are thankful for) and thank you for having (insert name of someone you love in your life here) in my life who makes living a*

*true joy. Please watch over and protect them as well as I and keep us safe from all harm. I have need of (insert those things you know you need here) and I would also like a few things such as (here you insert two or three things you would like to have). I am thankful for another wonderful day and multiple opportunities that I may partake of this life. I know soon enough I will join the ranks of the ancestors. Thank you."*

Now, in the invocation you will notice there are some aspects that you typically do not find in most ritual formula. First off we are calling on the powers of the gates, crossroads, and cemetery. Unless you are baptized into a particular spiritual tradition, it is ideal to simply refer to these beings as I have outlined them here without using any names. This will keep you out of trouble.

The first break is where you recite a litany of names of your deceased ancestors, if known. Many folks claim they do not know who their ancestors are. With the paper trails in today's society, it is rather difficult within the last thirty years for anyone to conceal a birth or death from a governmental database. And with some online sites utilizing these databases, we can find out who our parents and grandparents are for a small fee. Thus, you name the ancestors you are related to here, preferably ones who actually knew you, but if you grew up without knowing them, it is not the end of the world if they never met you.

You are also going to offer a small white unscented tea-light, household, or votive candle and a glass of water to the ancestors. It's protocol and respectful. You should have the candle holder and glass on their shrine anyway, so this should not be any surprise. Just fill, light, and begin.

You then list several things you are thankful for. Often I have thanked the ancestors for good health, a roof over my head, food in my pantry, money to pay my bills, the companionship of my cat, and so on. This is where you are genuinely thankful for the things you truly need. For instance, I need a special leg brace to walk properly, so I often mention this to the ancestors because it is a very expensive item and insurance only covers so much as you well know.

By thanking the ancestors for what you already have, you show courtesy and respect for what they have given you. This is opposite of what most want to do, which is complain about what they don't have. Before you ask, be mindful and thankful of what has been given to you already. Even if you had to pay for it out of pocket, that does not matter. The ancestors gave it to you. If you're a hard head who feels otherwise, then *pretend* for the sake of argument they gave it to you. Trust me on this one.

Now mention someone in your life you are thankful for having there. This could be a lover, a dear friend, a companion, a spouse, an animal, someone that makes your heart feel at ease and full of joy when you're around them. It should be someone you have strong feelings for rather than just the guy at the corner pub.

Now list those things you know you need. These are the things you truly want such as a fulfilling relationship or career, an education, or something that you know deep down inside is not a mere want but a need that has been unfulfilled in your life. Why ask? Ask and ye shall receive as the prophet stated. The ancestors listen and will process this for you.

Finally we come to the fun stuff. Here is where everyone wants to jump to immediately — the "gimme stuff" part. Here you name several things you'd like to have but can live without. Seriously. If you want a PS4 or Xbox One, ask for it. If you want a new Harley Davidson motorcycle, this is where you ask for it.

The idea is that the ancestors won't simply drop the item into your lap, usually; rather, they will drop the opportunity/ies to make the money necessary so that you can afford these items. The difference between your needs is that they will move heaven and earth to help you get into that career that will help you live a better lifestyle or raise you up from where you were.

Wants need to be differentiated from needs so that you're not crossing your wires with the ancestors. Try mixing them up and nothing will happen. Your ancestors are not stupid nor are they thick-headed. They can see things down the road ahead of you that you cannot see. This is why you will begin to notice more hunches, intuitions, gut reactions, and other instincts coming to your notice as you progress forward.

## THE DEMAND

Now, here is where we make the ancestors sit up and take note, giving them what is referred to in my Vodu House as a *demand* but elsewhere most folks refer to it as a *request*. The demand is written down on a piece of clean, unused paper in your own hand.

For a simple working, you would lay a good demand face up on a saucer or plate with a cup of coffee, glass of red wine, or shot glass of liquor on top of it. You could also just sit a glass of water on top of it as well.

Now, if you have a demand where you need someone to leave you alone, say some jerk at work, then after you write that out, lay it face down, and sit the cup or glass of liquid on top of it, because it is not a good demand.

Earlier when I mentioned the hamburger? Same thing here. Write your demand out on paper and then place it either face up if the demand is positive or face down if the demand is negative on a white ceramic dinner plate and place the hamburger on top of the demand.

Once you have positioned the food or liquor on top of your demand, then you offer the food or liquor on the white plate to the four corners as explained previously.

# In Summary

What I've attempted here is to help you with a simple system that will give you a leg up on other practitioners who either refuse to work with ancestors or who feel it is somehow beneath their status.

This is a system that works if you apply and use it. The concepts are simple enough that anyone with half a brain should be able to figure out how to use the invocation structure, what sorts of offerings are pleasing to the ancestors, how to give them to the ancestors, and then how to get the ancestors involved in your work.

The final thing to remember is to let all offerings sit on your ancestor's shrine for twenty-four hours then dispose of them either by pouring the liquids down the drain or putting the food items into a brown paper sack along with three pennies and dropping it at an intersection as the old folklore goes.

Hey, it's just as simple to put the sack with the pennies into the garbage and be done with it.

# The Back Yard Path
## toward the
### *Summum Bonum*

*Frater Rufus Opus*

s I've gone through the process of creating and projecting the Stone of the Wise over the years, I've learned a lot of amazing things from really smart people. Jake Stratton-Kent, Brother Moloch, Aaron Leitch, Jason Miller, and many others too numerous to list by name have been there teaching and saying, speaking and spelling the things they've presented in this anthology in conversations both public and private, and I will always be grateful for the opportunities I've had to appropriate and use their experience to my benefit. Magicians are great, and everyone should cultivate friendships with the best minds of their generation. Shortcuts and tech you just don't think of on your own get bandied about in passing. Other Magicians are a great resource.

That said, the best teachers of the art and science of making offerings over the years have always been *the spirits themselves*. Working with the Archangels and the elemental hierarchies of the terrestrial Kingdoms, with my head in the heavens and my feet in the chthonic realms, I've received an extremely wide range of requests for specific offerings from the spirits over the years. I've been asked for everything from scents of flowers to specific flavors of scotch that have a very particular degree of smoked peat flavor that can only come from a particular Scottish isle that rhymes with Mmmmmm-Islay. It was, however, my work with the spirits of place, the *Genii Loci*, that taught me the most subtle methods of conjure communion.

These spirits include the spirits of local flora, fauna, and the landscape around us. In my back yard, I've met some of the coolest and most powerful spirit familiars. In my early commercial-spiritual work, I had a client in San Antonio, Texas, who needed some very special personal Work, while I was stuck in Maryland. Fortunately, in my youth I had lived in Del Rio and had made friends with the local spirits of place near the Amistad reservoir. Because they remembered me, and I'd spent so much time with them, I was able to have my client get some material from the reservoir and form a physical link that I could work through with those spirits I had gotten to know so well to dissolve the spells levied against her.

I received my elemental initiations at the hands of the Genius Loci. I don't talk too much about it, but suffice it to say, Frater Ashen Chassan is not the only one who has had amazing experiences in spite of the source when working with *The 21 Lessons of Merlin*. It was a dark and stormy night, and it was me against the elements as I raced from one part of Aurora, Colorado, to another; Knowing, Willing, Daring, and Silently (because I could barely fucking breathe) completing my race against the spirits of Earth, Water, Wind, and Fire, and being welcomed into their ranks as a spirit of the Terrestrial Realm after completing the obstacle course I'd set for myself.

Since that evening, I have continued to learn a great deal from the local spirits of place. From them, I received boons and wisdom, and I continue to learn lessons about community, time, and place, and the intimate relationships between the offerings you make and the opportunities you receive as a result.

And that is the primary intent of this conversation: the subtle relationships between the offerings we make and the results we receive. I'm going to focus on meeting and greeting spirits of place through the provision of offerings, but beneath that, the hidden occult mystery of working with spirits I would most like to convey is the essence of how the things we offer in exchange for benefits received become key to the manifestation of the things we conjured the spirits to manifest on our behalf in the first place.

I'll wait a minute for that to sink in, because it's pretty convoluted.

Did you re-read it? Ok, good. Let's move on to making friends with the locals.

The best way to make friends with the locals is to go on a walk. Chances are you've been walking for a while, so I'll skip over the basic instructions in ambulation. However, when you're going on a spirit walk, it's different. Start out with some meditation, or prayer to your source. Open your spiritual senses. Meditate on the Orange Catholic Bible quote, "*Think you of the fact that a deaf person cannot hear. Then, what deafness may we not all possess? What senses do we lack that we cannot see and cannot hear another world all around us? What is there around us that we cannot know?*" Anoint yourself in holy oil or holy water, have a shot of something that softens the edges a bit, and assume an attitude of inner silence and observation.

Then go for a walk. I like to go out my back door and down the alleyways of my neighborhood. There you can see what's really going on in people's lives, who they really are, what they really stash next to the garbage pails that they haven't really gotten ready to get rid of yet. And people tend their back yards differently than they tend their front yards. Some people have really ornate gardens that no one passing by the front of their houses will ever see. These are my favorite people, who create majestic beauty for themselves, for their own sakes.

But also in the alleys, you get a feel for the spirits of the neighborhood. If there are a lot of active spirits, you get a sense of weight, pressure, and power. You get a feel for the elements that are strong on the block you're walking, and you sense where the invisible boundaries of spiritual influence have been drawn. Around my current house, there are a lot of Aerial spirits. We get birds, and the overall flow of the block is verbal, intellectual, conversant. We talk and think at each other.

Not far, there's another block that is all Earthy. The yards are verdant and overflowing in flowering vines, and there's a pressure in the air that isn't around here. There's a ponderous feeling of immense power in the earth, and you get a feeling that the trees are watching you, and that they do not necessarily approve of your presence.

As you take a walk, observe the flora and the fauna of the area. In cities, you'll see cultivated yards, but pay attention to that anyway. The people doing the cultivation are also being influenced by the spirits of place, and their efforts at gardening can tell you a lot about what the local spirits are like. Lots of orange and yellow flowers may indicate a fiery spirit sets the tone, while lots of fountains and ponds may indicate watery spirits are predominant. Look for patterns, themes, tones.

When you've figured out the types of spirits local to you, you can then begin putting together your offerings. Spirits of nature tend to prefer natural things, flowers planted, or nuts and seed left out for birds and squirrels. They like breads and meats. Set up a part of your yard, or set up a little table on your back porch or patio or balcony or whatever you have close to home that is outside, and place some things that match the theme and tone of your neighborhood on a plate in that space. It doesn't have to be extravagant. You are just trying to get their attention.

Watch for signs that the offering is being accepted. If it's being eaten, it's being accepted. If it's being left out untouched, try something else. Watch for other signs, like an offering decaying too quickly, or not at all when it should. Watch for anything out of the ordinary.

As you make contact, and you are feeling that you've managed to find the right approach to the local Sprightly Spirits, start to make verbal contact. Let them know what it is you're interested in, like developing a closer relationship. Let them know you have things for them to do and that you're willing to make offerings in exchange for their help.

Then, when you need something that an elemental spirit can help with, go to the place you've set up with an offering and announce what you have in mind while leaving the offering out. Repeat this process for nine days, and on the ninth day make a more formal ritual out of it. Light a candle and some incense, write up your statement of intent, leave it with the offerings you've placed around you, and then watch for the opportunities that will come your way.

For example, suppose I was looking to get something to happen more quickly in my life, and I wanted to enlist the aid of a fire elemental to heat things up a bit; I might make an offering of tiger lilly and a tiki torch lit at the same time each evening or morning for a certain amount of time. I might scatter some dried red pepper around the offering space or plant some mustard greens or some other flowers of the appropriate fiery color. For nine days, I'd talk about what I wanted unstuck, and then on the ninth day, I'd light a red candle, write up my statement of intent, light some incense, ask the spirits who have gathered to receive my offerings to now turn their attention to my problem as it is written on the paper, then burn the paper and let them take care of things.

Then I'd look for signs of success, for signs of opportunity. I'd watch for the colors of my offerings to show up in signs, portents, omens. For example, I'd talk to people who started conversations with me who were wearing the colors of the offerings. Or if I found myself reminded of the smell of the flowers I'd left out or planted when I met someone new, I'd take that as a sign that they were part of the solution I am looking for. Being open to see, to hear is important, and the offerings we make can serve us well to keep us from missing the opportunities we get when they appear.

Spirits of place and community are also good at conjuring us when they need us, and like any community, you must be aware that there will be times when you are needed the same way you need spirits. Being new to a community, you might ask for an opportunity to meet and greet your neighbors and receive an invitation to a block party. Then at the block party, you'll be introduced to a community activist who happens to be looking for someone with your skill set to publish a newsletter, or a local business leader who is looking for entrepreneurs who will help get the local economy pumping. You'll find opportunity to excel and get what you want, but it will end up being through service in ways that help contribute to the egregore of the community you're working within.

And that's how it ends up working, twelve times out of ten. Offerings made lead to opportunities to make more offerings that lead to more opportunities. As you get what you are looking for, the spirits you work with get what they also need, and our interaction with them becomes a dialogue, an ecosystem of giving and receiving that builds synergy and shifts paradigms . . .

Er . . . I apologize for that moment of 1990s-speak. It won't happen again.

But there's a pretty big and certainly important reason this kind of thing happens, Hermetically speaking. The system is built so that spirits and humans interact in a synergistic way, because humans are not, in spite of what we may think, separate from the spirit realm at all. We are spirits in a material world, as St. Sting sang so long ago.

He was only a more recent evocateur of something Dionysius the Areopagite pointed out in his *Celestial Hierarchies*, that humans are a "Choir of Angels." In each sphere between the Source of All that Exists and the Infernal Realms of Hell Beneath Us, there are Intelligences and Spirits, Archangels and Angels, Kings and Dukes and Prelates and Presidents and the infinite foot soldiers under them called Legionnaires. Every sphere has a main big guy that leads it, and under that guy there are servants who do their will.

Dionysius points out that Human Beings (that's you) are the "Angels" of the material world. We have a place in the hierarchy of entities, and we are supposed to work with the spirits "under" us the same way Buné leads his thirty legions of spirits.[82]

This is not the kind of thing a lot of people talk about. In fact, there may be some people out there who disagree with my conclusions, but they can go pound sand. It's sort of all laid out there where anyone can read it for themselves in the *Divine Pymander* of the Corpus Hermeticum (yes, Hermeticum,

---

82   Bune is a spirit found in the *Goetia of Solomon*, one of the books of the *Lemegeton*. All the spirits of the *Goetia* are said to command several legions of lesser spirits. -ed.

as in the holy books of Hermetics, and yes, I'm referring to *that Hermes*). Read it, read it again, and then read what it says. It's not that long, or that hard to figure out, but basically, we're little manifestations of God with privileges, and the Great Work is entirely about reminding you of that, because you forgot.

We work with spirits to help us remember. They know right away by looking at us who we are and what it's going to take to get us to remember how things work. Most of them are pretty cool about teaching us what we need to learn to take on our full responsibilities here on planet materialized Earth. All of them are eager to get us up to speed, because they all are looking for some help.

They are looking for a little guidance from anything resembling the First Father (a.k.a. "God," in whose image you happen to have been created, Hermetically speaking) and are more than willing to take you under their wing/hoof/claw/flaming appendage of doom to bring you the wisdom, insight, understanding, and skill so you are qualified to help them with their current situation, their needs, and their desires.

"But R.O.," you might find yourself saying, "What about the mugger-filching demons, for Frank's sake? They aren't, like, avuncular professors in the school of life with your personal attainment as their main goals; there are real spirits that really hurt you out there, man!"

Yes, you're right. All the spirits in your neighborhood aren't going to be particularly pleasant to work with. I didn't say it would be fun; I only said they will help you get to the point where you can help them do what they think needs to be done. I also didn't say they would be right. They have limits to their vision the same as everyone else who isn't fully one hundred percent consciously the SOURCE OF ALL THAT IS.

You don't have *carte blanche* to check out your brain just because you're part of an overall system that works together for the good of itself and its participants. You'll see what I mean as you go along, but there's a reason you're in God's image with a Ruach and the ability to discern between what you want and what you don't want. Consciousness is not optional, and choices will have to be weighed and made, and it's all on you. No excuses.[83]

If it's all starting to seem a little more complicated than you wanted it to be, I apologize, and commiserate. I wanted this all to be easy too, but it's not. I mean, it is pretty simple in practice, but figuring out what you want to

---

83    See the introduction of this book for important warnings about *staying in charge* of your spirit relationships. -ed.

do and whether doing what you want will actually bring you what you want is harder than it looks.

And before I go any further, I'd like to talk about the dead. Agrippa lists the *Ishim* as one of the choirs of angels. You and I know them as "Saints," which are the holy dead. The holy dead humans: people who have died and gone over to the spirit realm but are still influencing the material realm regularly.

In the Olde Dayes (think Persians and Greeks, not Saxons and Nords), the Genii Loci were not just the local plant and animal spirits. They included the local Heroes, the Honored Dead. Many communities had shrines to the local main big guy who died fighting off lots of the enemies, and they made regular offerings to this guy to get his favor. He was usually a spirit you would go to for help in defending your city from attack or to receive blessings and aid in getting made and paid through barter and trade.

Today we still have the dead among the Genii Loci, but in our American culture, there isn't a lot of veneration going on. Our psychopompery sucks. There aren't yearly rites to the local *Agathosdaimon*,[84] and hardly anyone leaves out black beans to clean out their dead. Worse, the echoes of those killed in terrible ways, by vehicles, murders, or long, slow diseases are as influential in our local spiritual neighborhoods as any other type of spirit.

Working with the dead is not the subject of this particular essay, but it's worth noting that in your travels, you may well run into this type of spirit. Offerings left out and about for elementals may well attract the hungry dead. There's nothing wrong with working with these spirits if you're into that kind of thing, but if you aren't an initiate of the Saturnian side of things, it might behoove you to put some time and attention in becoming familiar with this side of the realms of the Genii Loci. I haven't read the offerings of the other contributors to this compendium, but the writings of Jake Stratton-Kent spring quickly to mind if you're looking for a resource to work with in this vein. Brother Moloch's had a lot of useful things to say on the subject over the years I've known him as well.

Bear in mind always this: offerings matter, and words said. Most of our interactions with spirits of any type can be boiled down to those two things, and offerings, "payment" to spirits can almost always be understood as a physical manifestation of our paying attention to them in ways they can understand. In my experience, all Hermetic magic can be understood as the

---

84   "Good Spirit" — the term is used to indicated a very powerful personal helper/ guardian. -ed.

expression of our intent or Will and our reception of the resulting experiences. It's all summed up nicely in the Thoth Deck's Universe card. We express, we experience, and in between we dance with the multitudes of manifest spirits, taking our will and fill of love as we see fit.

So assume your role, take your place in the hierarchy of spirits in your neighborhood, in your community, in your world. Start small, or large, with an evening's walk or an all-out evocation. Make your offerings and expect it to bring you closer to the accomplishment of something you're still figuring out.

Whatever you do, pay attention to whatever you do. It's pretty key to figuring out what you want.

# RITUAL OFFERINGS IN
# NEW ORLEANS VOUDOU

*Denise M. Alvarado*

Change itself does not destroy a culture. All societies are constantly evolving. Indeed a culture survives when it has enough confidence in its past and enough say in its future to maintain its spirit and essence through all the changes it will inevitably undergo.

~ Wade Davis, *The Wayfinders: Why Ancient Wisdom Matters in the Modern World*

he term *ritual offerings* is typically not clear when discussed among people without a background in religion or the magickal arts. Many times the concept is conflated and confused with *sacrifice*, which has a similar, albeit different function and meaning when considered within the context of the African Traditional Religions (ATRs). Further, when it comes to pairing the words *Vodou, Voudou, Vodun, Voodoo,* or *Voudou* with the term *ritual offerings*, the non-practitioner will likely get images in their heads of blood spilled from the killing of animals — and even humans — by savages, for the purpose of appeasing a heathen god.

All forms of African-derived traditions practice animal sacrifice to some degree, including New Orleans Voudou, which enjoys the unfortunate notoriety of the sacrificial black cat rituals (Hurston, 1932; Tallant, 1946). The practice of animal sacrifice did not begin or end with African traditions, however. Western traditions (including Christianity) are well known for their history of human and animal sacrificial practices; yet, the manner in which it is viewed and presented in popular and scientific literature is often not offered in equal measure, no doubt a function of colonialism and prejudice. Whereas the offering of a ritual sacrifice is viewed as an extreme act of faith and devotion to the biblical God, the ritual act of offering an animal sacrifice to an African God is presented as savage and inhumane.

In New Orleans Voudou, animal sacrifice has been slowly but steadily fading away into a tradition of the past, and in its place bloodless sacrifice or ritual offerings, such as food and libations, are the primary method of feeding the diverse pantheon of spirits. This natural evolution has differentiated New Orleans Voudou from her religious counterparts and is the topic of controversy amongst practitioners of closely related traditions. The controversy stems from the belief that bloodless sacrifice holds less *aché* (divine energy) and is thus a less powerful offering.

For some traditionalists, the lack of offering an animal in sacrifice denigrates a religion to an inferior status and makes ceremonies that previously called for it incomplete. Of course, this is a matter of perception. The argument can be made that all living things have aché if all things are created by an all-powerful and divine Creator. The assignment of degree of aché and categorization of sacrifice type is a function of the participant's motivation that supports "sacrificial rituals; the traditional categories of praise, thanksgiving, impetration and satisfaction would correspond here" (Eliade, 1995, p. 545). In fact, in the traditional African religions there are two types of sacrificial or ritual offerings: petitional and remembrance. Petitional sacrifices can consist of blood or bloodless offerings, while remembrance sacrifices are typically bloodless as they concern the Ancestors.

This essay focuses on the concept of ritual offerings in New Orleans Voudou. I will begin by offering a description of New Orleans Voudou as a religion and defining the differences between *ritual sacrifice* and *ritual offering*. I will discuss the natural evolution of many practitioners of New Orleans Voudou to bloodless temples and a "no harm to animals" practice. A protocol for ritual offerings in graveyard work is then discussed. The essay culminates with a discussion of three major spirits of the New Orleans Voudou pantheon — Marie Laveaux, St. Expedite, and Black Hawk. These spirits are discussed and their appropriate ritual offerings are identified and described in detail. Finally, special recipes for favorite food offerings to these spirits are given.

# WHAT IS NEW ORLEANS VOUDOU?

New Orleans Voudou originated from the ancestral religions of the African Diaspora, specifically Vodun. A direct link to West African Vodun is easily traced through slave records that indicate the first Africans who set foot in New Orleans in 1719 were from the Bight of Benin, who brought the Vodun religion with them (Hall, 1992). The other two-thirds of the first slave arrivals were from Senegambia (Hall).

Subsequent African cultural groups that arrived in Louisiana during the slave trade include the Bambara, Mandinga, Wolof, Fulbe, Nard, Mina, Fon (Dahomean), Yoruba (Nago), Chamba, Congo, Ibo, Ado, Hausa, and Sango.

Each of the regions from which the slaves were stolen had their own religious and magickal practices, and these traditions were all brought to the shores of Louisiana with the enslaved Africans. After the United States purchased the Louisiana territory in 1803, there were several influxes of immigrants from Saint Domingue (Haiti) as well, who brought with them their version of Caribbean Vodou and their own pantheon of Spirits, many of whom were adopted into the New Orleans Voudou pantheon.

New Orleans Voudou is a religious system based on three levels of spirit: God, the loa, and Ancestors. Voudou believers accept the existence of one ultimate god referred to as *Bon Dieu* (Good God), below which are the powerful entities referred to as loas, spirits and saints. These powerful entities act as intermediaries between Bon Dieu and humans and are responsible for the daily matters of life in the areas of family, love, money, happiness, wealth, and revenge. As in African Vodun, veneration of the Ancestors is considered to be the foundation of the New Orleans Voudou religion.

Voudou in New Orleans has consistently undergone change as a result of the intermingling of the various African tribal groups and the influence of Native Americans who often shared the same slave masters, or who, in some instances, were slave masters. Since the city was a major port where multiple cultures converged, influences of European, Canadian, and Caribbean cultures were inevitable as well. The ultimate gumbo of cultural influences on colonial Louisiana included people of French, Canadian, Spanish, Latin American, West Indian, German, Irish, English, Scottish, Jewish, Native American, and African descent. Some of these cultures have left their mark on New Orleans Voudou as well.

New Orleans Voudou is also noted for its marked Catholic influence. It became syncretized with the Catholic religion as a result of the massive forced migrations, displacements of the slave trade, and especially during the implementation of Louisiana's Black Code in 1865.[85] It was African ingenuity that resulted in the incorporation of saints into the New Orleans Voudou pantheon of spirits — the similarities between some of the saints and Voudou spirits (*loas* and *orishas*) were such that a saint could act as a sort of stand in for public worship of the loa. Since a person could be whipped, branded with a *fleur de lys*, and killed for practicing African traditional religions, the saints were used to cloak the spirits in Catholicism, allowing the African traditions

---

85   Through the Black Code laws, slave owners forbade Africans from practicing Voudou under penalty of torture and death and forced them to convert to Catholicism.

to survive.[86] This process is referred to as *syncretism*. While this syncretism no longer serves the same function of preservation and protection as it did in the past, it nonetheless remains popular in practice today — although both spiritual entities (i.e., saint and spirit) are recognized as individuals and unto themselves.

Finally, the term *Creole Voudou* is commonly used by Louisiana locals to describe our unique brand of Voudou. It refers to an acknowledgment of many cultural influences and a blending of religious and magickal elements. Because of the multicultural influences on New Orleans culture and Voudou specifically, New Orleans Voudou never did follow the same manifestation and evolution as its sister religions Haitian Vodou, Santeria, and Palo, for example. Influences of each of these religions can be found in New Orleans Voudou; but, because of the sociopolitical climate, the formal, community-driven rites of the religion were lost. When devotees of the religion went underground to avoid persecution subsequent to the Black Codes, so did its rites. What has emerged are what was retained in individual families. And, because many New Orleans Voudouists are also initiated in other ATRs, many times all of the religions are included under the umbrella term *Voudou* in New Orleans, furthering the confusion to outsiders.

# Ritual Offerings vs. Sacrifice

Sacrifice and the drinking of blood were integral parts of all Voodoo ceremonies. Usually it was the blood of a kid that was used, but often it was that of a black cat. (Tallant, p. 15)

For the most part, the words *sacrifice* and *offerings* are used interchangeably in everyday speech. But, there are important differences between the two acts of devotion when discussed in the context of the African traditional religions.

Almost always, when the word *sacrifice* is used in the context of the African religions, it insinuates the offering of the life of a sentient being to a Spirit in exchange for divine assistance in satisfying a personal need. Complicating

---

86    The Lucumi teacher Ochani Lele once related to me that the Saints are honored and revered today for *protecting* the Orishas (Santeria) and Loas (Voudou) during the dark days of slavery. -ed.

the issue is a lack of an agreed upon definition of *sacrifice* amongst academics, leaving modern religious studies to couch such discussions "in the context of the Latin concept of *sacrificium*: sacred action" (Eliade, 1987, 544). According to the Merriam-Webster online dictionary, *sacrifice* is "the act of giving up something that you want to keep especially in order to get or do something else or to help someone; an act of killing a person or animal in a religious ceremony as an offering to please a god; a person or animal that is killed in a sacrifice," while *offering* is "something that is given to God or a god as a part of religious worship; an act of giving a religious offering." These differences are summed up by Van Baal (1976) who posits an "offering [is] every act of presenting something to a supernatural being, a sacrifice [is] an offering accompanied by the ritual killing of the object of the offering" (Van Baal, 1976, p. 161). These definitions — while incomplete and somewhat ambiguous — provide a starting point for the present discussion.

One dimension the stated definitions do not account for is bloodless sacrifice, which is especially pertinent to the discussion as it pertains to New Orleans Voudou. Blood sacrifice is the killing of an animal and offering it or its organs, bones, or other parts in ritual. Bloodless sacrifice is the offering of food, plants, bread, and liquids, for example.

Two major spiritual leaders of New Orleans Voudou, Louis Martinie and Sally Ann Glassman, have openly stated they do not practice animal sacrifice. Glassman, who is a vegetarian, has stated she never did practice animal sacrifice. Martinie, on the other hand, has discussed his evolution from a practitioner who engaged in frequent animal sacrifice to someone who does not, nor does he participate in ceremonies that engage in animal sacrifice. This choice, he states in his book *Talking to God with Food: Questioning Animal Sacrifice,* is the result of conversations and contact with Tibetan Tantric Elders who "caused me to reexamine not so much my love for the loa as the ways in which that love is expressed" (Martinie, 2012, p. 13).[87]

On the other hand, in an interview with *The Southerner* by Brooks Boliek (n.d.), Priestess Miriam Chimani of the New Orleans Voodoo Spiritual Temple stated there are rituals that include animal sacrifice; however, "It is not done in the Voodoo order until one understands what's going on," she said. "It can be a big part of a ceremony, but not today until people fully understand and

---

87    For more on this, see Jason Miller's *Severed Head Cakes and Clouds of Dancing Girls.* -ed.

use it properly."[88] There are other practitioners who decline to comment on the practice due to the inflammatory nature of and public reaction to the issue.

# RITUAL OFFERINGS AND GRAVEYARD WORK

Working in the graveyard is a common and primary activity for many New Orleans Voudouists, especially among those who also practice rootwork. Thus, there are important protocols to observe when working in graveyards, because cemeteries are the domain of the *Guede*, the spirits of the dead. The Guede are traditionally led by the Barons (La Croix, Samedi, Cimitière, Kriminel) and Manman Brigit, and are loud, rude, crass, sexual, fun-loving spirits. When entering their domain, it is customary to make an offering to the head Guede, Baron Samedi. (He is syncretized with St. Expedite in New Orleans Voudou.)

In New Orleans Voudou, offerings are left at three different times during graveyard work, depending on the nature of the work being done there. If you are entering a cemetery for the purpose of buying graveyard dirt, for example, offerings must be made upon entering the cemetery, at the point of buying the dirt, as well as upon leaving the cemetery. Each of these offerings are made for specific reasons. Primary is the fact that graveyards are alive with spirits and haints. Many spirits just linger around and are quite opportune in behavior; they will attach themselves to you while you engage in your ritual activities if you are not careful and do not take certain precautions. Observing proper graveyard procedures will prevent hauntings and spiritual hitchhikers from following you home and wreaking havoc.

Prior to entering a cemetery, one must ask permission. Consider that the cemetery is the home of the Dead and the one in charge, Baron Samedi, is the caretaker. Before barging into their home, it is common courtesy to knock, provide an offering, and ask permission to enter. There are many variations on this theme, but a general rule of thumb is to stand at the gate and knock three times on the ground. Then, leave three pennies to the gatekeeper and ask if it is okay to enter. Tell him what your business is there. If all feels good, then proceed.

---

88    Also see the section on blood offerings in *Liber Donariorum*. -ed.

Leaving a cemetery is just as important as entering. When you are ready to leave, pour some rum on the ground and back out of the cemetery.[89] Thank the gatekeeper for allowing you to visit and do your work.

The other offering one should make in a graveyard is during whatever activity one is there to do. Common activities include visiting an ancestor or loved one, gathering grave or graveyard dirt, and hiring a spirit. There are different offerings that can be left, and there is no hard and fast rule of thumb. That said, there are common practices that hold special cultural meaning in African American cultural history:

## Candles

Among the most common offerings to the deceased are simple candles. Candles are said to represent the souls of the departed. Catholics will often leave candles on graves as a way of showing that prayers have been said for the deceased.

## Shells

Some of the offerings found on African American graves hold ancestral memories. White shells and conch shells are a common sight. Prior to being placed on a grave, however, conch shells are bleached completely white. They are then placed at the foot and head of the grave with smaller shells decorating the border. The border serves to delineate the realm of the dead from the realm of the living. Shells also represent the sea. The sea was the means of transporting slaves to the Americas, and it is believed to be the way back home (North by South, n.d.).

## Coconuts

Coconuts are another traditional offering. Offering a coconut to a spirit in a grave symbolizes food for the spirit. Coconuts have been a cash crop and a source of food for a very long time in areas in Africa where they grow. In addition, leaving letters, photos, and other personal possessions are other ways of communicating with the dead.

---

89    Apparently this is done to fool the spirits of the graveyard. They will think you are *entering* the property, and will therefore not be motivated to follow you home. -ed.

## Coins

A very common offering is that of coins of various denominations. Fifteen cents is commonly offered to the spirit of any grave where any activity is conducted. In addition to coins, a small bottle of rum is also offered. Offering coins as a means of payment has its roots in African traditions. Coins were placed on the eyes of the deceased to keep them closed. They were placed in the palms of the deceased to represent their contribution to the ancestors, as well as for payment for crossing over in a good way. Coins were also placed around the gravesite for the same reasons. Clearly, a connection can be seen between this old custom and the ongoing practice of leaving money at the gravesite as payment for services rendered (Alvarado & Angelique, 2012, p. 32).

## Buying Grave Dirt

The means of collecting graveyard dirt is what gives it its power. Grave dirt is dirt collected from an actual grave and is always purchased from the spirit of the deceased who lies in the grave. A magical contract is made with the spirit, and the dirt is usually paid for with coins and rum or whiskey. Graveyard dirt is purchased from the guardian of the cemetery and gathered from the general cemetery grounds. Nine pennies, fifteen cents, and a silver dime are common coin combinations offered as payment for grave and graveyard dirt. Some Voudouists offer a dime to the entire cemetery and all of its inhabitants; others just leave it at the one grave where the dirt was collected. If you are collecting dirt from the cemetery at large and not a specific grave, leaving your offering at the gates for the entire cemetery and its inhabitants is appropriate. It is also appropriate to place a dime into the hole you dig to get your dirt and then cover it up.

Graveyard dirt is traditionally used in many ways. It is used for ancestor reverence, protection spells, coercive love spells, court case spells, harming, and enemy tricks. Graveyard dirt can be used as an offering itself on altars of various spirits having to do with the dead. It is also kept on ancestral altars (particularly if the dirt is from the grave of an ancestor), and it is kept in prendas (Palo) and spirit pots (New Orleans Voudou).

## Hiring a Spirit

When dirt is collected from a grave, it is possible to hire the spirit of that grave to perform a job for you. Sometimes spirits cooperate and other times they don't. Hiring spirits can be a dangerous activity if you don't know what you are doing. Doing any kind of work in a graveyard is not a frivolous affair and requires mindful intention, especially when hiring a spirit to assist you in a given work. A good rule of thumb is to get to know the spirit before hiring it. Do some research on the spirit by looking into the history of the cemetery and the various people buried there. Take some time to walk around and observe the signs and symbols, and listen (Alvarado & Angelique, 2012, pp. 33–34).

In the book *Workin' in da Boneyard*, Madrina Angelique provides some direction for hiring a spirit:

Take some offerings of food, flowers and whiskey or rum with you to the graveyard. If you know a particular spirit was a teetotaler, leave out the alcohol. You may also want to bring a candle and walk around the graveyard by candlelight if you are working at night. As you approach a grave, set the candle down and meditate for a few moments. Ask the spirit if it is willing to do the work you ask. Listen quietly for your answer. If they agree, tell them exactly what you want them to do. Tell them what you will pay them for the work. After you have reached an agreement with the spirit, proceed with taking a little dirt from the head, heart and foot of the grave. It is only necessary to dig a couple of inches deep. (Alvarado & Angelique, 2012, p. 35)

Offerings can also consist of an activity as opposed to an object. For example, if it is needed and you are so inclined, take some time to tidy up the grave where you are working. If there are weeds growing up around the grave, pull them, and if there is dirt on the gravestone, brush it clean. Prayer can also be an offering. Informal prayer in the graveyard can be addressed to the spirit of the grave, the spirits of all the Dead who reside there, as well as to the Guede or Baron Samedi. The important thing is that it is a heartfelt prayer, said with meaning. Whatever you do, be sure to thank the spirit of the grave and leave the cemetery going a different way from whence you came.

# RITUAL OFFERINGS TO THE SPIRITS

New Orleans Voudou altars come in many sizes and shapes. Some spirits prefer their altars and offerings to be on the ground as parterres, while others require three-tiered altars. The parterres are arrangements of offerings that are spread out on the floor if inside, or on the ground if outside, and are reminiscent of a festive picnic. A white cloth is laid down, and offerings of food, flowers, candles, and incense are placed on top of the cloth in a variety of arrangements. The candles are placed on the four corners of the cloth if outdoors, and in the four corners of the room if indoors, and are of a color or colors specific to the type of work being done (i.e., green for money, white for blessings, red for love or power). In the book, *Voodoo in New Orleans* by Robert Tallant (1946), there is a detailed description of a parterre layout for offerings:

Then, he spread the tablecloth on the floor in the center of the room . . . Green and white candles were stood on the end on the cloth and other candles of various colors were placed beside these, in a circle around the picture. On each side of this circle he placed a quart bottle, one containing cider, the other raspberry pop. He laid saucers and small dishes here and there, one filled with steel dust on the right side of the picture, another holding dried orris root in front of it. A plate of dried basil was placed on the other side of the picture and another plate, containing the flat hard cakes called "stage planks," was put in front of the dried basil. Behind the picture he laid a five-cent box of gingersnaps. Around the edges of the cloth he laid dishes containing mixed birdseed, cloves and cinnamon, and on each side a bowl of congris. A small bottle of olive oil was placed at the very far edge of the cloth on the left side, and behind this was placed a small paper sack of sugar. On the far right he put a hand of bananas with a saucer of small red apples nesting close to it. A branch from a camphor tree was carefully laid in front of the picture. Then, in front of all, he placed a pint of gin and a bottle of beer. (Tallant, 1946, p. 157)

Aside from the parterres and the three-tiered altars, there are some spirits who prefer their offerings be in cast iron (such as Iron Joe and Annie Christmas), sea shells (La Sirene and La Baleine), or in a bucket of sand or dirt (Ancestor pots and Black Hawk). In fact, the diversity of altars and accompanying offerings is quite remarkable. As it would be impossible to describe all of the ritual offerings for the spirits in the New Orleans Voudou pantheon here, I have chosen to highlight three major spirits that represent well the diverse and idiosyncratic nature of the religion: Marie Laveaux, St. Expedite, and Father Black Hawk. These spirits are unique to New Orleans Voudou and differ in significant ways from each other, driving home the point that New Orleans Voudou embraces the spirits of the cultural traditions that surround her, and calls her own those who come knocking.

## Marie Laveaux

The legend of Marie Laveaux was kept alive by twentieth-century conjurers who claimed to use Laveaux techniques, and it is kept alive through the continuing practice of commercialized voodoo in New Orleans (Salzman, 1996).

Marie Laveaux is the iconic Voudou Queen of New Orleans who has risen to the status of loa within the New Orleans Voudou pantheon. People from all walks of life went to Marie Laveaux for all kinds of things. There was never a situation she couldn't handle, though she did not take all cases. Like most professional practitioners, she had her own criteria for the jobs she took on, and one of those criteria was payment. She was a consummate businesswoman and, in fact, is credited for singlehandedly making a business out of New Orleans Voudou and Hoodoo.

Marie Laveaux was a remarkable woman, both for her time and even by today's standards. Her shrewd business sense had her serving the bourgeoisie, comforting the sick, and counseling the rich and the poor. Her charms were known for their efficacy and are said to have sold for thousands of dollars. That said, she is known for her charity and pro bono work with the incarcerated and the sick.

Marie Laveaux's influence and contribution to New Orleans Voudou and Hoodoo is extremely significant. She smiles favorably upon those who know how to serve her correctly. Others who try and fall short do not have her favor, and it is not unheard of for her to wreak a bit of havoc upon their lives as a result. She is a strong female Spirit who knows her worth and commands respect in spirit, as well as in life.

Marie Laveaux's altar is a three-tiered altar. Three-tiered altars are a traditional style of altar in Louisiana for those who work with the saints and candle magic. As with all loas, Marie Laveaux is best served with her favorite things and colors. She was a hairdresser, so offerings related to that profession are desirable. She was a devout Catholic, so Catholic iconography and prayer items are good. Here are some of her attributes to get you started:

**Feast Day:** June 23–24th, St. John the Baptist Day — the most important Voudou holiday in New Orleans

**Birthdate:** September 10, 1801

**Colors:** Blue, white

**Offerings:** Fresh flowers, candles, healing-related items like mortar and pestle, herbs, beauty-related items like mirrors, combs, head scarves, gris-gris, images of saints, rosaries, chaplets, money, cigars, white rum, French wine, candy, Voodoo dolls, incense, perfumes, silver and gold jewelry, donations to charity in her name. A photo of her tomb in a nice picture frame is nice to have on her altar. Blue candles are used and you can leave New Orleans themed items, such as beads, doubloons, Mardi Gras keepsakes. Pumpkins are good, as are seven-day hoodoo candles, cakes, and money. Catholic items are good; images of saints, crosses, and rosaries are especially good. What she likes the best is for us to donate to the poor and volunteer our time in her memory as a humanitarian to help those who are less fortunate. Some people say that leaving her pennies is insulting to her; she requires a LOT more than a few pennies.

**Snake figurine** — King Snake, Water Moccasin, Rattlesnake, Python, or Boa Constrictor.[90]

**Foods:** Hoppin' John, congris, money greens, gumbo, jambalaya, all Creole foods and soul foods.

### Creating Marie Laveaux's Altar — First Tier:

This is the bottom tier. Most often the bottom tier is the floor. Spread out a blue cloth. On either side of the tier, place fresh flowers in blue or white vases. Place four candles at the four cardinal points of the lower tier. Place your various offerings on this level. Place a plate for her food offerings on this level.

### Creating Marie Laveaux's Altar — Second Tier:

Place the elevation shelf or table on top center towards the back. Drape this layer with another blue or white cloth. On either side of this level, place images of St. Anthony and St. Peter (or you can substitute Legba for St. Peter). Place three more white candles — two on either side and one in the middle. You can place more flowers on both sides of this level.

### Creating Marie Laveaux's Altar — Third Tier:

Place the third elevated shelf on top center and drape with another blue cloth. Place a doll or figurine of Marie Laveaux in the middle of the top layer, with a snake figurine at her feet and the special blue candle next to her but not in front of her. Keep a chaplet or rosary on this level.

Note that these are basic guidelines, and you will want to personalize it by placing other items from the offerings list on the altar as well.

Once you have all of your offerings placed on her altar, say to her: *"Mam'zelle Laveaux! Do you see these offerings I have given you? You are the most powerful and most beautiful of all the Vooudous! Come and partake of these gifts I have for you!"* Then, ask her for what you need. Be sure to thank her when all is said and done.

---

90    The Python or Boa Constrictor represents *Li Grande Zombi*, and the others represent her signature snake conjure — they are two separate things and are NOT interchangeable.

## The Wishing Tomb

Though not a traditional New Orleans Voudou ritual per se, the tomb where Marie Laveaux is buried has become a pilgrimage site for Voudouists and others interested in paying homage to the infamous Voodoo Queen. Referred to as the Wishing Tomb, it is located in St. Louis Cemetery No. 1, the oldest graveyard in New Orleans, Louisiana. As a pilgrimage site, it is a major location on the map of New Orleans' sacred geography.

Indeed, the magickal properties ascribed to Marie Laveaux's final resting place is one of the most intriguing pieces of New Orleans folklore. Miracles have reportedly occurred after performing the rite associated with the tomb. The most remarkable story is of a Missouri woman who won two million dollars in the state lottery after reportedly making her wish there.

On any given day, Mam'zelle Laveaux's tomb can be found with a cornucopia of gifts on the ground next to it. People customarily leave offerings of coins, Mardi Gras beads, doubloons, candles, Voodoo dolls, gris-gris, flowers, written letters, and a host of other things. The tomb is almost always covered with graffiti consisting mostly of X's written with pieces of broken red brick confiscated from neighboring tombs.

Mam'zelle Laveaux's presence can often be felt strongly at her graveside. She reportedly responds to the types of offerings left for her, so it behooves a person to learn what her favorite things are (refer to the above list and you will do just fine). Some report being slapped when leaving certain offerings at the foot of Marie Laveaux's tomb, presumably due to the inappropriate nature of the offerings. I once saw a dead water moccasin someone left at her gravesite. This is the epitome of the wrong type of offering and is actually beyond disrespectful. Just because New Orleans Voudou has the serpent at the center of its pantheon, and Marie Laveaux is famous for her boa constrictor named *Zombi* that accompanied her in ceremonies (after the loa *Li Grand Zombi*), it does not mean she wants dead snakes as offerings. In the eyes of Voudouists, this kind of offering is akin to leaving a dead Jesus at the steps of a Christian Church.

There are a number of versions of the actual ritual for making a wish at the Wishing Tomb. This is the way I learned it. First, you place your offerings at the foot of her tomb. Then, knock on the tomb three times, calling out her name each time: "Mam'zelle Laveaux! Mam'zelle Laveaux! Mam'zelle Laveaux!" Then, you can state your wish either out loud or to yourself. Then draw three X's on the grave with your finger (I was originally taught to use red brick, but have since abandoned that practice in response to the preservation efforts of her tomb). Turn around three times after doing so. Then go across the street to the Our Lady of Guadalupe Chapel where she used to do her charity work and light a candle in her honor. Doing some charity work is also highly recommended as an offering to her for helping you.

Some spirits are only given part of their offerings when petitioned and then given the remainder after they have helped. This is never done with Marie Laveaux. Always give her all the offerings you can upon making your petition. She is, after all, the Queen.

## Recipe for Hoppin' John

Hoppin' John is one of Marie Laveaux's favorite offerings. Here is a recipe that was handed down to me from my mother:

*Ingredients*
- 1 lb. black-eyed peas
- 8 slices bacon, cut into fourths
- 1 ½ cups onions, finely chopped
- 1 cup celery, finely chopped
- ½ cup bell pepper finely chopped
- 2 ½ quarts water
- 2 cloves garlic, minced
- ⅛ teaspoon Creole spice seasoning blend
- ⅛ teaspoon thyme
- 1 bay leaf
- ⅛ teaspoon rosemary
- ½ teaspoon salt
- ¼ teaspoon black pepper
- 2 cups raw jasmine rice

Soak black-eyed peas overnight in water. Fry bacon in a heavy skillet until crisp. Add 1 1/2 cups onions and cook until the onions are transparent. Add 2 1/2 quarts water, bring to boil. Add garlic cloves, Creole spice blend, thyme, bay leaf, rosemary, salt, and pepper. Drain peas and add to the boiling mixture. Barely simmer mixture, partially covered, for 1 1/2 hours. Add 2 cups cooked jasmine rice. Serve with crisp French bread and butter.

## St. Expedite

*Long live our protector, St. Expedite, Warrior martyr of Christ,*
*Long live our protector, St. Expedite, Loyal and blessed shield,*
*You call on the Lord to assist us today!*

St. Expedite is one of the most popular and beloved saints in New Orleans. He is a major figure in both Catholic worship and Voudou in New Orleans, and has become quite popular among non-Catholic hoodoo and rootwork practitioners nationwide. He is the patron saint of those who need fast solutions to problems, who strive to put an end to procrastination and delays, and who seek financial success, among other things. He has recently been coined the *Patron Saint of Nerds* due to his association with computer programmers and hackers—a designation that upsets the apple cart of St. Isadore, who had previously been named Patron Saint of Computers and the Internet and who is not nearly as popular.[91] St. Expedite is also known as one of the lawyers of impossible causes with St. Rita and San Judas Tadeo, and as such, is petitioned for court cases and legal issues. As has already been mentioned, St. Expedite often represents Baron Samedi, the spirit of Death in New Orleans Voudou.

---

91    Ah, but let us not forget the patron saint of programmers: Ada Lovelace. -ed.

According to legend, *Saint Expeditus* was a Roman Centurion in Armenia who decided to convert to Christianity. Before he did so, it is said the Devil appeared to him as either a crow or a snake and told him to put off following through with his decision until the next day (hence, his association with procrastination). Instead, Expeditus stomped on the animal and killed it, proclaiming, "I'll be a Christian today!" Unfortunately, St. Expeditus met with the same fate as many Christian converts preceding him and was one of a group of martyrs beheaded in Melitene (modern day Malatya, Turkey) on April 19th, during the Diocletian Persecution in 303. As a result, he became known as *Sant'Espedito di Melitene,* or *Saint Expedite of Melitene* and his feast day is April 19.

But how did St. Expedite end up in New Orleans? The answer to this question is said to be related to the construction of the Our Lady of Guadalupe Chapel, International Shrine of St. Jude (Old Mortuary Chapel). Built in 1826 as a funeral chapel for victims of yellow fever, it was strategically constructed near St. Louis Cemetery No. 1 so as to minimize the spread of disease throughout the French Quarter. The unknown dead were moved through the mortuary's back door directly into the cemetery right across the street.

According to legend, some priests sent off to Spain for a large statue of the Virgin Mary, and months later, two crates arrived by ship. One crate contained the statue of Mary, which was expected. The other crate, however, had the word ***ESPEDITO*** (EXPEDITE) stamped on the outside. When the priests opened it, they found the statue of a saint depicted as a Roman Centurion. Apparently dimwitted, the priests did not recognize the identity of the saint and mistook the stamp indicating "expedited delivery" to be the name of the saint. And so, the unidentified statue of the Roman Centurion has been known as St. Expedite ever since, or so the story goes.

While the above explanation makes for an interesting urban legend, I doubt that the priests of New Orleans made such an ignorant mistake. For one thing, there are reports of identical stories coming out of Sao Paulo, Paris, and Haiti. In addition, priests were highly educated, making it hard to believe that they would not have known the stamp **ESPEDITO** referred to an expedited delivery, as opposed to the name of the saint.[92]

---

92    Besides, St. Expedite is mentioned in martyrologies before that time, and his cult apparently goes back to the Middle Ages. Originally, the Latin word *Expeditus* indicated a Roman soldier who was traveling lightly. -ed.

The famous statue of St. Expedite in New Orleans is still located in Our Lady of Guadalupe Chapel on the right hand side, just inside the door. On the other side of the chapel is a statue of St. Jude, Patron Saint of the Hopeless. There are a number of practices engaged in by locals and tourists alike that involves one or both of these statues. Those who may be more straightforward Catholic in their beliefs will go to St. Jude and pray for his intercession, then head on over to the other side of the chapel and ask St. Expedite to make their request happen fast.

Prayers, offerings, and requests are made by visitors to the chapel in quite creative ways since the Missionary Oblates of Mary Immaculate, who maintain the Our Lady of Guadalupe Chapel, do not allow devotees to leave offerings at the feet of the statues. As a result, Voudou devotees and Hoodoo practitioners leave offerings for St. Expedite in the care of Marie Laveaux, whose famous tomb is located just a hop, skip, and a jump away in St. Louis Cemetery No. 1. It is believed that Marie Laveaux will accept gifts on behalf of St. Expedite for those who wish to compensate him for his services. People do manage to covertly leave written petitions in the chapel at his feet, however.

Even more of a mystery than how St. Expedite became such a popular saint in New Orleans Voudou is his association with Baron Samedi. This seemingly unusual association can be explained by examining his iconography. In one hand he holds the Christian symbol for martyrdom, the palm frond. His other arm stretches above his head and in his hand is held a cross inscribed with the word *Hodie*, which is Latin for "Today." He stomps on a crow or raven with a ribbon in its beak, upon which is written the word *Cras*, meaning "Tomorrow" in Latin. The crow is considered in the folklore of many cultures to be harbingers of death; hence, his association with death, dying, killing and Baron Samedi. Two headed doctors[93] and sorcerers strongly identify with these aspects of his character. In addition, it is the message of the Baron to remind people to live for today because you never know when your time will come to be escorted to the world of the Invisibles by the Spirit of Death himself.

Moving away from New Orleans into the largely Sicilian and Italian community of Independence, Louisiana, we find St. Expedite by the name of *St. Expedito*. He became popular in the community when a chapel was built in his honor after he helped someone in an apparently big way. Celebrations

---

93    "Two headed" means a practitioner who works both light and dark elements of the tradition. -ed.

were held every second Sunday in June in his honor. According to Karen Williams (2011):

> In the '50s and '60s the pavilion was packed with people eating and drinking. Differing from New Orleans' custom of feeding the saint, the Italians made sure to feast with him, not limiting the food to one simple cake to leave for the saint's benefit, but feasting on hotdogs garnished with a local specialty, Hi Ho barbeque sauce, made in the community, along with soft drinks and beer, while the festivities included dancing and music by local bands like the Rhythm Kings. (Williams, 2011)

Offerings to St. Expedite are straightforward and simple: candles, red flowers, water, Sara Lee pound cake, charity work, and public recognition. In fact, anyone who works with St. Expedite on a regular basis in the context of New Orleans Voudou should keep a Sara Lee pound cake in the freezer. Sara Lee pound cakes even come pre-sliced, so all you have to do is reach in and grab a slice, place it on a plate, and you are good to go. If you are the sort of person who likes to bake/prepare your own offerings, that is certainly okay to do, but it is entirely traditional to go with the Sara Lee in New Orleans. It is, after all, the quick way of procuring the offering. Unfortunately, I do not know the origin of this tradition, only that it has been done this way for as long as I can remember.

The manner in which offerings to St. Expedite are done is a little different than other spirits due to Catholic influences. In Catholicism, it is customary to make both an offering for help and an offering of thanks. The flowers, candles, and water are offered during the petition, while the pound cake is offered in gratitude after he has granted your request. After the pound cake is offered, it is customary to make a public statement of gratitude and acknowledgment. He is believed to grant any request within his power provided the petitioner recommends his invocation to others. Many people also do charity work as an offering of thanks.

## St. Expedite's Altar

St. Expedite's altar should be set up in a triangle pattern. Use red candles, except when asking for money, in which case you would use green candles. You can also use a glass-encased candle with his image on it. Whichever candle you use, place it at the back of the altar; this is the tip of the triangle formation. In the front and to the left, place an ordinary glass of water, and in the front and to the right of the triangle, place the statue or image of him in the form of a picture or holy card. His offering of flowers is set next to the glass of water, and pound cake is placed in front and in between the water and his image.

Petition St. Expedite on Wednesdays, Thursdays, and Fridays. Wednesday is also the day dedicated to Mercury, the messenger god of the Romans. It is fitting to have a Roman Soldier and a Roman deity honored on the same day. Burn red candles on Wednesdays. Fridays are payday for a lot of people so this would be a time to give him thanks or ask for financial gain. Burn green candles on Fridays. Yellow candles are burned on Thursdays.

## St. Expedite's Pound Cake

For those of you who prefer to make your own offerings, here is a southern recipe for a basic pound cake that St. Expedite will surely love.

*Ingredients*
- 4 cups all-purpose flour
- 3 cups sugar
- 2 cups softened butter
- ¾ cup milk
- 6 large eggs
- 2 teaspoons vanilla extract

Preheat oven to 325°. Combine all of the ingredients in a large bowl and mix well. Pour batter into a greased and floured ten-inch tube and bake for one and a half hours or until a knife or wooden skewer inserted in the middle comes out clean. Allow to cool for ten minutes.

# BLACK HAWK

Courage is not afraid to weep, and she is not afraid to pray, even when she is not sure who she is praying to. ~ Black Hawk

His Indian name is *Ma-ka-tai-me-she-kia-kiak*, or *Black Sparrow Hawk*, and he was born in 1767 at Saukenuk, the principle city of the Sauk tribe located along the Rock River. Called Father Black Hawk by devotees, he was born into the Thunder clan. He chose to have only one wife, *As-she-we-qua*, or *Singing Bird*, although in Sauk culture polygamy was the norm. Black Hawk and Singing Bird had five children—two girls and three boys. He is best known as the historical War Chief (though he was not a chief at all but a medicine man) who fought fearlessly for his people, the Sauk and Fox, until the bloody massacre at Bad Axe River, where he escaped but was captured shortly thereafter by the United States federal government and held as a prisoner of war. He is considered a Voudou loa in the New Orleans Voudou pantheon.

The Indian Spirit Guides, such as Black Hawk, White Cloud, and Sitting Bull, came to New Orleans via the spiritualist movement. Black Hawk in particular was brought to the church by its founder, Mother Leafy Anderson. She called him the Spirit of the South, while White Hawk was the Spirit of the North. When Mother Leafy Anderson died, Mother Catherine Seals carried on the Black Hawk tradition as head of the Spiritualist Church, relating to Black Hawk as her spirit guide, as well.

Spirit guides are incorporeal entities acting as protectors and assistants to human beings. In general, Spirit Guides have a couple of functions. Whenever you have a problem, you can call upon your Spirit Guide to intercede for you.

As long as you know you have your Spirit Guide looking out for you, then nothing can get you down for long.

Spirit Guides also provide protection from earthbound spirits. These are the spirits of the deceased who have yet to pass over. Earthbound spirits are in spiritual limbo—they cling to the living because they can't deal with where they are. Earthbound spirits often manifest during séances even if they don't know anyone present.

The Indian Spirits are called upon for help with the problems and challenges we faced in daily living. Whatever they did when they were alive is the kind of thing they are expected to do when they are Spirits. For example, Black Hawk was a warrior who defended his people to the very end. He stood watch from a watchtower and so he is called the "Watchman on the wall" who will "fight your battles for you."

In the Spiritualist Churches, Black Hawk is considered to be a saint. Anyone who is recognized as doing the work of the Creator is considered a saint, whether or not they have been officially canonized by the Catholic Church. To spiritualists, Black Hawk fights injustices and will come to your aid when called upon, even fighting battles you are too weak to fight for yourself. According to Spiritualists, Black Hawk is a saint sent by God. It is said that when Black Hawk comes to help, God is right behind him.

December 17 is observed as the feast day of Black Hawk in the Spiritualist Churches who celebrate him as a spirit guide. It is also his celebrated feast day among New Orleans Voudouists. The feast of Black Hawk consists of testifying, hand blessings, prophesying, and readings. Some folks who speak in tongues are said to be speaking an "Indian language."

At some of his feasts, tripods made out of sugar cane and representing teepees stand over multiple plates of incense. A special healing oil is passed out along with plastic Indian toys, while people rub the leg of an Indian statue for his blessings.

His altar usually consists of red cloth and red candles, photographs of other Indians, bows and arrows, tomahawks, images of Jesus, St. Michael, and sometimes Dr. Martin Luther King. Like these three figures, Black Hawk is a champion of the oppressed. He is the one who justifies fighting for what is right and standing up to your enemies — righteous retribution. He can help with virtually any problem. He is the consummate warrior and it is said he will come to those who have enough patience to sit still and listen.

While he is most commonly served as an Indian bust in a bucket of sand, Black Hawk does not have to be confined to a bucket. This is a practice that has been adopted most commonly by conjure workers; though, in the churches themselves he is usually not in a bucket. Sometimes, his altar consists of a teepee with a plate of incense on the floor in front of it. Other times, he is on a long table covered with a red and white checkered, picnic-style table cloth. Still other times, a three-tiered altar is constructed for him, where he sits at the top.

## On the Issue of Offering Alcohol to Black Hawk

When Black Hawk walked this earth, he followed the traditions of his people. He did not dress in White man's clothes, nor did he drink alcohol. He understood alcohol to be a Spirit that energized the worst in his people. He saw it used as a weapon of war against the Indians. This is why I never offer Black Hawk alcohol when serving him. He does not need to be offered alcohol to "fire him up" as is the common misconception.[94]

In fact, the popular practice of giving Black Hawk alcohol to "fire him up" is deserving of specific attention. It is completely contrary to both Native American spiritual traditions and Black Hawk's belief system (not to mention horribly stereotypical). He tells us how much he hated alcohol because of what it did (and continues to do) to his people. Consider the following passages from his autobiography where he states in no uncertain terms exactly how he feels about alcohol:

> "Why did the Great Spirit ever send the whites to this island to drive us from our homes and introduce among us poisonous liquors, disease and death?"

> "I found several barrels of whisky on the captured boat, knocked in the heads and emptied the bad medicine late the river."

> "Our people got more liquor from the small traders than customary. I used all my influence to prevent drunkenness, but without effect. As the settlements progressed towards us, we became worse off and unhappy."

---

94    As I warned in *Liber Donariorum*, you must know what items will offend the spirit you wish to work with! -ed.

Perhaps, this passage from his autobiography is the best example for not offering Black Hawk alcohol:

> The white people brought whisky to our village, made our people drink, and cheated them out of their homes, guns and traps. This fraudulent system was carried to such an extent that I anticipated serious difficulties might occur, unless a stop was put to it. Consequently I visited all the whites and begged them not to sell my people whisky. One of them continued the practice openly; I took a party of my young men, went to his house, took out his barrel, broke in the head and poured out the whisky. I did this for fear some of the whites might get killed by my people when they were drunk.

So, in the above passage, he refers to those who brought the alcohol as fraudulent. Knowing how strongly he felt about alcohol, why would we give it to him? To do so would make you fraudulent in his eyes. He doesn't want it and he doesn't need it. In fact, he is likely to ignore you and not fight for you at all, or fight against you. He is a warrior spirit — warriors do not need alcohol to fight their battles.

While giving spirits alcohol as an offering is commonplace in New Orleans Voudou, it is not a blanket practice. Not everyone gets rum and whiskey. So the inevitable argument that alcohol is an appropriate offering to Black Hawk is an irresponsible and disrespectful excuse on the part of the practitioner, especially in the context of ancestor reverence.

## Appropriate Ritual Offerings for Father Black Hawk

As I described previously, there are different ways of setting up an altar to Black Hawk. Once you prepare his altar or bucket, you will be able to add things to it that relate to him. I find that the ritual offerings for Black Hawk are of four different categories: 1) utilitarian, 2) medicinal, 3) conjure, and 4) sustenance. Each of these types of offerings are needed for him to do his work for you, and it is up to the devotee to provide him with what he needs to take care of business.

### Utilitarian Offerings

The first category of offerings are those things he will need to assist you with your petition. If you are asking him to fight a battle for you, then he will need weapons: a hatchet, a knife, and an arrowhead, for example. If you need his assistance for obtaining a long term goal, he will need his spear, because it is thrown to reach a distant goal. The hatchet is for chopping through obstacles and breaking chains that bind us. Arrowheads provide direction and can pierce an enemy. Each of his weapons can also function as a tool, the manner in which it is used is up to him. It is our responsibility to provide him with what he needs.[95]

### Medicinal Offerings

Black Hawk was a medicine man, and to the Native American, every living thing is a source of spiritual power and as such should be revered. This is similar to the African concept of *aché*. From the native worldview, however, all living things are also our relations — our relatives — aunt, uncle, sister, brother, and cousin. We look to our plant, animal, and mineral relations as Bird people or Winged Ones, Fish people, Snake people, Four-leggeds, Animal people, and Tree people. The rocks and minerals are our grandfathers and grand-mothers. The elements Lightning and Thunder, Wind and Rain, Earthquake and Fire — all are powers of nature with the ability to transform and teach, as well as to destroy and put us, the two-leggeds, in our place when necessary.

You will need to offer Black Hawk some herbs and roots so he can do his healing work. Hold the herb or root in your hands and pray or meditate on the power of the root. Before placing them in his bucket or on his altar, hold them to your mouth and whisper to them what you need and want from them and tell them where they will be residing. Tell them they will be assisting Black Hawk as needed.

Following are the primary plant medicines that should be offered to Black Hawk for his spiritual medicine bundle. You can also keep your extra herbs and roots on his altar to empower them until you need to use them.

**Tobacco:** In the Indian way, tobacco is medicine and medicine is tobacco. Tobacco is a sacrament. All tobacco — and there are many kinds — are sacred. It does not have to be smoked when used as an offering and for many purposes it is not smoked. Tobacco smoke is said to be the pipeline to the Creator. The

---

95    See *Liber Donariorum* for more on gift and tool offerings. -ed.

elders always say to be very mindful of the words you speak when smoking tobacco because your words are a prayer carried directly to the Creator. Words are believed to have activating power; one can manifest situations through the spoken word. Your words can imbue the tobacco with positive or negative energy. As an intermediary Spirit, Black Hawk requires tobacco to send your petitions to the Creator. He also needs it to activate his Thunder medicine.

In the Indian way, all tribes have their own sacred tobaccos, each of a different kind of plant, bark, or herb. None is better than the other; all is sacred. Lobelia, for example, is a sacred tobacco that can be smoked for respiratory problems, and can be used as an offering whenever tobacco is called for in a work.

**Sage:** Sage is one of the most sacred herbs among Native American peoples and is the primary herb used in the cleansing ritual called *smudging*. Sage is burned in leaf form or as a bundled smudge stick to bless a person and their environment. It has the ability to nullify negative energies attached to people, places, and things and can clean any contaminated object. As well as being burned, sage is often held, worn, or kept with sacred objects to ward off negative influences. Native American tradition says that wherever sage is, evil spirits cannot enter.

**Cedar:** Cedar in its many varieties is one of the most widely used and versatile plants among Native people. Cedar is found to be used as cordage, as fiber for making mats, rugs, blankets, clothing, canoes, boats, decorations, bows, and other hunting and fishing items. In certain Native American traditions, cedar is used to carry prayers to the Creator. It is used to connect heaven and earth.

Cedar is burned to banish negative energies from a person and their environment, thus opening the door for good spirits and energies to enter. It can be used as loose leaf or as a smudge stick and burned in an abalone shell. Cedar is often used in the sweat lodge ceremony (*inipi*) to bless the lodge and prepare the space for the Spirits to enter. In folk magic, cedar is used for healing, purification, money, and protection.

**Sweetgrass:** Sweetgrass is an aromatic grass and is considered to be a sacred herb among indigenous peoples. The smoke of burning sweetgrass is said to purify and clear people, places, and things. It feels lighter than sage and is often burnt after using sage. Its sweet smell has drawing properties and encourages positive vibrations to enter an area or room. Sweetgrass is also used in sweat lodges to invite the powerful Spirit beings to enter the ceremony.

**Bloodroot (*Sanguinaria Canadensis L.*):** A favorite rheumatism remedy among the Indians of the Mississippi region. Also called: *Red Root, Red Indian Paint, Tetterwort, Blood Root, Indian Paint, Pauson, Red Paint Root, Red Puccoon,* and *Sanguinariat.* The Algonquin used it as a love charm and to make a red dye for skin, clothing, and weapons (Bradley, 1936). The Micmac also used bloodroot as a love charm (Rousseau, 1948). Single Ponca men rubbed bloodroot on their palms as a love charm (Gilmore, 1919). Among the Iroquois, a decoction of dried roots was taken for ulcers or for women that were ugly (Herrick, 1977). Other interesting uses of bloodroot among the Iroquois include using smoke from the plant to cleanse a person who has seen a dead person and a cold infusion of roots that was made to take as a remedy for sickness caught from a menstruating girl (Herrick). The Cherokee used it as a respiratory aid by sniffing the pulverized root (Hamel and Chiltoskey, 1975). The Menominee used the fresh root to paint the face of a warrior. The Ojibway used juice as face paint for the medicine lodge ceremony or when on warpath (Smith, 1932).

**Black Snakeroot (*Aristolochia serpentaria*):** Also known as *Virginia Snakeroot, Virginia Dutchmanspipe,* and *Virginia Serpentary.* The dried rhizome is a popular herbal tonic. Some old Cherokee Indian remedies consist of a decoction of black snakeroot blown upon a patient for fever and feverish headache, and drunk for coughs; root chewed and spit upon a wound to cure snake bites; bruised root placed in a hollow tooth for toothache, and held against a nose made sore by constant blowing in colds (Mooney, 1891). As a tea, "Blacksnake root is good tuh nuse [use] in de homes fo' heart trouble, nerves, broken down systems an' any bad feet dat chew have tuh de body" (Hyatt #3, p. 2195).

**Devil's Shoestring (*Tephrosia Virginiana*):** Also called *Catgut, Turkey Pea, Goat's Rue.* An Indian remedy used a decoction drunk for lassitude. Women wash their hair in a decoction of its roots to prevent its breaking or falling out, because these roots are very tough and hard to break; from the same idea ball-players rub the decoction on their limbs after scratching, to toughen them (Mooney, 1891). In folk magic, devil's shoestring has multiple uses including protection from gossip and crossing, gambling, luck, power, employment, uncrossing and tripping up the devil.

## Offerings of Sustenance

Like all spirits, Black Hawk has his favorite foods. Black Hawk is offered red beans and rice on Mondays and spaghetti and meatballs on Wednesdays. Any other days, he is offered fruits and nuts, water, corn, cornmeal, wild meats like venison, Indian stews, fry bread, and water.

## Mama D's Fry Bread

Fry bread is a sacred food to many native peoples. It is found at every celebration, every feast, and nearly every meal. It is sold at Pow Wows and art shows and carnivals. It is said that fry bread will be consumed by Indian people until the earth is again pure.

*Ingredients:*
- 1 cup unbleached flour
- 1/4 teaspoon salt
- 1 teaspoon powdered milk
- 1 teaspoon baking powder
- 1/2 cup water
- Vegetable oil for frying

Combine flour, salt, powdered milk, and baking powder into a large bowl. Add water and mix the dough until it starts to form one big clump. Rub a little oil into the palms of your hands. Begin mixing the dough, trying to get all the flour into the mixture to form a ball. Mix well, but do not knead it. The resulting dough should be pliable. Add a little flour to the outside of the dough so it is not sticky. Allow the dough to sit for about five to ten minutes.

Break off sections of the dough to form round balls about four inches in diameter. Using your floured hands, stretch the balls into flat discs about five to seven inches wide. It works well to pinch the edges and turn clockwise to start, then stretch a little, pinch, turn, and stretch until the disc is formed. Some folks find it easier to lay the dough on the counter and stretch and flatten.

Add about an inch of vegetable oil in a frying pan (I prefer cast iron but any heavy duty pan will do) and heat until it's ready. Indians don't test the temperature with a thermometer . . . instead we drop a little piece of dough in the oil to see if it is ready. It is ready when the dough begins to fry immediately. Take the formed dough and gently place it into the oil, being careful not to splatter the hot oil. Using a spatula or metal tongs, press down on the dough as it fries so the top is submersed into the hot oil. Sometimes big bubbles will form in the dough . . . that's okay; just gently press it down into the oil.

Fry until brown, and then flip over to fry the other side. Each side will take approximately three to four minutes to cook. Remove from the oil and place the cooked Fry Bread on a paper towel to absorb excess oil. Fry Bread is best when served immediately, though it can keep in the refrigerator and be reheated later.

## Conjure Offerings

There are specific types of works that Black Hawk does. Indian head pennies and buffalo nickels can be offered to him to empower them for future use. He has a special kind of medicine called Thunder medicine and will require lightning-struck wood to activate it when needed. He will also require some rocks and minerals.

**Indian Head Pennies:** Spiritual workers who work with Black Hawk will fix and prepare the pennies as protective talismans for the home and business. They are also widely used in Law Keep Away Spells. Indian Head Cents act as spy boys or scouts who will warn you when danger approaches. It is said if you dream of an Indian person or come in contact with one in waking life that you have been duly warned. You then have an opportunity to take other evasive or defensive measures to protect yourself.

There are countless simple works using Indian Head pennies in conjure. Most of these works have to do with bringing luck, business success, and keeping the law away. In all instances the penny is face up so that the Indian scout can keep watch according to his assigned purpose. In most cases, the penny is placed at the entryway of the home or establishment, and sometimes at the back door and windows.

**Buffalo Head Nickels:** Buffalo nickels can be employed in a similar manner as Indian Head pennies; however, they have a dual function. The Indian Head side can serve as a personal warrior and protector, as opposed to serving as a scout and warning system. The buffalo side draws on the spirit of the buffalo to plow down any enemy that dares approach the home or business where it stands guard.

**Arrowheads:** Interestingly, the historical and archaeological evidence suggests African Americans used Native American artifacts for magical and ritual purposes. This theory is based on ethnographic studies of objects, such as arrowheads, found on the Oakley Plantation in West Feliciana, Louisiana, a tenant house in South Carolina (see Orser, 1985), King's Bay Plantations in Georgia (see Adams, 1987), and other locations. Indian arrowheads are considered to be lucky charms. Although they are called *Indian arrowheads*, they are believed to have been made by the Creator. This belief can be traced back to the Akan-speaking people from the African Gold Coast who believed prehistoric stone projectile points had magic powers. They called arrowheads *nyame akuma* (God's axes) and believed they formed from lightning bolts that hit the earth. Add an arrowhead to any work to cut through any confusion or obstacles getting in the way of making a decision.

**Stones:** Rocks and stones, from the Native American perspective, represent the ancestors. They are often referred to as grandfathers and grandmothers because they hold the wisdom of the ancients. You will also need to get a special stone or stones to place in Black Hawk's bucket or on his altar. This can be any kind of stone — from a crystal to an ordinary rock. You can use one of the minerals of the medicine wheel: jet or black onyx, turquoise, red jasper, or shell. Fossils are a good idea if you intend to ask for any kind of divinatory assistance from Black Hawk.

**Lightning-Struck Wood:** Lightning-struck wood can be added to any work to increase its power. It is particularly good for commanding spells, sex spells, and spells of destruction, which draw on its fire energy to destroy. Fire also has a dual nature to transform, hence its ability to be used in positive works as well. Add to mojo bags and gris-gris to provide a serious boost in power. One way to use lightning-struck wood in candle magic is to take some splinters and stick it into the candle wax. The second way is to grind some of it down to a powder and sprinkle the tops of glass-encased candles or roll candles in the powder.

# References

Alvarado, D. (2011). *The Voodoo Hoodoo Spellbook*. Red Wheel Weiser and Conari Press.

Alvarado, D. & Angelique, M. (2012). Workin' in da Boneyard. Prescott Valley, AZ: Creole Moon Publications.

Animal Sacrifice, retrieved from: http://en.wikipedia.org/wiki/Animal_sacrifice

Berry, J. *The Spirit of Blackhawk: A Mystery of Africans and Indians*

Blier, (1995). African Vodun: Art, psychology and power. University of Chicago Press: Chicago.

Bradley, W. T. (1936). Medical Practices of the New England Aborigines. *Journal of the American Pharmaceutical Association 25*(2):138–147 (p. 142)

California Folklore Society (1964) *Western Folklore, Vol 23.*

Densmore, F. (1928) Uses of Plants by the Chippewa Indians. *SI-BAE Annual Report #44*:273–379 (p. 336)

Eliade, M. (1986). *The Encyclopedia of Religion*. Macmillan Library Reference

Guiley, R. E. *The Encyclopedia of Witches and Witchcraft*. New York: Facts on File, Inc.

Hall, G. M. (1992). *Africans in Colonial Louisiana: The development of Afro-Creole culture in the Eighteenth century.* Baton Rouge and London: Louisiana State University Press.

Hamel, P. B. and U. Chiltoskey, M. U. (1975). *Cherokee Plants and Their Uses -- A 400 Year History.* Sylva, N.C. Herald Publishing Co. (p. 25)

Herrick, J. W. (1977). *Iroquois Medical Botany.* Doctor of Philosophy. Dissertation. State University of New York at Albany.

Herskovits, M. J. (1964). *Life in a Haitian Valley.* New York : Octagon Books

Hohman, J. G. (1856). Pow Wows or the Long Lost friend. Harrisburg, Pa. : T.F. Scheffer

Hurston, N. Z. (1932). *Mules and Men.*

Hyatt, H. M. (1970–78). *Hoodoo-Conjuration-Witchcraft-Rootwork,* 5 vols. Hannibal, MO: Western Publishing.

Kieckhefer, Richard. *Magic in the Middle Ages.* Cambridge: Cambridge University Press.

Lang, A. (1901) *Magic and Ritual.* New York: Longman's Green & Co.

Marie-Jose Alcide Saint-Lot (2003). Vodou, a Sacred Theatre: The African Heritage in Haiti. Educa Vision Inc. p. 14.

Mooney, J. (1891). Sacred Formulas of the Cherokees. *7th Annual report, Bureau of American Ethnology.*

North by South, (n. d.). Conch Shells - North by South/Great Migrations Page. (n.d.). Retrieved from http://northbysouth.kenyon.edu/1998/death/conchshells.htm

Offering. (n.d.). Retrieved September 20, 2014, from http://www.
merriam-webster.com/dictionary/offering

Rousseau, J. (1948). Ethnobotanique Et Ethnozoologie Gaspesiennes.
*Archives de Folklore 3*:51–64 (p. 56)

Russell, J. B. (1972). *Witchcraft in the Middle Ages.* New York: Cornell
University Press.

Salzman, Jack, et al., eds. (1996). *Encyclopedia of African-American Culture
and History, vol. 3.* London: Simon & Schuster and Prentice Hall
International, 1581.

Smith, H. H. (1932). Ethnobotany of the Ojibwe Indians. *Bulletin of the
Public Museum of Milwaukee 4*:327–525 (p. 414)

Tallant, R. (1946). *Voodoo in New Orleans*

Turner, N. J. and Efrat, B. S. (1982). *Ethnobotany of the Hesquiat Indians
of Vancouver Island.* Victoria. British Columbia Provincial
Museum, p. 33.

Baal, Jan van. (1976). Offering, Sacrifice and Gift. *Numen 23*: 161–178.

Williams, K. (2011). St. Expedito's Role in South Louisiana Catholicism,
in New Orleans and in the Italian-American Community
near Independence, Louisiana, *Louisiana Folklore Miscellany,
Volume 21.*

# Severed Head Cakes and Clouds of Dancing Girls
## *Offerings in Tibetan Buddhism*

## Jason Miller

ther than meditation, there is no single practice that I place a higher value on than the making of offerings. Students in my Strategic Sorcery Course report that regular offerings yield the largest changes and biggest results — even acting as a catalyst for other magic that they do. Given that most of us with full lives need to make the most of our time, offerings are a high ROI exercise. Those readers familiar with the Pareto principle[96] can be assured that offerings are part of the 20% investment that yields 80% of the result.

I have been overjoyed to see offerings take an increasingly important role in western magic over the last twenty years or so, especially in the "old magic" grimoire revival. When looking for living traditions from which to take their lead with offerings, most writers and practitioners have been taking their lead from various African Traditional Religions. Back in the 90s, many of us started making offerings inspired by Louis Martine and his writings on *Vodou* in the *Cincinnati Journal of Magic* and *Black Moon Chapbooks*[97]. Later Aaron Leitch focused on Santeria and Palo in his *Secrets of the Magical Grimoires*. Jake Stratton-Kent, meanwhile, has turned his eye to Brazil and *Quimbanda* in his writings about the *Grimoirum Verum*.

My own training in magic is largely informed by Tibetan *Tantra*, which also places a heavy emphasis on offerings but can be very different from African traditions both in terms of what is offered and who the offerings are for. I am not claiming these practices are *better*, only that they are different. Those of

---

96    Or the "80-20 rule," which states that 80% of the effects (of anything) comes from 20% of the causes. For example, in business it is known that 80% of sales will come from 20% of the customers. -ed.

97    You can read about my own first experiment with offering to Papa Legba in "Words of Power, and Anthology of O.T.O Local Body Publications"

us integrating practices into western magic from other living traditions may benefit from a look to Asian as well as African offering practices.

# SUBSTITUTES FOR SACRIFICE

Being Buddhist, most Tibetans do not offer blood sacrifice to spirits. This goes back to the introduction of Buddhism to Tibet in the mid-8th century. In the year 760 the King of Tibet, Trison Detsen, a strong proponent of Buddhism, had invited Santaraksita the abbot of Nalanda to build a monastery in Tibet. This upset the local lha-dre (local demons and gods) who survived off blood sacrifices and were not terribly keen on the idea of Buddhism taking hold in the land of snows, as Buddhism does not allow for animal or human sacrifice. Every night after the workers finished for the day, the spirits would come and tear down everything that was built, as well as causing floods, storms, and disease. Being a simple Abbot, Santaraksita was no match for the spirits arrayed against him, and he recommended the king summon Padmasambhava, a great Tantric Sorcerer who could overpower both gods and demons.

Padmasambhava was at the Asura Cave in Yang-le-shod (Pharping) Nepal practicing sex yoga with his Nepali consort Shakyadevi[98] when he sensed that he was needed in Tibet and flew off to be of assistance. Upon crossing the border into Tibet, he was attacked by the Yul-lha (mountain god) Yarlha Shampo who took the form of a giant white yak with lightning emanating from its eyes and blizzards issuing from its nose. As it charged down Mount Sotang Kangbori at Padmasambhava, Padmasambhava simply grabbed him by the nose, twirled him around his head three times, and slammed him on the ground so hard that it created an earthquake that was felt as far as Kathmandu.

Yarlha Shampo transformed into a humanoid form and asked Padmasambhava to spare him. Padmasambhava made him promise to stop creating problems for the people in the Yarlung Valley and to become a protector of the Buddha's *Dharma* and all practitioners that come down Padmasambhava's students. He became the first Tibetan Dharmapala (Protector). Yarlha Shampo agreed but there was a problem: He subsisted on *mar-chod,* the "red-offering" of sacrificed animals and humans that Buddhists do not practice.

---

98    As opposed to Mandarava his Northern Indian consort, or Belwong Kalasiddhi his Western Indian Consort, or Mangala his other Nepali Consort, or Yeshe Tsogyal his Tibetan consort. Padmasambhava got around . . .

Padmasambhava said that this was not a problem and established the tradition of Red *Tormas*, cakes that stand in for, and sometimes are shaped to look like, blood sacrifices. These cakes get packed with *prana* during offering rites, and multiplied through meditative visualization so that they function for the recipient the same way that a blood sacrifice would.

Padmadambhava eventually got to Samye where he subdued the demons blocking the building of the monastery. He then traveled all over Tibet and recruited more Dharma Protectors. Some, like the Nagaraja Angkusha of Chimphu Cave, had to be subdued and forced to become a protector. Others, like Dorje Lekpa (literally Vajra Good-Guy), happily agreed to it over a glass of beer. The Tormas and other types of Buddhist offerings were so attractive to some spirits that it even attracted Gods from outside of Tibet. Pehar supposedly came from Turkey and agreed to become a Tibetan Protector in exchange for a wife[99] and regular *puja* offerings. Pehar still serves as the main spirit that speaks through the Nechung Oracle to this day.

# SEVERED HEAD CAKE

Today there are many types of tormas that get offered to different spirits and dieties: White ones are offered to peaceful spirits and vegetarians like *Nagas*, red heart-shaped tormas for rishi-wrathful or semi-wrathful gods, and wrathful tormas that are triangular and red or shaped like actual sacrificed people and humans.

You can see one example of this type in the photo to the right. This torma is typically shaped to represent an upturned skull cup (*kapala*) with five sense organs inside it: a heart representing consciousness, two or three torn out eyes representing sight, a tongue representing taste, a nose representing smell, and ears representing sound. Sometimes severed hands or feet are attached as well. The torma in this photo was offered during a three-day *Vajrakilaya Puja* in Kunzang, Dorje Rinpoche's personal temple

99    Metsum Karmo

in Pharping. I took the photo as we were walking it outside the boundary of the rite to be enjoyed by wrathful and harm-causing spirits just as Padmasambhava did in the 8th century.

The cake itself is usually made from kneaded barley flour, butter, and water, to which have been added the three sweets of molasses, sugar, and honey and the three whites: butter, curd, and milk. In addition to this are added various medicines and herbs, such as the twenty-five vase substances: five medicines, five fragrant substances, five "essences," five grains, and five precious substances, such as gold, pearl, coral, crystal, and lapis. The essences are usually sesame seed, salt, ghee, molasses, and honey. After the torma is complete, it is colored with vegetable and natural dyes to give it whatever color is needed.

In other words, a lot of care and effort goes into the construction of these tomas. Except when it doesn't . . .

Just as the torma pictured above is a stand-in for actual blood sacrifice, there are stand-in's for actual tormas. If you have a daily practice that requires a torma, it would certainly be a pain to make one from scratch every day, what with all the *dril-bu* (medicine pills) and precious substances required. Lacking the ability to make a physical torma, people can do one of three things: use a normal cake or pastry without all the symbolism, purchase a re-usable permanent torma, or visualize the offerings without physical support.

# TASTYCAKE: FOOD OF THE GODS?

I have been on retreat where we offered store-bought cakes to the Nagas.[100] We found some white cakes at the local bakery, stuck it on a plate with incense, and did the ritual. We purified it with Fire (*RAM*), Air (*YAM*), and Water (*KHAM!*). We blessed it with the syllables of Body (*OM*), Speech (*AH*), and Mind (*HUM*). We mentally multiplied it so that it filled all space. We prayed and meditated, pumping it with prana, waved it around regally as we chanted the mantra of offering: *OM NAGARAJA SAPARIVARA AKARO MUKHAM SARVA DHARMANAM ADYANUTPANNATVATA . . .*

On the plate it was still a cake, but in our minds it was an inexhaustible substance of enjoyment for the Nagas of the lake we were practicing at. What was it to them? I am not sure, but I can tell you that even though it was supposed to, it did not rain during our teaching. Instead it started raining the

---

100    Also see Denise Alvarado's *Ritual Offerings in New Orleans Voudou*. -ed.

very second that Rinpoche finished the puja, but stopped again right before the next session began. It did this over and over several times — stopping for the teaching. If that was not a sign of acceptance, I don't know what is.

# Torma Toys

If you have an altar and wish to keep a Torma on it without having a piece of rotting food around, you can purchase a permanent Torma that can be re-used over and over again. These can range from very expensive metal Tormas filled with all manner of precious substances to very cheap resin tormas made in China that can be purchased from *Feng-Shui* outlets.

The one pictured here is a resin torma that stands in for the wrathful torma described above but stands only six inches tall. Though it can look a little like a Pokémon Toy or something like that, it has all the same features for the senses that are traditional: the skull, tongue, eyes, heart, nose, and ears, as well as the decorative jewels and such on top. In ritual this is cleansed, consecrated, multiplied, and offered just like any other torma, and serves its purpose for regular offerings. If I was doing a major working with some specific end that I wanted to materialize, or a large and important gathering, I would probably pay to have monks make a torma from dough with all the necessary substances.

# Clouds of Dancing Girls

Whether or not you are using a physical support, such as Torma, *Sang* (incense), or *Serkyem* (liquor or tea offering), you are supposed to visualize it as well, multiplying it and making it fill all space with clouds of offerings. For many practices visualization alone is enough of an offering, and the prana that rests in the visualization gets enjoyed by the spirits the exact same way. After all, in Buddhism everything is essentially empty of self-nature, including the spirits and the offering. Besides, since when you do offer physical offerings, the spirits seem only to be able to feed on the spiritual essence of the offering, leaving the physical materials for you to clean up and dispose of afterward, might they not be pleased with an offering of energy and intent with no physical basis?

When doing practices with no physical offerings, *mudras* (hand gestures) are often employed to trigger the proper result. Gestures for the outer offerings of drinking water, washing water, flowers, incense, light, perfumed water, food, and music are all represented by hand gestures. These are followed by mudras for the inner offerings of *Amita* (Nectar), *Rakta* (Blood), and Torma.

Because things are much more mutable in the realms of spirit and mind, you occasionally find instructions for very wild phantasmagoric offerings. One *Sadhana* I have for Rigdzin Dhupa, a form of Padmasambhava, requests that you emanate clouds of coquettish dancing girls[101] in the sky as an offering. Some Chod practices, where you meditate on your own body being offered, request a *dakini*[102] to pour nectar in through the top of your skull until you are blown up like a water balloon, then slice open your belly so you pop and spill your guts and *amrita* all over the place, eventually covering the whole world.

Sometimes, when the offering is made to a *Yidam* or Tantric Diety, the inner offerings symbolize qualities that you are offering up: *Rakta* represents desire, Amrita represents anger, and Torma represents ignorance. Of course this level of the offering would only be perceived by enlightened beings[103]; to ordinary spirits of the eight classes[104] they would appear as offerings that are most desired.

---

101    Again, Padmasambhava clearly likes the ladies.
102    A female spirit, also called a sky walker or sky dancer. -ed.
103    There is a Western equivalent to this concept. See Sam Webster's essay *Offerings in Iamblichan Theurgy*. -ed.
104    Since there are actually many classes of spirits, the list of what actually constitutes the eight classes differs depending on who you talk to, yet they are always referred to as the eight classes. Most often the list is: Devas, Yamas, Mamos, Rudras, Tsen, Gyalpos, Yakshas, and Nagas.

# So What Does This Mean For Me?

Like it or not, western magic has been in a simultaneous state of recovery, reconstruction, and further evolution all at once. Offerings have been a severely neglected aspect of magic in the west that is just now getting the attention it deserves. As I mentioned earlier, western magicians are increasingly looking to ATRs as examples for how to integrate offerings into our practice. *Vajrayana* offers a view of offerings that can be similar in some ways, but a stark contrast in others. This is not a *better* way, just a different way. There are three aspects that I would specifically like to draw your attention to: Visualizations, Offerings to Enemy Spirits, and Blood Replacements.

Recently a grimoire-based magician shared with me the opinion that visualizations in magic were an invention of the Golden Dawn and not at all part of traditional magic anywhere. This is patently false, as Vajrayana has been relying upon visualizations for over a thousand years. Everything from inner channels to Buddha bodies to offerings get visualized. Even when there is a huge pile of physical offerings, visualizations are used to multiply and bless the offerings. When performing short rites in public places like a forest or state park, it may not be desirable to leave a physical offering, but quite easy to make a vast visualized offering with only some liquid and incense as a physical basis. After all, when you do offer food to the spirits, the physical substance remains even after they have taken their fill, doesn't it? Therefore, is it such a stretch to offer up something that has little or even no physical basis?

In my own practice I offer physical substances when I am looking for a physical result, but often use visualizations, direct prana, mudra, and so on in daily offerings. Western magicians can and should integrate such methods into their practices. Some people in ATRs that are cross initiated into Tibetan Buddhism are already doing this with their Orishas.

## Offerings to Harmful Spirits

While I think that many western magicians have gotten used to the idea of making offerings to spirits that they want to worship or ask for some kind of intercession, the idea of making offerings to beings that are out to kick your ass is less popular. Tibetans have a tradition of recognizing four types of guest at offerings:

1) Higher Guests: that constitute Buddhas, Bodhisttvas, Deities, etc.

2) Guests of Quality who are your protector spirits and other powerful worldly spirits.
3) Guests of Compassion which basically includes everyone caught in the cycle of incarnation.
4) Lower Guests: beings that we owe a karmic debt to or who are harm-causing demons and such.[105]

It is this last group that is actually the most useful to make offerings to. In daily practices like *Riwo Sang Cho* smoke offerings, spirits that we offend by our human lifestyle, and all the pollution and destruction that comes with it, get supplicated and asked to please forgive our actions. When doing practice in a new location we might offer a *gek-torma* to the local spirits to warn of our presence and so that the land gets turned over to us. In cases of sickness, spirit obsession, and even curses, often an offering of supplication can be a much easier cure than an exorcism. Might as well try the olive branch first — you can always shift into ass-kicking mode later.[106]

## BLOOD REPLACEMENTS

The topic of blood replacements is a hot topic with lots of strong feelings on all sides.[107] Let me state here that while Buddhism overall has prohibitions against animal sacrifice, I am perhaps a bad Buddhist because I am not really against it. I eat meat, as do most Tantrics, and I find it a little hypocritical to be against animal sacrifice when you are chomping down on a steak. That said, most of you reading this will not have had the regular experience of killing your own food as a part of normal life. Someone who is used to that existence can perform the act efficiently and nearly painlessly; someone like me would make a bloody and unholy mess of it without proper training.

Whether it is due to lack of space, lack of know-how, or ethical objection, there are many people even within ATRs that look for bloodless alternatives

---

105 Usually these offerings are made outside the working space (or temple), after which the main ritual is held inside. I have used this very technique when the planet I am invoking is negatively aspected by another. Offerings were made to the opposing planet before the main ritual, so as to negate its influence. -ed.
106 This is a technique I have adopted directly from Eastern sources. When I am called to clear a place of a haunting spirit, I always bring an offering. I tell the spirit I am not there to harm it or cast it into darkness, but that I have come to feed it and take it to a better place (usually to be poured out in the local river). -ed.
107 See *Liber Donariorum* for more on blood sacrifice. -ed.

to supplicating spirits that ordinarily request it.[108] The Blood Red Torma is one alternative to this, and I know of some people in the Bronx who use Red Palm Oil and dough to create their own versions of them for their spirits. Some feel it is ok to do this, but others certainly do not. A few years ago, someone commenting on one of my rituals said something along the lines of: "It's fine to do this in Buddhism with Buddhist spirits because you have emptiness as a basis. If you were to offer Eleggua a rubber chicken and call it sacrifice, I don't think it would go well." Fair enough, except that the practice of Blood Red Tormas arose specifically out of making offering to spirits that were NOT Buddhists. It is a practice that arose out of traditions and cultures bumping up against one another and adopting practices to suit new needs. Kind of like what is happening now.

I have really not even scratched the surface of offerings in Tibetan Buddhism, where offerings can get used as weapons, as medicine, and as tools for transformation. Given the availability of Lamas and Dharma centers throughout Europe and the United States, it is easy enough to get teachings and texts for this kind of work. The innovative Sorcerer should have no trouble adapting it to his practice.

*Lha Gyalo!*
May the Gods Prevail!

---

108    This is also discussed in Denise Alvarado's *Ritual Offerings in New Orleans Voudou.* -ed.

# Offerings In Roman Deity Magic

*Nick Farrell*

For the last six years, I have been living in Rome and adapting my magic to suit the local conditions. While there is nothing new about neo-pagan reconstruction, the use of ancient gods magically is not something that is often talked about. A magician does not want to worship gods so much as work with them, and this means that issues like sacrifices and offerings need to be clearly understood in both an Ancient and a magical context.

Understanding Roman magic requires a slightly different understanding of how Roman religion worked and evolved. It is a misconception that Roman gods and goddesses were just stolen from the Greeks and need to be treated in the same way. Once entering the Roman mindset you can start to understand how the magic might have worked, and how you can recreate it.

## THE CHILDREN OF THE FLAMES

Before the arrival of the Greek or Etruscan gods, the Early Romans were fire worshippers. Archaeology shows that each house had a sacred flame at its centre, and all the early myths of Rome involve fire spirits, such as Cacus and Caca and especially Vulcan. In the 7th or 8th century BC, Rome cleaned out an area of ancient graveyards (where is now the Roman Forum) and built a shrine or *Vulcanal* to Vulcan.

The Romans identified Vulcan with the Greek smith-god Hephaestus, and he became associated with the constructive use of fire in metalworking. However, Vulcan was more destructive and people worshipped him to protect them from harmful fires. On the positive side, he was a fertility and military god to whom the arms of the defeated enemies were dedicated. The Etruscans who ruled Rome considered it unwise to place his temple within the city boundaries. It is thought that Vulcan's shrine contained an ever-burning flame and that the bodies of the dead were cremated there. Vulcan worship was replaced by that of Jupiter, making the fire god the Uranus of the Romans. His temple was covered over as his importance was forgotten.

The other important fire Goddess was Vesta, whose cult appears to be extremely ancient and was an extension of the hearth fires of each household. Her temple, in the heart of the Forum, was the flame of Rome itself, and when it was to be extinguished on the orders of the Christian Emperor Theodosius I in 391 AD, it was carried to the temple of the Sacred Fire of Vesta. When that temple was closed, the flame was moved to a Temple of Cybele, which was served by a solitary Vestal.

In 408 AD, Serena, the wife of Patrician Stilicho and the niece of Emperor Theodosius, directed her servants to quench the Sacred Fire. She was cursed by the Vestal who was dragged from her temple. Serena, Stilicho and their son were executed within a year and the City of Rome fell to the Visigoths led by Alaric. This was the first time the City had been sacked in 800 years, and it was linked in popular culture as a sign that the Gods had abandoned Rome for following Christianity. Augustine's City of God was designed to dismiss this point, even if it failed to provide a good argument.

For this reason anyone seriously using Roman god magic must use many candles for nearly every ritual they do. Candles have the advantage of not only being a traditional form of sacrifice, but they are also representative of the divine spark in matter itself. In modern times it is harder to keep an ever-burning flame as an offering to the Earth-Fire spirits, but a daily offering of a tea-light appears to appease Vesta and the house spirits.

Vesta also had a special salt flour, dubbed *mola salsa*, which was made for her by her Vestal Virgins three times a year. Caroline Tully from the University of Melbourne carried out some interesting research into mola salsa.

Mola salsa consists of two ingredients, flour and salt. The flour is made from prematurely harvested spelt. After the spelt is harvested, it is parched over the Vestal fire, ground, and then stored. Spelt wheat is not difficult to find. I toasted it on a grill and then ground it with salt in a coffee grinder. The salt is refined already, but I would bless it ritually using a traditional Golden Dawn method, to make it "holy."

It is harder to get the slightly green version, but what I found was that Vesta did not appear to mind. On three occasions, I scattered Mola Salsa on the ruins of Vesta's temple in the forum. Twice I saw what appeared to be smoke coming from the ruins, as did the people who were with me.

Mola Salsa was seen as food for the gods and is given as an offering in most rituals. It can also be dusted on objects which are going to be sacrificed. If you were making a food offering, you would scatter the Mola Salsa over the food before giving it.

In his *Fasti* 1. 337–53 Ovid tells us that this libation of grain and salt was regarded by the Romans as the earliest form of offering to the gods, and Horace, *Odes*. 3. 23. 20, claimed that mola salsa can be used alone as a sacrificial offering in itself.

In later Roman animal sacrifice, mola salsa was poured over the animal's head and on the sacrificial knife. It was seen as a critical part of the ritual when the animal was transferred to the ownership of the gods.

Besides mola salsa, the Vestals also made *suffimen*, which consisted of a mixture of the ashes of unborn calves from cows sacrificed to Tellus (Earth) and the blood of the October Horse. These were alchemically calcified on the Vestal fire and reverted to dust. It is fortunately less important, as a cow which has been sacrificed to the Earth God is hard to find in Rome and October Horses are thin on the ground. Its function appears to have been to unite the influence of the different fire festivals under one umbrella.

## CULTUS SECRETUM

The Romans considered the city itself sacred and everything that went through it was holy. One thing which was especially holy was the underworld of drains and sewers that passed underneath it. One of the oldest Fire Goddesses ruled this domain, the appropriately named Caca.

Caca was an important Goddess who was possibly a proto-Vesta, and indeed much of her fire aspects were taken over by that Goddess. However, as Rome developed its sewer network, Caca became connected with Venus Cloacina, which translates as "Venus of the Sewer," or more subtly "Venus the Purifier."

This was a triple fusion between the Roman Venus with the Etruscan water goddess Cloacina. What this means is that offerings to this Goddess are actually going to the toilet (and flushing). If you think I am making this up, one of the Roman Kings, Titus Tatius, who establishing altars to many deities at Rome including Ops, Flora, Veiovis, Saturn, Sol, Luna, Vulcan, Summanus, Larunda, Terminus, Quirinus, Vertumnus, the Lares, Lucina, and Diana, had a shrine dedicated to Caca in his private toilet.

While the Roman's did not think their poo was generally holy as an offering, they did know it was the sort of thing that Caca wanted and there was pretty much an infinite supply.

What the magician is doing in making such an offering is giving part of themselves to be purified in the fires (and, thanks to Cloacina, the sacred waters of the underworld).

It also means that getting rid of used offerings to other gods and goddesses, such as wine, charcoal, babies' hearts, etc., by flushing them down the loo is entirely appropriate. Once you get into the Roman mindset, you end up thinking, "What is wrong with that?"

## LARES AND ANCESTORS

Already we have seen how much the house was the centre of Roman worship, and none was more involved and confusing as the house spirit — or *Lares*.

Lares are spirits of a particular place. The Romans had one or two for each house. Traditionally they were beings from the underworld. They are sometimes seen as two young children holding cornucopias with a large snake. This image helps them to act as protectors of the home. Sometimes the image is painted and hung on the wall; other times a special shrine is created with statues of them. But this was a later development as the Lares were also connected with Ancestor Worship. In fact, the two children could be seen as representatives of the ancestors of everyone who lives in the house. The Romans had special rooms for the Ancestors and would take their death masks out on important occasions, but daily interactions came with the Lares.

The advantage for a magician is that they help bring power into the place where they work and live. In some respects, they are the missing link between the Planetary Forces and the earth. Too many magicians invoke Jupiter to bring them happiness and wealth but have no spirit locally on hand. By doing this invocation, you are acknowledging the powers of those spirits to operate for you.

Once you have a lare or two, you must honour them daily. This could include leaving out food offerings for them, lighting a candle or incense stick. You should proceed each offering by saying:

*Enos Lases iuvate, Enos Lases iuvate, Enos Lases iuvate.*[109]
*Salve lar familiaris (salute). I (full name) the Pater (Mater) familias make this offering to your honour. Strengthen and bless this family so that we may extend your powers into this generation. Stat Fortuna Domus (good fortune to this house) Macte esto (Be thou increased).*

The Romans would often put a plate of food and wine on the Larum so that the Lares would share the meal with them. At other times they would place the statues of the Lares on the dinner table and invite them to join them. Sometimes this role was carried out by the Panes or Penates which were earth spirits connected to the larder. They are supposed to have a special shelf where candles are offered to draw more food into the house. They are especially connected to the physical house and do not tend to move when the family does.

Although this all seems bizarre to a modern mind, it creates an interesting magical effect. Not only do the Lares offer to protect the house from nasty astral spirits, they also help "earth" ritual magic by bringing it into your home. If you did a Jupiter ritual, the Lares would often be responsible for making sure that the energy manifests as cold hard cash.

Sharing food or lighting candles to them daily links the magician to them, and as they grow in strength so too does your ability to "earth" your magic. Psychically they appear as two dancing children or a large snake or a house pet.

The Roman approach to Ancestors was similar, and sometimes the Lares fulfilled their function. In ancient Rome ancestral spirits were believed to have influence on mortal life and to return to visit their relatives when rites were held in their honour. The spirits of dead ancestors were believed to live in statuettes or funeral masks and were known as *Manes*. The Manes were worshipped during a festival known as *Parentalia*. During the festival, sacrifices were made to the Manes. The sacrifices (which usually took the form of flower garlands, wine-soaked bread, wheat, and salt) were placed at family tombs. It was believed that unless the festival of *Feralia* took place, the spirits of the dead would rise from their graves and roam the streets.

But a Roman family was expected to pray to them daily. The Ancestors were also supposed to be acknowledged on significant dates, such as

---

109 This is archaic Latin and was recorded in the Second Century AD, by which time its meaning had been lost. It was chanted by the Arval Brethren as part of a rite of Mars and calls upon the Lares to protect the city.

anniversaries, weddings, and birthdays. Again, these were often offerings of fire, wine, and food.

Acknowledging the Ancestors can be a considerable source of power and teaching, and this does not need to be restricted to any particular time of the year.

For example, it can be worth building up a cupboard or small wall with pictures of your Ancestors before which a candle can be lit or an offering made. It is extremely important that as an offering is made to name each Ancestor and identify them clearly. This naming also awakens and invigorates the spirit in the afterlife and renews their energy.

Romans thought it important that the spirits were prayed to and worshipped properly. It was believed that if a spirit was not shown the proper respect or if a family forgot to pray to it, it could become wrathful or mischievous. Spirits who became unhappy were known as *Lemures*.

Ancestors are very concerned about preserving the family and insuring their continuance. Although you might be the first in a couple of thousand years to pray to them, it is an indication that the family still exists and their line of evolution has not died out.

After contact has been made and a regular pattern of offerings made, ancestors are good at helping bring family members together, curing illnesses, and other useful things. It is possible to see them as a database of all your DNA and knowledge which can be tapped in the modern age. Remember also that whatever they are, at least part of you will be in the future.

Offerings to the ancestors can be also sent directly to them in Hades by digging a trench in the earth and pouring wine, blood, or food offerings within it. This does not have to be done where the dead are buried, but if you are after some form of contact with the dead, it should be done after dark. The Romans believed that offerings to underworld gods and goddesses and the dead should be conducted at night.

Here is a ritual formula that I have used, which is based on the Greek Magical Papyrii which works well when summoning the ancestors:

## INVOCATION

*I invoke you, spirit of the dead, whoever you are, by the mighty names SALBATHBAL AUTHGEROTABAL BASUTHATEO ALEO*

*SAMMABETHOR. Come forth into this place, oh ancestors of my family, root of my roots. I entrust this spell to you, gods of the underworld, to Pluto and Prosephone Ereschial and Adonis, and BARBARITHA and Hermes in the Underworld and Thoth PHOKENSEPSU EREKTATHOU MISONKTAIK and to mighty ANUBIS PSERPHTHA who holds the keys to the Gates of Hades, to the infernal gods, and my ancestors, to youths and maidens, from year to year, month to month, day to day, hour to hour, night to night I conjure all spirits in this place to stand as assistants to the great spirit the Mater Larum.*

*Come forth into this place by the blood in my veins which was forged by you.*
*Come forth, oh beings, whose names are forgotten by time but remembered by blood.*
*Come for these offerings of wine (pour wine).*
*Come for these offerings of flame (light candle).*
*Come for these offerings of food (pour mola salsa onto a plate).*
*Come for these offerings of incense (put frankincense on the altar).*
*For it is not just [your name] who calls thee, but Mater Larum who calls thee.*

# OFFERINGS TO LARS OF A PLACE

The Romans saw spirits as pretty much everywhere — some were bigger than others. A lake would have a single spirit, but different bays around that lake would be served by minor ones. A forest would have one ruling spirit, but groves of trees would have lesser ones. These spirits were called *numina* (singular, *numen*). Some of them, such as Vulcan, would later get merged with foreign gods or just be "promoted"; others would just stay small. Some trees were said to contain a numen.

Their role was more important in the agricultural areas of Roman society where the numina could control the weather and wild animals. Appeasing these gods was done by animal sacrifice. Animal sacrifice was said by Hesiod to have been first performed by Prometheus, and because of this it has been performed by people ever since (Theogony 535–60). This is not an option in modern society so other methods have to be found.

A New Age approach is to tidy up a spot and remove any rubbish from the area, on the sound basis that a spirit would appreciate it. Tree spirits tend to like having their seed planted elsewhere in a place so it has a chance to grow. Offerings of sacred water or wine are usually accepted. I have also buried old coins in the roots of trees or placed sacred stones from other sites into rabbit holes.

Water Numina like objects to be cast into the water with the prayer, *I offer this to the Numina of this place so that there may be peace and understanding between us.* Earth Numina like objects which are buried in the ground. You find a way, and just occasionally you get a sign that it has been accepted.[110]

# GODWORK

Working with the Roman gods has been an experiment on my part which has involved offerings but also some strange agreements too.

It is a huge mistake, made by many Neo-pagans, to assume that the Gods are going to form personal relationships with them and will do something for them merely because they ask. To the ancient Romans, the gods were something that you wanted on your side. If something went wrong in your life, it was because you had angered some god or goddess. Thus, the Romans piously attended festivals and made sacrifices mostly to avoid pissing off a god or a goddess. Reading the prayers of pious Romans, they are very legalistic. The person drafts a contract between the two — effectively saying, "If I do this, you will do this."

It was this lack of intimacy that made foreign Gods and Goddesses so appealing to the later Romans. The mystery religions, such as Mithras, Isis, and Christianity, allowed a more direct connection to the Gods and Goddesses. One of the advantages was that you knew exactly where you stood and what you had to do.

Later pagans recognised this, and some of the writings of the Neo-platonic schools feature the best of both worlds. But the relationship is nothing as close as the modern Christian idea of having a god you chat to as a mate.

To a magician this is not a bad thing. Magicians, to quote Terry Pratchet, work with the Gods but they do not believe in them — it is as pointless as believing in the postman. Gods have to be seen, as they are — centres of archetypal ideas and force. They have a persona, but that has been given

---

110    Also see Frater Rufus Opus' essay *The Back Yard Path to the Summum Bonum* for more information on working with local spirits, or *Genii Loci*. -ed.

to them by humanity. They can have a form, but then that is to help them communicate with you rather than a nature of their reality. In fact, the early Roman's did not anthropomorphize their gods much at all.

This level of abstraction makes it easier for a magician to work with. All sorts of atrocities are committed because people think that a God or Goddess is their invisible friend.

# GETTING ONSIDE

So if the relationship is not one of worshipper, then how may a magician hope to get onside with the being invoked? Offerings are a good way of getting the attention of a being. It is a little like ringing the God on its landline — you know where it is and how it was traditionally contacted. Making appropriate offerings is a way of the magician showing that he respects the deity he or she is calling. One thing that is important with Roman gods is that you show respect.

It is not entirely possible of course. Jupiter Optimus Maximus is not going to get a white bull slaughtered to him in the High Street anymore, and Magna Mater is not allowed to castrate males either. However, one thing I have noticed is that the old Gods are surprisingly willing to overlook that and are keen to adopt new technology. Vesta, for example, has no problem in seeing electricity as an extension of her hearth fire, and Venus likes the new forms of roses and has a tendency to like chocolate as an offering. It requires a lot of lateral thinking, but it is not difficult.

If you were Jupiter, what would you like as an offering? I have not tried it, but I would think Venus might like a nice pair of shoes. Mercury likes poems and invocations composed to him on the Internet that people can find and use. The idea of dedicating a book to a divine inspiration means much more to an Ancient deity than simply a few oranges absent-mindedly put on an altar.

All these serve to get the God onto your side. Any ritual must also be developed to feature some form of sacrifice. This is more simply done with multi-coloured candles which can stand in for a sacrifice to a specific god.

Recently I was working with the Roman gods as part of a series of rituals involving astrological patterns in a natal chart. In the ritual the Gods were not only invoked and given offerings but were each given an appropriately coloured candle which was allowed to burn down, as a sacrifice to the god or goddess. The flame of the candle is a sacrifice to the God and it becomes a magical act in its own right.

Another form of sacrifice is to build an astral temple for the God or Goddess to use. This is an exercise which developed from the Dion Fortune stream of magic, and it works rather well. What you do is construct a ritual and pathworking which visualises the creation of a temple to the God or Goddess you are working with. This is best tried with a vision journey to a particular place on the astral where you, and any astral helpers you might have, construct an authentic looking temple for the Godform. You then perform a ritual to consecrate it to the being. You can tell people where it is by writing a pathworking to get there and describing what you have built. This means that anyone might, if they wish, visit the Inner Temple and meet with the God or Goddess.

Even if you do not tell anyone the inner location of the temple, the fact that the temple has been created on the lower astral gives the godform a chance to work closer to the mind of modern humanity. In my experience, they tend to like it.

# BUILDING AN ASTRAL BODY

Another offering is a little more complex but has a similar concept to the Inner plane temple. One of the difficulties that the Ancient Gods have in making themselves useful in modern society is that they often fail to understand the "kids of today." A way around this is to provide them with an astral body formed from the matter of modern people. This is something which happens to all established religions anyway because they have legions of worshippers constantly re-inventing them. But Ancient Gods and goddesses have fewer connection points with modern humans, and creating an astral body for them to inhabit does help.

The sacrifice of Astral energy is managed using a middle pillar but only drawing down energy as far as Yesod and allowing it to leak into the temple. You will find that you can control and shape it into a form of the God or Goddess.

A final ritual for Magna Mater might look a bit like this:

On the altar are three candles in a triangle. In the centre is a black stone and the image of the goddess. Perform an opening of the quarters with the statement:

*Creatures of [element] build a body to assist the Magna Mater. The purpose of this working, if it please the One Thing, is to assist the Magna Mater to walk again amongst the people of [country] and protect the country from destruction and harm. For the people have forgotten her ways, forgotten hers powers, and she has slept in the Void. We have awoken her and now assist her as she manifests in our Aeon.*

*IMMINET LEONI VIRGO CAELESTI SITV SPICIFERA IVSTI INVENTRIX VRBIVM CONDITRIX EX QVIS MVNERIBVS NOSSE CONTIGIT DEOS: ERGO EADEM MATER DIVVM PAX VIRTVS CYBELE LANCE VITAM ET IVRA PENSITANS*

*The Virgin in her heavenly place rides upon the Lion! Bearer of wheat, Inventor of law, Founder of cities, by Whose gifts it is mankind's fortune to know the gods: therefore She is the Mother of the gods; Peace! Virtue! Cybele, weighing life and laws in her Balance. Walk the streets of [country] again and protect the Nation from fall.*

Perform the middle pillar and the sacrifice of energy to create the body of the Magna Mater. See her as huge, flanked by two lions, standing above the capital city.

*We have sacrificed our astral energy for the Mother of the Gods and now she is able to draw from the energy of the people of the Age. She has awoken and now we assist her work.*

Light the incense in the south.

*We offer thee incense as a sacrifice to give thee strength in this generation.*

Go to the West.

*We offer thee wine as a sacrifice to give thee strength in this generation.* (Pour wine into bowl.)

Go East and breath out to the Godform.

*Mother of Gods, thou Wife of starry Heaven,*
*We offer thee our breath as a sacrifice to give thee strength in this*
*generation.*

Go North and place the Mola Salsa.

*I have partaken from the Tympanum; quaffed from the Cymbal.*
*We offer thee sacred salt as a sacrifice to give thee strength in this*
*generation.*
*(Pause.)*
*SALVE MATER DEVM MAGNA IDAEA SALVE O DEA MAIOR*
*SANCTISSIMA*
*TE PRECOR BONAS PRECES O CYBELE BERECYNTHIA*
*MATER DINDYMENE*
*TE QVAESO IN CVSTODELAM NOS TVAM VTINAM*
*RECIPIAS ET TVTERE*
*TIBI OFFERO HANC ORATIONEM VT DES PACEM*
*PROPITIA SALVTEM*
*ET SANITATEM NOSTRAE FAMILIAE VTI SIS VOLENS*
*PROPITIA NOBIS*
*ET NVNQVAM DESOLES LIBEROS TVOS HARVM RERVM*
*ERGO MACTE HAC LIBATIONE ESTO FITO VOLENTE*
*PROPITIA NOBIS*

*Great Goddess of women, protector from enemies, healer of grave*
*illness, guardian of the dead, and mistress of prophecy and the*
*future. Bring thy powers to [country] as you did to Rome of old and*
*Protect it in this generation. Transform and bring it to life. Forgive*
*those who have forgotten you and heal them so they will know you*
*again. Let there be violets where there were pain and may you love*
*the city as you have loved and resurrected the spirit of Attis.*

Visualise the Goddess saying the following as you do:

*"I am awake in a new generation and stand my guard over [country]*
*again, from my new home in the Pantheon. Let all who would do*
*[country] harm, pay grievous penalty, and to all who do her tribute*

*accrue fitting reward. From my place in the Centre of Spiritual Rome . . . I return to all my old temples. I light them with the sacred flame once again. I bring my power to a new generation*
(Long pause for visualisation.)
*Magna Mater is in her place and in her new home in [country], bringing her blessings and protection to another age. The elemental gates which have built her body are closed in piece.*
*Sybil has returned.*

# Summary

In an article like this, we can only scratch the surface of Divine Magic using the rich and detailed Roman gods. Central to it is the process of offerings and sacrifice which requires a degree of lateral thinking to bring it up to date and make it useful. However, once we have gotten beyond that point, and rejected our Christian worldview of the Roman gods, we can find ourselves at the centre of a world controlled by divine beings who have been here for a lot longer than us. We can find a way to communicate with spirits which have been worshipped in one form or another by our ancestors and access those deeper aspects which make us human. At the centre of all this is a process of offerings as old as humanity.

# OFFERINGS IN IAMBLICHAN THEURGY

*Sam Webster, M.Div., Ph.D.,*
*founder OSOGD*

hile the term "Theurgy" was voiced by Julian the Theurgist, son of Julian the Chaldean, both authors of the Chaldean Oracles, it was Iamblichus that wrote the single most thorough explanation of the spiritual practice.[111]

Iamblichus of Chalcis (Northern Syria today) was born *c.* AD 240 and died *c.* 325.[112] He was a student of Porphyry, who was himself the student, scribe, and biographer of Plotinus, the founder of Neoplatonism, the religious form of Platonism that developed in the second and third centuries of the common era. Iamblichus is credited with fusing theurgy with Neoplatonic philosophy. He is known principally through fragments of his work quoted in later writers which are mostly commentaries on the Platonic dialogues, and sections from his work *On the Soul*.

One exception to this is his longest surviving work, given the title *De Mysteriis*[113] (*DM*) in the Renaissance. It was written as an extended reply to his teacher Porphyry's *Letter to Anebo,* a work critical of the general cultic practices of the day and explicitly those of theurgy. Iamblichus defends theurgy in *De Mysteriis* and presents a rationale for cultic worship, divination, divinization through divine possession, the art of sacrifice and allied practices, generally termed "magic" today. This work and the rest of his writings and teachings integrated worship and philosophy in a way previously unseen and came to dominate Neoplatonic philosophy thereafter.

---

111    This essay is substantially drawn from my doctoral thesis, *The History of Theurgy from Iamblichus to the Golden Dawn*, submitted and defended at the University of Bristol in June 2014.
112    The current best biography of Iamblichus is found in the introduction to Iamblichus, *Iamblichus, de Mysteriis*, trans. Emma C. Clarke, John M. Dillon, and Jackson P. Hershbell (Boston: Brill, 2004), pp. xvii and following.
113    Iamblichus, *Iamblichus, de Mysteriis*, trans. Emma C. Clarke, John M. Dillon, and Jackson P. Hershbell (Boston: Brill, 2004).

# Sacrifice: the Engine of Theurgy

Sacrifice was the basic experience of the sacred in the pre-Christian Greek world and so is vital to understanding any religious practice of the time.[114] Libations were poured, objects were dedicated, and animals were killed, burned, and in most cases, eaten.

The Neoplatonic theurgy of Iamblichus was no exception. Sacrifice was central to Iamblichus' method and so important that he devotes the entirety of Book Five of *De Mysteriis* to it. This work as a whole can be seen as a justification of the ancient practice of sacrifice in the face of challenges by skeptics, possibly by Christians, and most importantly by his own teacher, Porphyry.[115] In responding, Iamblichus created a new explanation for sacrifice that legitimates it and sets it in the context of theurgic practice.[116]

In *DM*, Iamblichus discusses many phenomena associated with theurgic practice, and as the results of that practice. But when we turn to the practice itself, only one action is named, albeit a complex one: sacrifice. By means of correctly performing sacrifice all of the other phenomena associated with theurgy arise, such as purification, divination, possession and oracles, ascension, and so forth.

Studying this "engine" of theurgy, in its centrality, will therefore disclose the character of theurgy, its path of advancement, and eventual attainment. The focus of this essay is on the nature of sacrifice or offerings in theurgy, with some thought as to how this manifests in the three order structure of the Golden Dawn.

# *Qui Bono?* — Not Reciprocity . . .

In *De Mysteriis* Iamblichus speaks in the guise of an Egyptian Priest named Abamon as a way of replying to his teacher Porphyry's *Letter to Anebo* without,

---

114   Walter Burkert, *Homo Necans: The Anthropology of Ancient Greek Sacrificial Ritual and Myth*, trans. P. Bing (Berkeley: University of California 1983), (German original 1972).

115   Porphyry, *On Abstinence from Killing Animals,* trans. Gillian Clark (London: Gerald Duckworth & Co. Ltd., 2000).

116   Clarke, Emma, *Iamblichus's De Mysteriis: A manifesto of the miraculous* (Ashgate: Aldershot, 2001), p. 31.

Shaw suggests, formally contradicting him.[117] In this epistle, Porphyry dispar-ages traditional cult as unnecessary and verging upon harmful.[118] Porphyry claimed, for a start, that sacrifice is just feeding the Daemons (*DM* 5.10 p. 243). Daemons, properly, are the lowest-but-one divine beings who invisibly manipulate the machinery of the universe and *are* such varied forces as momentum or growth, and bind souls like ourselves into our bodies. Human souls are the lowest of all divine entities.

Also, he claimed that sacrifices pollute the higher with (low) matter (*DM* 5.2 p. 227). Iamblichus fired back that, besides not being able to pollute the higher since matter cannot pass beyond the moon (*DM* 5.4 p. 231), Daemons don't need food (*DM* 5.10 p. 243), and certainly not from what is lower than Them, namely us. And if not the Daemons, how much more so the higher Beings right up to the Gods. None of them *need* sacrifice. The Gods, as well as all other divine beings, are "unchangeable and impassible, luminous and free from needs" (*DM* 5.10 p. 243). So then, *qui bono?* Who benefits?

We, the ones *offering* the sacrifice, benefit. For Iamblichus, sacrifices "contribute to the purification or the perfection of the soul [of the sacrificer] or to its freeing from the bonds of generation" (*DM* 5.6 p. 235). He dealt with and defended the validity of sacrifices for material needs later in *De Mysteriis* (5.16 p. 233), but his primary focus was on its spiritual benefits. The fires of sacrifice, he states, "render us also impassive; they assimilate what is in us to the gods . . . and [the fire] leads us up by means of sacrifices and sacrificial fire towards the fire of the gods . . . [which] draws up downward-tending and resistant entities to divine and heavenly ones" (*DM* 5.12 p. 247).

This view is contradictory to the common and ancient understanding of sacrifice as an exchange or a gifting in hope of helpful response from those offered to. But the idea that the Gods cannot be affected by sacrifice is con-sistent with an understanding of the Gods as truly Divine. This principle was disclosed through the theology of the day, called philosophy, in this case (neo-) Platonic. The Gods would not be Gods if they could be affected by humans.

---

117    Gregory Shaw, *Theurgy and the Soul: The Neoplatonism of Iamblichus* (University Park: Pennsylvania State University Press 1995), p. 21 n.1.
118    Porphyry, II 36.5, II 42.1.

# WHAT IS OFFERED

The power of sacrifice for Iamblichus comes fundamentally from the united life of the cosmos and the fact that the Gods are the primary causes in it (*DM* 5.7 p. 235–7). In accord with Plato's *Timaeus* and contemporary Stoic doctrine, for Iamblichus the cosmos is "one single living being possessing a common life in all parts of itself" (*DM* 5.7 p. 237). The Gods as "primary causes" are the structures and functions of the cosmos, and it is the *philia* (love) They have for the materials offered due to Their presence in the materials (DM 5.9 p. 239) that makes the materials effective offerings. This framework appealed to Iamblichus because it permits the Gods and other divine entities to remain uncompromisingly pure while presiding over the entity to be offered: The Divine Ones are not attracted to or corrupted by the fumes of the sacrifice, as Porphyry claims.[119] Also, it frees the theurgist from the charge that she is coercing the Gods. They come because They made, and thus love, what is being offered. A brief explanation of this in Neoplatonic terms is in order . . .

# MAKING THE OFFERINGS

In Neoplatonic cosmology matter itself is formless and devoid of characteristics like color, shape, or weight, etc. All qualities come from the primordial Forms (*Eides*) which are originally part of the One, the primary creative cause. As the Demiurge fashions the Cosmos, per Plato's *Timaeus*, these Forms become instantiated as the Gods. The Gods, continuing creation, emanate Their constituting Forms into the Cosmos as a *Logos* or Word, which descend from the *Noetic* (the proper Realm of the Gods), through the *Psychic* and the Celestial worlds to the Terrestrial (our world), giving form to the unformed at each step of the way.

This structure is none other than the four Worlds of the Qabalah, familiar to the Golden Dawn.[120] As the Words descend, they blend or breed with the

---

119    Porphyry, II 42.3.

120    Gershom Scholem, the father of the modern study of Kabbalah, concisely provides the connection: "Inasmuch as early Kabbalah needed a theoretical foundation it was largely influenced by neoplatonism" (Scholem, Gershom. *Kabbalah* [New York: Dorset Press, 1974], p. 96). As an example, the early Kabbalist Rabbi Azriel provides a direct conceptual connection in his writings between the Kabbalistic stages of emanation called the *Sepherot* and the intermediate substances of Neoplatonism and, according to Scholem, is the instigator of this

other Words producing the manifest complexity of the World and the characteristics of all things. In this way all of the qualities of objects and persons in the world are derived from the Gods, which is to say that everything in the world has several Divine Parents or Makers. Or, in more modern language, each thing in the world instantiates a complex union of the Words of a number of the Gods (a sentence?). Thus, we offer back to a God that which has as part of its constitution the Word of that God. As Iamblichus notes, Creators most love their creations (*DM* 5.24 p. 271).

This notion of the Maker's intent being present in the materials offered provided the single most important technical principle in theurgy, justifying the use of "stones, plants, animals, aromatic substances . . ." (*DM* 5.23 p. 269). "Immaterial beings are present in material natures immaterially," as Shaw[121] translates *De Mysteriis* 5.23.10 (p. 266). The intent of the Maker of the item is revealed in it symbolically as its characteristics (*DM* 3.15 p. 157). Shaw explores this extensively throughout *Theurgy and the Soul*, explaining the anagogic (upward lifting) value of this kind of symbol to the theurgists, using them as a means to perfect their souls and ascend to the Gods.[122]

In the Golden Dawn, this kind of thinking produces tables of correspondences culminating in that published by Aleister Crowley under the title *777*.[123] This document presents a large, diverse array of material and immaterial items arranged by and indexed to the Qabalistic Tree of Life, the primary symbol system and structuring element in Golden Dawn ritual and practice. By reading horizontally across the tables the practitioner is able to find a set of objects, symbols, and meanings that all embody the same *sunthemata*, and by employing them able to compose a ritual to invoke the principle they all contain. Unfortunately, the very existence of the tables can lead to dogmatism and dependency on written materials. Perhaps this is why Iamblichus does not provide any.

---

important bridge between the two systems of thought (Scholem, Gershom. *Kabbalah* [New York: Dorset Press, 1974], p. 100ff). Scholem then goes on to discuss the technical differences between Neoplatonic and Kabbalistic notions of emanation, which only concerns us here in that it reinforces the stimulus the philosophy provided.

121    Shaw, p. 48

122    Shaw, pp. 162–5.

123    Crowley, Aleister, *777 and other Qabalistic Writings of Aleister Crowley* (York Beach, Maine: Samuel Weiser, 1983), 336 pp.

# Three Grades of Offering

In theurgic practice objects are offered not for their physical natures, which is itself void of characteristics, but for their immaterial "content," which grants those characteristics. Thereby the offerings bridge the material-immaterial divide between the physical Cosmos and the Realm of the Gods in the *Noetic*. Iamblichus explains that "for each part of the cosmos there is on the one hand this body that we can see, and on the other hand the various particular incorporeal forces associated with bodies" (DM 5.20 p. 261).

A corollary of this is that if we are really offering the immaterial Word back to its Divine "Speaker," why can't we just offer that without all the matter? While it can be done, most can't do it. All persons can make material sacrifices but not all can make immaterial ones, at least properly. But those who have studied philosophy and know that the material object is a complex instance of Divine Form can see past the cow or libation to the anagogic and Divinely given token, the *sunthemata*, and knowingly make offering of the immaterial form while the material body is consumed by flames.

Out of the interaction of these two "things," formless Matter itself and the incorporeal Word derived from a Divine Form ("spoken" by a Deity), is produced a threefold gradation of offerings:

1. objects offered for their materiality (a cow, barley, a libation, incense),
2. purely immaterial or *noetic* offerings (geometric forms, etc.), and between them
3. quasi-material objects offered for their immaterial content, such as a divine word spoken (its materiality being sound) or a geometric form sketched in the air (its materiality being gesture).

These latter offerings which Shaw calls "intermediate" *sunthemata* are of special interest to the theurgical practitioner because they give her the opportunity to make equally profound sacrifice but without the same degree of materiality. Yet more important is that all invocation, in the sense of words spoken, constitutes intermediate *sunthemata*. Skill in the practice of invocation is crucial to the theurgist's success.

Shaw describes this gradation at length in his notions of **material, intermediate**, and ***noetic*** *sunthemata* and we adopt his schema here.[124] It is important, following Shaw, to stress that the *sunthemata* in and of themselves are not to be distinguished by their degree of materiality. *Sunthemata* are essentially *noetic*, purely objects of the mind, what we might call "information" today. As above, "Immaterial beings are present in material natures immaterially," informing them and giving them their distinct characteristics (*DM* 5.23.10 p. 266, tr. Shaw). It is the bodies upon which they are impressed and to which they impart their causal efficacy as manifest by the characteristics of those bodies that vary with respect to their materiality. They are "wondrous deposits" sent by the Demiurge to our world and through them "the inexpressible is expressed through ineffable symbols."[125]

There is also a general scaling of the *quality* of the *noetic* impression on the "substance" in inverse proportion to its materiality. Thus, the less material the item, the better the copy is in the medium and therefore the more pure the *sunthemata*. Some are fully material like animals, plants, and stones,[126] and some are subtly material like vapors, sounds, and graphics.[127] The *sunthemata* in purely *noetic* offerings can be considered the pure *sunthemata*, shorn entirely of body, no doubt accounting for their profound, if subtle, impact.[128]

From this comes Iamblichus' "double mode of worship," part material and part immaterial (*DM* 5.15, p. 251) and available to those in the median between those "governed by universal nature," the common folk, and "those who conduct their lives by intellect alone" (*DM* 5.18, p. 257–9). While she cannot expect the same degree of material effect, since one must make material offering to the material gods to gain material effect (*DM* 5.17, p. 255), the theurgist of the first or second grade of theurgic practice can simply burn some incense, perhaps draw a character, or just pray, which after all is a word offering, and thereby achieve divine union of some degree.[129]

---

124    Shaw, p. 162–228. Shaw dedicated six chapters to the subject of *sunthemata* in detail, two each on the intermediate and *noetic* kinds.
125    DM 1.21, p. 79–81, tr. Shaw, p. 163.
126    Ibid. p. 162–169.
127    Ibid. p. 170–188.
128    Ibid. p. 189–215.
129    See the Cicero's *Ritual for the Declaration of Maa Kheru* for examples of these kinds of symbolic offerings. -ed.

Theurgists of the third grade would not even use this much materiality but in a purely *noetic*[130] manner make offering and attain to union.[131] But a caution must be raised here as *noetic* worship is not "something immediately available to those beginning theurgy, nor yet those who have reached a middling degree of proficiency in it; for even these latter endow their performance of cult with some degree of corporeal influence" (DM 5.21, p. 263).

# Three Grades of the Order

While a caution, this statement is useful to us as it may allude to one of the most vexatious notions in the Golden Dawn: What is the nature of the Third Order?

The threefold division of beginning, middling, and transcended theurgic practitioners, as characterized by the kinds of offering they can make, may provide explanation for the three orders of the Golden Dawn. It shows what they are, their purpose, and how they work, but rooted in the source material of the Kabbalah: Neoplatonism.

Space does not allow a more detailed exploration of the first and second orders than that alluded to above, except to say that the beginning ranks are still characterized by a predominance of materiality. This manifests in the First Order of Golden Dawn in the advancements, which are traditionally unexplained to the aspirants, thus leaving the rites' inner work to be the province of the Second Order. In the Second Order, the material rites have been passed and the work proceeds with the various other Order rituals, typified by the Z Document rituals which, being based on the Neophyte Hall, have dematerialized all of the officers and equipment. All that is left on the physical plane is the solo practitioner and her tools. The vast majority of the work has been transferred into the realms of spirit/energy and mind/astral. Following this pattern then, the Third Order can be mapped to the practitioners of wholly immaterial sacrifice and offerings.

The characteristics of such practitioners are that they have transcended the "Abyss," the gap in the geometric regularity of the Tree of Life between Chesed and Binah. While Crowley makes much of this in the *Vision and*

---

130    *Noetic*, meaning mental, imageless, and incorporeal, and of the highest level of existence.
131    I am reminded here of biblical imagery (see the *Revelation of St. John*) where the prayers and praises of the Saints are collected into a spiritual censer and, in and of themselves, offered to the Highest. -ed.

*the Voice,* his *Confessions,* and elsewhere, the source data in the Kabbalah is thin. But it does have a place in Neoplatonic Cosmology: the gap between the *Psychic* and the *Noetic,* mapping to Briah and Atzulith, respectively.

# USING THE PHAEDRUS

Plato discusses the soul in a number of his dialogues, like the three parts of the soul in the 4th book of the *Republic,* but it is in the *Phaedrus* (along with the *Timaeus*) that the Neoplatonists turned to understand the structures of the soul and whole human constitution. In the *Phaedrus* (245c–249d) Socrates tells the tale of souls as being like "the composite nature of a pair of winged horses and a charioteer" (246a). In the midst of this narration, Socrates also inserts the term *Kubernetes,* or Helmsman, as a part of the soul that sees what is "visible only to the mind" (247d), "the colorless, formless, and intangible truly existing essence, with which all true knowledge is concerned" (247c). These parts or entities, that in composite form the soul, will be explicated by the Neoplatonists, and in particular, Iamblichus.

Iamblichus analyzes the Pheadrus myth of the soul to integrate the One and the *Nous* with the soul. It is worth quoting the fragment at length:[132]

> The divine Iamblichus takes the "helmsman" as being the One of the soul; its Intellect is the charioteer; the term "spectator" is used not to signify that it directs its gaze on this object of intellection as being other than it, but that it is united with it and appreciates it on that level; for this shows that the "helmsman" is a more perfect entity than the charioteer and the horses; for it is the essential nature of the One of the soul to be united with the gods. (Dillon 1973, *In Phaedrum* Fg. 6, p. 97)

This gives us two important notions. First it plainly shows how Iamblichus assigns the various entities of the Pheadrus myth to the cosmological hypostasies on the one hand and the parts of the human experience of the soul on the other. The otherwise brief reference in the myth to the Helmsman is seen as the instantiation of the unifying power of the One in the human

---

132    The following extended quotes are taken from John M. Dillon, tr., ed., *Iamblichi Chalcidensis in Platonis Dialogos Commentariorum Fragmenta* (Leiden: Brill, 1973).

soul. The Charioteer is identified as the Intellegence of the Soul, here clearly meaning the *dianoetic* or discursively reasoning part of the soul. The horses, perhaps, are the passions, and the chariot itself the "soul vehicle" or the body. Second, and more importantly, it points to the vital nature of the One of the (individual) soul, the Helmsman. This is the faculty of the soul that achieves divine union. It is its "essential nature [. . .] to be united with the gods."

We are told here something about the nature of that union: The Helmsman "directs its gaze on this object of intellection [not] as being other than it, but that it is united with it and appreciates it on that level." Elsewhere Iamblichus describes this kind of union with the Gods as "sharing in Their intellect, *homionoeticos*, or being 'of one mind' with the Gods."[133] This kind of union is consistent with the Aristotelian principle that mind is identical with the object of its contemplation. But elsewhere we learn that this gaze or contemplation is not a result of any effort, but rather something aporetic or even gracious. In Iamblichus's commentaries on the *Parmenides*, he says:

> That neither by opinion, nor by discursive reasoning, nor by the Intellectual element of the soul, nor by intellection accompanied by reason is the Intelligible to be comprehended, nor yet is it to be grasped by the perfect conning-tower of the intellect, nor by the flower of the intellect, nor is it knowable by a mental effort at all, neither along the lines of a definite striving, nor by a grasping, nor by any such means as this.
> (Dillon 1973 *In Parmenidem* Fg. 2A, p. 209)

In this fragment, Iamblichus dismisses all of the intellectual entities in the soul from even being capable of comprehending the Intelligible and further denies that any effort at all results in such comprehension. One can only conclude that it is by the grace of the Gods that the One of the soul, the Helmsman, is at all able to achieve that comprehension and that it is done though passive contemplation and the gift of divine union. This is entirely in keeping with Iamblichus's doctrine that it is the Gods who do Theurgy and that humans have no such power to attain to divine union, leastwise in

---

133    Iamblichus, *De Anima*, tr. and ed. John F. Finamore and John M. Dillon (Leiden: Brill, 2002), Fg. 44, p. 71 & Commentary, p. 201. See also John F. Finamore, *Iamblichus and the theory of the vehicle of the soul* (Chico, Calif.: Scholars Press, 1985).

its final stages.[134] Our offerings make the connection and open ourselves to change. Then the Gods work the change.

Now that we have a sense of the nature of the *Noetic* realm and the states of mind in which it is experienced, let us turn to the individuals who attain to this state.

# The Plotinian Third Order?

The path of theurgy is anagogic, leading one up into the heavens, and so from the Material Gods we are to turn to the Immaterial Ones. Yet in truth few practitioners can make exclusively immaterial offerings, only "one, or some small easily counted number of men," can make them (*DM* 5.15 p. 253). This is a point Iamblichus makes so many times that we must remember that one purpose of *De Mysteriis* is to correct his teacher Porphyry.

Porphyry in *On the Abstinence from Animal Food* stresses the preeminence of immaterial offerings and discounts material ones strenuously, except for a few minor purposes, none of which are appropriate for philosophers.[135] This clearly irritates Iamblichus, for by his theory few can perform this kind of immaterial worship, and even of them, if anyone is still in the body there is a legitimate purpose for material worship in that it provides for the body and material needs (DM 5.16 p. 253). To end this would be to cut off whole cities and the mass of humanity from the providential care of the material Gods (DM 5.15 p. 253).

Iamblichus is not satisfied with saying this only once, but rather five times in Book 5 of *De Mysteriis*.[136] His statement that one should not generalize from the condition of one person, saying all should behave as he did, draws our attention to his motivation. The following selection will give us a clue to whom Iamblichus is referring and further delineate the strata of the theurgic path:

> [W]hen one makes contact in a hypercosmic mode with the gods of theurgy (which is an exceedingly rare occurrence), such an individual will be one who has transcended the bounds of bodies and matter in the service of the gods, and who is united to

---

134    See *DM* 1.21 for limits of human capacity to grasp the Gods through reasoning.
135    Porphyry, II throughout but especially 43.2.
136    DM, 5.15 p. 253, 5.18 p. 257 & 259, 5.20 p. 261, 5.22 p. 265.

the gods through hypercosmic power. One should not therefore take a feature that manifests itself in the case of a particular individual, as the result of great effort and long preparation, at the consummation of the hieratic art, and present it as something common to all men, but not even as something immediately available to those beginning theurgy, nor yet those who have reached a middling degree of proficiency in it; for even these latter endow their performance of cult with some degree of corporeal influence.
(DM 5.20 p. 263)

As Plotinus' student, scribe, and biographer, ever before the eye of Porphyry is his master, who clearly had attained to such a state that immaterial worship was available and even primary to him. Iamblichus insists that just because this one superlative individual was capable of immaterial worship, "a feature that manifests itself in the case of a particular individual," one should not discount the value of material worship for everyone else. I believe that Iamblichus is criticizing Porphyry for over-generalizing from his teacher.

On a practical basis, Shaw suggests that disdaining material offerings may have contributed to Porphyry's ongoing struggle with depression, weakening his relationships with the material Gods and rendering him unable to be at peace in the world.[137] The Material Gods are the gateway to the Immaterial Ones and if not properly integrated through material theurgies, troubles arise. In a theurgist's mind this might also account for Plotinus' slow, painful, and mortal illness.[138] Neglecting the Gods responsible for corporeal things by not making material offerings would either cause the ailments or be the consequence of not taking the appropriate "medicine."

Since the purpose of theurgy is to make us more like the Gods and to be ultimately in communion with the One, the Supreme Being and Source of All in Neoplatonic thought, the theurgist will have to ascend from the Material Gods through the Immaterial Ones to the One. This process places the aspiring theurgist in a median position, neither fully of the herd nor having completely attained to immaterial worship like Plotinus (DM 5.18 pp. 257–9). Therefore, Iamblichus will have them make offerings that are in part material

---

137    Shaw, p. 155.
138    Glenn W. Most, "Plotinus' Last Words" *The Classical Quarterly, New Series*, Vol. 53, No. 2 (Nov., 2003), pp. 576–587.

and in part immaterial, and have a suitable set of intermediate entities (DM 5.19 p. 259) for them to address.

In the quote above, Iamblichus also alludes to a beginning level of theurgic practice and a middling degree, each distinguished by more and less material components in their cultic observances. At the beginning, immaterial worship is "not even . . . something immediately available" to the theurgist, and even the middling "endow their performance of cult with some degree of corporeal influence." Only one who has "transcended the bounds of bodies and matter in the service of the gods, and who is united to the gods through hypercosmic power," can be meaningfully said to engage in incorporeal worship, the third grade of theurgic attainment.

Our translators, Clarke et al., were puzzled by why Iamblichus needed to introduce the median set at all and discussed it in a footnote.[139] It is necessary to account for the developmental process in the practice of theurgy and bridges the gap from the herd to the Plotinian heights. This is the likely position of the First and Second Orders of the Golden Dawn. The beginners in theurgy are "members" of the First Order, making physical offerings, knowing of the immaterial essence of the offering but unable to produce the offering without the very material substance. The Second Order "members" can produce the *sunthemata* with a word or a symbol drawn in the air, but not yet wholly and solely of mind. Those who can work entirely in the mind would be members of the Third Order.

We may well be seeing here, in this debate between Porphyry and Iamblichus, a very early discussion regarding the nature of the mysterious "Third Order" and the almost god-like beings who attain to it. Having "transcended the bounds of bodies and matter" sounds a lot like the descriptions we will find in Mathers, Crowley, and others of the Magister Templi, Magus and Ipsissimus, the titles of the grades of that Order.[140]

The essence of the point is this: Iamblichus claims Plotinus is a member of the Third Order and what works for him won't work for everyone else.

---

139    DM, p. 257, fn. 326
140    Aleister Crowley, Desti, Mary, Waddell, Leila, Hymenaeus Beta, ed. *Magick: Book 4, Liber Aba* (Newburyport, MA: Weiser Books. 1998), Appendix II.

# Conclusion

Sacrifice, or the making of offerings, is a central part of theurgy which itself is the foundation of Golden Dawn practice. Offerings are made not to benefit the Gods, who have no needs, but to benefit the one making the offering, whether that person is a common worshiper, a theurgist, or one who has attained to the heights. The offerings themselves are part material, but more importantly part immaterial, and thus, the matter is the carrier of the immaterial and anagogic *sunthemata*. This divine token when properly apprehended gives us direct contact with the Deity as it is an instance of that Deity, however obscured by matter. The capacity to directly perceive the *sunthemata* in the substance, shorn of its materiality, is the index of one's grade.

From the beginner who just knows that the *sunthemata* is present in the object (1st Order) to the middling practitioner who is aware of the immaterial token and can produce it in graphical symbol or word (2nd Order) to, finally, those who are able to produce and offer the *noetic sunthemata* solely by mind, as apparently did Plotinus, we see the progression to the Third Order.

In the space allowed, this is only a sketch of the process that Iamblichus lays out. Making the correct offerings at the correct stage to the correct Beings is critical to the theurgists' success. Understanding the place of offerings in the development of *epitedeiotes*, fitness; the process of light-guiding or *photogogia* in the cultivation of the soul and its vehicle, the *Augoides*; solar worship and the personal Daemon; each of these, and so much more, has an important role to play in the theurgs' progress. This will have to await a longer work.

For now, I hope this sketch focuses practitioners' attention on the critical aspects of sacrifice and offerings, gives a sense of the developmental path in which they are crucial, and an inkling of the goal towards which they lead. Perhaps also, this will refine our understanding of the three order structure of the Golden Dawn and place Plotinus, the founder of late- or "neo-" Platonism, as an early, if not founding, member of the Third Order.

# Ritual for the Declaration of Maa-Kheru
## A Rite of Offerings to the Forty-two Assessors in the Hall of the Neophytes

*Chic Cicero and*
*Sandra Tabatha Cicero*

# INTRODUCTION

The Forty-two Assessors first appeared as a tribunal of Gods who judged the dead in the netherworld Hall of Justice or the Hall of the *Maati* (the "Hall of the Two Truths"). Early references to this divine committee may appear as early at the Pyramid Texts as well as in the later Coffin Texts of the Middle Kingdom. Once *The Book of the Coming Forth by Day* (better known today as *The Book of the Dead*) became the primary funerary text of the ancient Egyptians, the judgment of the deceased in the Hall of Justice was perceived as the central event in an individual's journey in the afterlife. After one's death, the Egyptians believed that the soul was escorted by the god Anubis into the Court of Osiris, where his deeds in life were recorded by Thoth, god of wisdom and writing, and examined for final judgment by Forty-Two Judges who acted in accordance with *Maat*.

Maat (or *Maet*), the Goddess of Truth, personified the physical and moral laws of the Universe. She also represented the ethical and moral principles of order, honor, truth, and Justice that Egyptians were expected to pursue in all areas of life — in matters relating to family, community, environment, country, and spirituality. In the *Book of the Dead*, she appears in dual form as the Maati in the Hall of Judgment, where she, along with the Forty-two Assessors who are under her charge, listens to the confessions of the deceased. The Assessors are often depicted seated in two rows of twenty-one.

The bulk of information on the Assessors can be found in the 125th Chapter of the *Book of the Dead*, in a section entitled "The Negative Confession."[141] This was testimony by the soul of the deceased addressed to each of the Forty-Two Judges. Each is addressed by name, along with their geographic area and other characteristics. The soul was expected to know the essential nature of each of the Forty-Two and to plead innocent of committing the specific sin or crime under the jurisdiction of that Judge. Within the courtroom the heart, representing the moral essence of the deceased, would be placed in a scale and weighed against the feather of Maat. The Assessors determined the destiny of the defendant. If their evaluation was unfavorable, the soul was devoured. If the judgment was favorable, and the heart's weight was equal to or lighter than Maat's feather, the individual was judged to be *Maa Kheru* ("Justified" or "True of Voice") — morally upstanding. Then the perfected soul went through the process of transformation and the subsequent rebirth into the *Aaru*, the pleasant "Field of Reeds" in the afterlife.

The Weighing of the Soul in the Hall of Judgment is the central motif upon which the Outer Order of the Golden in general, and the Neophyte Ceremony in particular, is based.

# THE FORTY-TWO ASSESSORS IN THE GOLDEN DAWN

The Golden Dawn system of magic is designed to gradually bring about a higher state of self-awareness, an increase in latent psychic faculties, and effect spiritual wholeness. In its initiation ceremonies the officers, like Jungian archetypes, represent the various component parts of the candidate's psyche all working together to effect change in consciousness. The Visible Stations belonging to the Outer Order Officers have Egyptian deities attributed to them, and the entire story of the Weighing of the Soul is employed to represent the advance and purification of the candidate in the Neophyte Hall. Much of this re-enactment of the Egyptian legend of the Hall of Judgment actually takes place on a magical and astral level that would not be perceived on the physical level.

---

141    Different versions of the Negative Confession exist, so none can be considered standard. The version used by the Golden Dawn is from *The Papyrus of Ani*, published by E.A. Wallis Budge in 1895.

There are also Invisible Stations or focal points of godform energy within the Hall that are attributed to Egyptian deities, but which do not have human Officers as counterparts to represent them. Among these are the Forty-two Assessors.

The teachings of the Golden Dawn only hint at the function of these Invisible Godforms in the Hall of the Neophytes. The Second Order document known as "Z-1: The Egyptian Godforms of the Neophyte Grade," tells us:

> The *Forty-Two Assessors*. These are not described at all save to say that they make the Sign of the Enterer as the Candidate is passed by them. They are Witnesses in the Judgment Hall of Osiris.[142]

More of their function is revealed in the paper "Z-3: The Symbolism of the Admission of the Candidate":

> The reception and consecration take place symbolically in the darkest part of Malkuth. The moment this is finished, the Candidate is conducted to the foot of the Altar, that is under the citrine part of Malkuth which receives the impact of the Middle Column. Now, the Hegemon throughout the Ceremony acts as guide, prompter and answerer for the Candidate. His office toward the Candidate is analogous to that of his Higher Soul — wherefore also, the Hegemon holds in his hand the mitre-headed sceptre to attract, since it is the sceptre of Wisdom, the Higher Self of the Candidate. At this moment, as the Candidate stands before the Altar, as the simulacrum of the Higher Self is attracted, so also arises the form of the Accuser in the place of the Evil Triad. This similarly attracts the simulacrum of the Evil Persona of the Candidate — *and were it not for the power of the 42 lettered name in the Palaces of Yetzirah (the Gods of which name are usually called the "Great Assessors of Judgment") the actual evil Persona would at once formulate and be able to obsess the Ruach of the Candidate.*[143] For, seeing that at this time, the simulacrum of the Higher Soul is attracting the Neschamah of the Candidate, the human will is not as powerful in the Ruach for the moment,

---

142    Regardie, *The Golden Dawn*, 358.
143    Italics are ours.

because the Aspirant of the Mysteries is now, as it were, divided. That is, his Neschamah is directed to the contemplation of his Higher Self attracted by the Hegemon. His natural body is bound and blinded, his Ruach threatened by the simulacrum of the Evil Persona attracted by Omoo-Szathan, and a species of shadow of himself thrown forward to the place of the Pillars, where the Scales of Judgment are set. At the same time that the first consecration establishes a semblance of the Pillars to his right and left, it also has drawn forth from him a semblance of himself to the place vacated by the Hegemon between the Pillars.[144]

Here then stands the shadow of the Candidate while the Scales of the Balance oscillate unseen. Unseen also and colossal, there is imaged before him Tho-oth) as Mettatron, in the Sign of the Enterer of the Threshold, ready, according to the decision of the human will, to permit or withhold the descent of the Lower Genius of the Candidate.

*Meanwhile, the Great Assessors of Judgment examine into the truth of the accusations formulated by the Evil and averse antithesis. The Assessors of Judgment come not under the head of invisible stations, but during the Obligation and circumambulation of the Candidate, until he is brought to the Light, they hover immediately about the limits of the Temple and their evil antithesis immediately below.*[145] Therefore, when the Candidate stands before the Altar before the Obligation, is the decision actually taken by the human will of the Candidate. Rarely in his life has he been nearer death, seeing that he is, as it were, disintegrated into his component parts. The process of symbolic judgment takes place during the speech of the Hierophant to the Candidate, the answer of the Hegemon and his consent to take the Obligation.[146]

---

144    Regardie has added a comment here: "(That is, the ceremony induces a species of schizophrenia so that the initiation may be effected. But see Jung's Commentary to *The Secret of the Golden Flower*, and also my book on alchemy *The Philosopher's Stone*.-I. R.)".
145    Italics are ours.
146    Regardie, *The Golden Dawn*, 365–366.

## Purpose

Various versions of the Negative Confession survive from antiquity. It is called the Negative Confession because the soul confesses what sins they have <u>not</u> committed. In reality few human beings could honestly make such a Negative Confession in such absolutist terms, for what human being has never lied or never caused another to cry? And yet it is important to strive for the ideals espoused by Maat. Theurgists strive and sometimes struggle to maintain the high principles required whenever a spiritual discipline is ardently pursued. That is the spirit in which this particular ritual has been written.[147]

The purpose of this ritual is to remind the Adept of the high goals to which he or she has pledged to live by — to become "more than human." Words are indeed powerful, and by orally listing a sin, a virtue, or a principle that one is working toward, the mere act of speaking makes the goal more real, more potent, and more present in one's consciousness.

The "confession" contained in this ritual has morphed from negative to positive. The Theurgist declares what he has <u>*not*</u> done, or what he or she has striven <u>*not*</u> to do, but follows this with what he or she *will* do, or what he *will* *strive to do* in the future. To accomplish this, the Adept makes an offering to each of the Forty-two Assessor gods from the Hall of Justice. Many of these offerings are personal, some intensively so. The final objective is for the magician to be found Maa-Kheru, True of Voice.

## The Truth Offerings

Make sure all the written offerings are on small pieces of paper to insure that they burn well and produce the least amount of smoke. The forty-two offerings to be prepared are as follows:

1. A personal vow[148] to always strive to act in accordance with Maat.
2. A piece of charcoal that has been anointed with consecrated oil.
3. This offering requires the replacement of something that was stolen (you don't have to be the one who stole it!). The important thing here

---

147   Honesty is very important to this ritual, so if the magician has committed one of the offences listed, the wording can be changed to reflect this. For example: "I admit that have caused someone sorrow in the past, but I have made amends, and I shall strive to not cause sorrow in the future."

148   It should contain your magical motto.

is to replace a stolen item and make the victim whole again. The offering here is a written testimonial.

4. This offering requires the magician to plant seeds. A leaf of a seedling is needed for burning.
5. A few kernels of grain.
6. Rose petals.
7. A small item of personal property *which you value*.
8. A written testimonial of a falsehood that you once made and later corrected.
9. A written testimonial of when you provided food to the hungry or to a charity.
10. A written, original hymn of praise to God that you have created.
11. A personal vow of Loyalty to a person or deity.
12. A personal symbol of what (for you) indicates happiness or laughter.
13. A written release of guilt, remorse, or old emotion that you are letting go.
14. A written statement of human rights that you ascribe to.
15. A statement of fact about yourself that few others know.
16. A written statement of appreciation (or thank you) to someone for their service. (A copy of such a document).
17. A whispered Vow to keep something a secret.
18. A written statement of praise for another person. (A copy of such a document).
19. A personal symbol of what (for you) indicates Justice.
20. A personal symbol of what (for you) indicates Union.
21. A small container of consecrated wine.
22. Censer of Incense (to be placed on the south side of the Altar.)
23. The Eye of Horus hieroglyph, drawn by your own hand.
24. The symbol of the Stone of Maat (hieroglyph), drawn by your own hand.
25. A written, original invocation to the deity of your choice.
26. The symbol of the Ear (hieroglyph), drawn by your own hand.
27. Intone (vibrate) three Divine Names.
28. A Dove's feather.
29. A written, personal prayer for peace.
30. The symbol of the Ieb (heart hieroglyph), drawn by your own hand.
31. The symbol of the Shen (circled rope hieroglyph), drawn by your own hand.

32. A moment of Silence.
33. A small vial of consecrated Lotus oil.
34. A written, personal incantation for the wellbeing of the community.
35. A Cup of Water (to be placed on the north side of the Altar.)
36. A humble statement spoken in whisper.
37. The symbol of the Ankh (hieroglyph), drawn by your own hand.
38. The symbol of the Waas (hieroglyph), drawn by your own hand.
39. Bread.
40. Honey Cake.
41. A written testimonial of your contribution to a place of worship.
42. The symbol of your totem animal, drawn by your own hand.

## SETUP

Prepare the temple in accordance with the Neophyte Hall of the Golden Dawn. The magician should dress in the regalia of the Second Order, with Rose Cross Lamen, sashes, etc. The primary implement will be the Lotus Wand. Elemental Altars should be set in each quarter with the four elements of the Mystic Repast distributed among them. Elemental candles should also be placed in each quarter. Elemental Tablets should be unveiled in each quarter. Upon the Central Altar should be the Cross and Triangle, the Tablet of Union, a Cup of Water, a Censer of Incense, and a large cauldron for the burning of offerings.[149] A white cloth is used to cover the cauldron. Have all offerings prepared ahead of time and place them in a box with the first offering on the top and last on the bottom.

---

149  Make sure that all offerings will fit within the cauldron. Charcoal may be placed in the bottom of the cauldron, but it is up to the magician whether to burn the offerings as each is dropped into the cauldron or to burn all the offerings later in an outdoor space. (This may be the more appropriate if space and ventilation is an issue — there will be a lot of burning and possibly a lot of smoke!)

# THE OPENING

## 1) THE OPENING DECLARATION:

Go to the Northeast corner of the temple and say: *"Hekas! Hekas! Este Bebeloi!"* ("Far, far from this place be the profane!")

## 2) THE BANISHING:

Perform the Lesser Banishing Ritual of the Pentagram (LBRP) to cleanse the area of all unwanted energies and set up a magic circle of protection.

## 3) THE INITIAL PURIFICATION AND CONSECRATION:

- Take up the cup and purify the room with water, starting in the east and moving clockwise around the room. Trace the cross and Invoking Water Triangle ▽ in all four quarters, going from east, south, west to north. Mark the three points of the triangle by sprinkling water thrice toward each quarter, starting from the bottom point and going clockwise. As you do so, say:

  *"So therefore, first, the Priest who governeth the works of Fire, must sprinkle with the lustral water of the loud resounding sea."*[150]

Return to the east, hold up the Cup and say: *"I purify with Water."*

- Take up the incense and consecrate the room with Fire, starting in the east and moving clockwise around the room. Trace the cross and Invoking Fire Triangle △ in all four quarters, going from east, south, west to north. Mark the three points of the triangle by waving the incense thrice toward each quarter, starting from the top point and going clockwise. As you do so, say:

  *"And when after all the Phantoms are banished, thou shalt see that Holy and Formless Fire, that Fire which darts and flashes through the hidden depths of the Universe, Hear thou the voice of Fire!"*

---

150  Optional: Insert *"Hear Thou the Voice of Water!"*

Return to the east, hold up the Incense, and say: *"I Consecrate with Fire."*

## 4) CIRCUMAMBULATION:
Circumambulate the temple thrice with a quick pace to build the energy.
Give the Projection Sign and the Sign of Silence whenever passing the east.

## 5) THE ADORATION TO THE LORD OF THE UNIVERSE:
Go west of the altar and face east.

> Say: *"Holy art Thou, Lord of the Universe!"* (Give the Projection Sign.)
> Say: *"Holy art Thou, whom Nature hath not formed!"* (Projection Sign.)
> Then say: *"Holy art Thou, the Vast and the Mighty One!"* (Projection Sign.)
> Finally say: *"Lord of the Light, and of the Darkness!"* (Give the Sign of Silence).

## 6) INVOCATION RITUAL:
Perform either the Supreme Invoking Ritual of the Pentagram (SIRP) or Israel Regardie's Opening by Watchtower.

## 7) INVOCATION TO THE HIGHEST:
Go to the West of the Altar and Face East. Say:

> *"Unto Thee, Sole Wise, Sole Eternal, and Sole Merciful One,*
> *Be the praise and glory forever.*
> *Who hath permitted me, who now standeth humbly before Thee,*
> *to enter thus far into the sanctuary of Thy mysteries.*
> *Not unto me, Adonai, but unto Thy name be the Glory.*
> *Let the influence of Thy Divine Ones descend upon my head,*
> *and teach me the value of self-sacrifice*
> *So that I shrink not in the hour of trial.*
> *But that thus my name may be written on high,*
> *And my Genius stand in the presence of the Holy One.*
> *In that hour when the Son of Man is invoked before the Lord of Spirits*
> *And His Name before the Ancient of Days."* (Pause)

# The Work

State your purpose:

> *"The Heaven is Above and the Earth is Beneath. And Between the Light and the Darkness exists the realm of blended natures. I supplicate the Powers and Forces under the Authority of Maat, the Lady of Justice, to look with favor upon this ceremony which I perform this day. I (state magical motto) open this temple to perform a working in the Magic of Light! I hereby dedicate this work to Maat. I seek to lead a Life dedicated to Truth! I wish to uphold the Principles of Righteousness! I strive to be a better man (woman) and to become more than human. I endeavor to be declared Maa Kheru — True of Voice in the eyes of the Divine! To that end, I will make offerings to the Forty-Two who sit in Judgment in the Hall of Two Truths! Grant me what I seek, so that through this rite I may obtain Greater Understanding and thereby advance in the Great Work."*

Perform the Qabalistic Cross.
Perform the Exercise of the Middle Pillar.

Once the Middle Pillar is completely formulated within your sphere of sensation, trace within your heart the letters of Maat's Coptic name **Thmê** (tah-may) in pure white. Then trace the letters and sigil of the name between the two Pillars in front of you.

Bring the Divine Light down from your Kether center to your Tiphareth center, and as you do so give the Sign of the Enterer, at the same time vibrating the name **Thmê** for as long as your exhalation of breath will last. At the end of the vibration give the Sign of Silence. Repeat this procedure of vibration a total of three times, once for every transliterated letter of the name (Tau Mem Aleph).

After the third vibration of the name, project a white ray of light from your Tiphareth center toward the throne between the Pillars and formulate the Godform of Maat there: The Goddess stands between the Pillars. Her serene face is golden yellow, and her calm expression seems as though it could soothe even the hardest of hearts. Her nemyss is striped yellow and violet and is surmounted by a white Shu feather. Her linen gown is yellow, and her collar is banded with red, yellow, and blue. Her right wristband is yellow and blue, while her left wristband is yellow and red. She holds a Phoenix Wand or Waa Staff, and her throne is yellow trimmed with violet upon a black and white pavement. Continue projecting the white ray until the astral figure is well formulated.

If you have charcoal in the cauldron, light them as you say the following invocation:

> *"Thou art Maat, the Great Goddess of Ultimate Truth! Your very name means Truth, Harmony, and Order, and you art the balance which existed before anything in the universe . . . before even the birth of the Gods! In your presence none remain unchallenged by the Gods, nor by their own heart. You weigh the hearts of all the dead and decree their Fates. You were before all things, for without Truth there can be no Order, and without Order there can be no form. All things before and without Truth are naught but chaos! I have called you to this Temple to give Truth to its works. Great Lady, I beseech you! Take the place of the balance point within this Temple, and show the way of balance towards the Light! In your Holy presence may I speak the Truth without fear. Wise and gracious Goddess, let my words be pleasing and let me be judged aright. Let me make Truth Offerings before the Forty-Two Judges who sit under your command. Let me be declared Maa Kheru!"*

Pause and briefly visualize the Forty-two Assessors around the limits of the temple. Then begin the Truth Offerings.

1. *Hail, Usekh-nemmet who comes forth from Heliopolis. Thou Whose stride is vast and who hates lies! I declare that I have striven to do no wrong. I am True of Voice! I have acted in accordance with Maat! I offer my vow to Walk in the Ways of Justice.* (Read your vow, then place it in the cauldron and trace a cross over it.)

2. *Hail, Hept-Shet, who comes forth from Kher-aha! Thou who art Embraced with Flame, and who hates theft! I declare that I have not committed robbery.*

*I have restored that which was plundered. I offer charcoal to kindle the Sacred Fire!* (Place it in the cauldron and trace a cross over it.)

3. *Hail, Fenti, who comes forth from Hermopolis. Thou of the Divine Breath, Long of Nose like Thoth! I declare that I have not stolen. I have replaced something that was stolen. I offer proof of my deed in the name of Restitution!* (You have the option of to read your document of proof or simply place the paper in the cauldron. Trace a cross over it.)

4. *Hail, Amkhaibit, who comes forth from Qernet. Thou who art the Swallower of Shadows, who hates the theft of Life! I declare that I have not slain men and women. I celebrate life. I have planted seeds. I offer seedlings in the name of Life!* (Place a leaf from the seedling in the cauldron and trace a cross over it)

5. *Hail, Neha-her, who comes forth from Rasta. Thou mighty Serpent who is Fearful of Face! Dangerous One! I declare that I have not stolen the grain offering from the gods. I offer grain to please the gods!* (Place some grain in the cauldron and trace a cross over it.)

6. *Hail, Ruruti, who comes forth from heaven. Thou Double Lions of Yesterday and Tomorrow! I declare that I have not stolen the sacred offerings. I have made offerings in the Sacred Temple. I offer Rose Petals to please the gods!* (Place the rose petals in the cauldron and trace a cross over it.)

7. *Hail, Arfi-em-khet, who comes forth from Asyut. Thou Whose Eyes are of Fire! I declare have not stolen the property of the gods. I offer something I value to the gods.* (Place some small item of property that you value, and which you are giving up, into the cauldron and trace a cross over it.)

8. *Hail, Neba! Thou who art the Sacred Flame that comes and goes! I declare that I have striven to not speak lies. I endeavor to speak truth. I offer the correction of an untruth.* (Place a statement of your deed into the cauldron and trace a cross over it.)

9. *Hail, Set-Kesu, who comes forth from Herakleopolis. Thou who art the Breaker of Bones! I declare that I have not stolen food from the hungry. I*

*have provided food to the hungry. I offer proof of my deed in the name of Charity!* (You have the option to read your document of proof or simply place the paper in the cauldron. Trace a cross over it.)

10. *Hail, Utu-nesert, who comes forth from Memphis. Thou who art the Green Fire that shoots forth strong flames. I declare that I strive to not utter curses. I have uttered praises. I offer a hymn of praise to God, written by my hand and spoken with my voice!* (Read the hymn, then place it in the cauldron and trace a cross over it.)

11. *Hail, Qerti, who comes forth from Amentet, the west. Thou of the Cavern and source of the Nile! I declare that I have not committed betrayal. I am faithful. I respect the dignity of others. I offer a vow of Loyalty in the name of Fidelity!* (Read your vow of Loyalty, then place it in the cauldron and trace a cross over it.)

12. *Hail, Herf-haf, who comes forth from the Cavern. Thou Whose face is turned back behind him! I declare that I have striven to not cause sorrow. I have brought laughter! I offer this symbol of happiness in the name of Joy.* (Place it in the cauldron and trace a cross over it.)

13. *Hail, Basti, who comes forth from Bubastis and the secret place. Thou who art of the Altar! Companion to Bast and adviser to Maat! I declare that I have striven to not grieve uselessly or pretend to be something I am not. I accept what I cannot change. I offer a release of guilt in the name of Forgiveness!* (You have the option to read your statement of release or simply place the paper in the cauldron. Trace a cross over it.)

14. *Hail, Ta-retiu, who comes forth at dawn from the darkness. Thou whose legs are of Fire! I declare that I have striven to not transgress anyone. I respect the rights of others. I offer this statement of human rights in the name of Liberty!* (You have the option to read your statement of rights or simply place the paper on the Altar. Trace a cross over it.)

15. *Hail, Unem-snef, Eater of Blood, who comes forth from the execution block. I declare that I am not a man (woman) of deceit. I am a man (woman) of Truth! I offer this statement of fact in the name of Truth!* (Whisper into

the cauldron some personal fact about yourself that few people know about. Trace a cross over it.)

16. *Hail, Unem-besek, Eater of organs, who comes forth from Mabet. I declare that I have not stolen or desolated cultivated land. I respect the hard work of others. I offer this document of appreciation for labor in the name of Service.* (You have the option to read your document of appreciation or simply place the paper in the cauldron. Trace a cross over it.)

17. *Hail, Neb-Maat, Lord of Truth, who comes forth from Maati, the city of the two Truths. I declare that I have not been an eavesdropper. I respect the privacy of others. I offer this vow of confidentiality — I swear to keep a secret.* (Whisper a secret into the cauldron. Trace a Cross over it.)

18. *Hail, Tenemiu, who comes forth from Bubastis. Thou who walks back from whence you came! I declare that I have slandered no one. I have praised men and women. I offer tribute in the name of Honor.* (You have the option to read your tribute or simply place the paper in the cauldron. Trace a cross over it.)

19. *Hail, Sertiu, who comes forth from Heliopolis. I declare that I have striven to not be angry without just cause. I have channeled my anger into honorable causes. I offer this symbol of Justice in the name of Maat.* (Place the symbol in the cauldron and trace a cross over it.)

20. *Hail, Tutuf, who comes forth from Ati. Thou who can cause double harm! I declare that I have not defiled the spouse of anyone. I respect the relationships of others. I offer this symbol of harmony in the name of Union.* (Place the symbol in the cauldron and trace a cross over it.)

21. (Repeat the previous affirmation but to a different god:)
    *Hail, Uamenti, who comes forth from the Khebt chamber of pain and the courthouse. Thou Mighty Double Serpent! I declare that I have not defiled the spouse of anyone. I respect the relationships of others. I offer Sacramental Wine in the Spirit of Friendship.* (Drink some wine, then put some in the cauldron and trace a cross over it.)

22. *Hail, Maa-Antuf, who comes forth from Panopolis. Thou who looks at gifts that are brought to him. I declare I have not polluted myself. I have sanctified myself. I offer this consecration in the name of Neter.* (Consecrate yourself with incense in the manner of the Dadouchos by tracing a cross in front of your forehead, then waving thrice with the incense. Then place some incense into the cauldron and trace a cross over it.)

23. *Hail, Heruru, who comes forth from Nehatu (Amemt), Thou who art Chief of the Mighty and Master of Divine Princes! I declare that I have terrorized none. I have comforted many. I offer this symbol of the Udjat, the Eye of Horus, the Protector.* (Place the symbol into the cauldron and trace a cross over it.)

24. *Hail, Khemiu, the Destroyer who comes forth from Kesiu. I declare that I have not transgressed the Law. I have upheld the Law. I offer this symbol of the Stone of Maat, the symbol of Justice.* (Place the symbol into the cauldron and trace a cross over it.)

25. *Hail, Shet-kheru, who comes forth from Urit. Thou who art the Disturber, Ruler of speech! I declare that I have not inflamed myself with rage. I have inflamed myself with Prayer! I offer my Invocation to God in the name of Prayer.* (Read your Invocation, then place it in the cauldron.)

26. *Hail, Nekhen, the Child who comes forth from Heqat. Jackal-headed ancestor of the Egyptian Kings! I declare I have not shut my ears to the words of truth. I have opened my ears to the words of Truth. I offer this symbol of the Ear that I might listen to Maat.* (Place the symbol in the cauldron and trace a cross over it.)

27. *Hail, Kenemti, who comes forth from Kenmet. I declare that I have striven to not cause grief. I have caused Joy. I have not blasphemed. I have sung praises! I intone the Holy Names of God.* (Vibrate three Divine Names into the Cauldron and trace a cross over it.)

28. *Hail, An-hetep-f, who comes forth from Sais, bringing Gifts and Offerings, I declare that I am not a man (woman) of violence. I am a man (woman)*

*of peace! I offer this Dove's Feather in the name of Peace.* (Place the dove feather in the cauldron and trace a cross over it.)

29. *Hail, Sera-kheru, who comes forth from Unaset. Thou who art the Disposer of speech and the Lord of Words! I declare that I have not stirred up strife. I am a peace-maker! I offer this Prayer of Peace.* (Read your Prayer of Peace, then place it in the cauldron and trace a cross over it.)

30. *Hail, Neb-heru, who comes forth from Netchfet. Thou who art the Lord of Faces. I declare that I have striven to not make judgments in haste. I have acted with forethought. I am open-minded. My heart is open! I offer this symbol of Ieb, the heart, the center of Balance.* (Place the symbol in the cauldron and trace a cross over it.)

31. *Hail, Sekheriu, The Accuser who comes forth from Uten. Thou who gives Knowledge. I declare that I have striven to not pry into inappropriate matters. I respect the boundaries of others. I offer the symbol of Shen, the encircling rope.* (Place the symbol in the cauldron and trace a cross over it.)

32. *Hail, Neb-abui, who comes forth from Sauti. Thou who art the Lord of the two horns! I declare that I have striven to not speak aimlessly just to hear myself talk. I have been thoughtful with my words. I offer a moment of silence in the name of the Ineffable One.* (Be silent for a least one minute before continuing. Trace a cross over the cauldron.)

33. *Hail, Nefer-Tem, who comes forth from Memphis. Thou lion-headed One who art the heat of the Sun in his seasons. I declare that I have striven to do no wrong. I renounce evil. I have righted what was wrong and have acted with Justice and Mercy. I offer Lotus oil in the name of Neter.* (Anoint yourself with oil by dipping your index and middle fingers in the oil and tracing a circle and cross on your forehead. Place a few drops of the oil into the cauldron and trace a cross over it.)

34. *Hail, Tem-Sep in his seasons, who comes forth from Busiris, I have not worked evil sorcery against others. I have performed magic for the benefit of my land, the people, and its leaders. I offer this Incantation for the protection*

*of my community.* (You have the option of reading your Incantation or simply placing the paper in the cauldron. Trace a cross over it.)

35. *Hail, Ari-emab-f, who comes forth from Tebu. Thou whose heart exists in Great Works and who acts with willful intention! I declare that I have not fouled water. I have purified water! I offer this purification in the name of Neter.* (Purify yourself with water in the manner of the Stolistes by dipping your index and middle fingers in water and tracing a cross on your forehead, then sprinkling thrice with water. Place a few drops of the water into the cauldron and trace a cross over it.)

36. *Hail, Ahi, who comes forth from Nu. Thou who art the Sistrum Bearer of the Abyss! I declare that I have striven to not raise my voice in arrogance. I have spoken with humbleness. I offer a whisper of humility.* (Whisper your statement of self-effacement and trace a cross over it.)

37. *Hail, Uatch-rekhit, who comes forth from Sais. Thou who art the Commander and Provider of Mankind! I declare that I have not cursed God. I have praised God. I offer the symbol of the Ankh, the Breath of Life — the most precious gift given by the Divine!* (Place the symbol into the cauldron and breathe into the cauldron. Trace a cross over it.)

38. *Hail, Neheb-kau, who comes forth from thy cavern. Thou who art the Provider of Powers and He Who unites the Soul! Serpent of Hermopolis who helped create the world by swimming around the Solar boat of Ra! Protector against snake-bite! I declare that I have not been consumed by an evil rage. I strive to act with mercy and love! I offer the Waas symbol of Power, in the name of Nefer.* (Place symbol in the cauldron and trace a cross over it.)

39. *Hail, Neheb-nefer, who comes forth from thy cavern of the lake. Thou who art Beautiful — the Bestower of Goodness. I declare that I have not stolen the bread of the gods. I offer bread to the gods.* (Place bread in the cauldron and trace a cross over it.)

40. *Hail, Tchesertep, who comes forth from his own shrine. Thou Serpent whose Raised Head is Sacred! I declare that I have not carried away the khenfu*

*cakes from the beatified Spirits of the dead. I offer honey cakes for the spirits of my ancestors.* (Place cake in the cauldron and trace a cross over it.)

41. *Hail, Anaf, who comes forth from Maati. Thou Serpent who brings and gives! I declare that I have not snatched away bread from children, nor treated the local deities with contempt. I have provided food for orphans and have treated the local religions with respect. I offer proof of my contribution in the name of Community.* (Place the proof in the cauldron and trace a cross over it.)

42. *Hail, Hetch-abehu, who comes forth from The Faiyum. Thou whose white teeth sparkle like those of Sobek! I declare that I have not slain the cattle belonging to the gods. I have not slaughtered the cattle belonging to the god. I honor all creatures who are sacred to the gods. I offer this image of my totem animal in the name of the Neteru.* (Place the image of your totem animal in the cauldron and trace a cross over it.)

Pause for a moment, then thank the goddess Maat for overseeing the ceremony:

> *Great Maat! Lady of all the Gods and Goddesses. You who stand with Thoth in the boat of Ra, the ship of the Sun! The scales and the feather belong to Thee! Your name is Justice and your word is Truth. You are the goddess of all that is upright, genuine and steadfast. Upon you rest the balance of the Hall of the Mysteries. Upon you depend the equilibrium of the universe. None can pass between the Pillars whose heart is not Maat, and whose voice is not True. Thank you, O Goddess! Take my hand, and let my heart, my soul, and my word be Maat.*

Withdraw the white ray of light from the godform back into your Tiphareth center. See the image of Maat slowly fade away.

Pause. Then say:

> *It is done. Behold! Things that are treated with low purpose are easily forgotten, but Whatsoever is Blessed and committed to the flames lives on forever in the Divine realm of ideas and powers!*

(If the offerings are to be burned later, cover the cauldron with a white cloth for the remainder of the ritual.)

Move the cauldron to the east of the Hall. Return the Elements of the Mystic Repast to the central Altar. Return the Cup of Water and the Censer of Incense to North and South of the Hall respectively.

# The Closing

## 1) Final Purification and Consecration:
Repeat Step 3 of the Opening sequence above.

## 2) Reverse Circumambulation:
Circumambulate the temple thrice anticlockwise. Give the Projection Sign and the Sign of Silence whenever passing the east.

## 3) The Adoration to the Lord of the Universe:
Repeat Step 5 of the Opening sequence above.

## 4) The Mystic Repast:
Put the Lotus Wand Aside. Go to the East of the Altar and face West. Give the Sign of Silence. Then recite the Prayer of Osiris:

> For Osiris Onnophris who is found perfect before the Gods, hath said:
> These are the Elements of my Body,
> Perfected through Suffering, Glorified through Trial.
> For the scent of the Dying Rose (+)[151] is as the repressed Sigh of my suffering:
> And the flame red Fire (+) as the Energy of mine Undaunted Will:
> And the Cup of Wine (+) is the pouring out of the Blood of my Heart:
> Sacrificed unto Regeneration, unto the Newer Life:
> And the Bread and Salt (+) are as the Foundations of my Body,
> Which I destroy in order that they may be renewed.
> For I am Osiris Triumphant, even Osiris Onnophris, the Justified.

---

151    Indicates that a cross is to be traced over the element with the hand.

*I am He who is clothed with the Body of Flesh,*
*Yet in whom is the Spirit of the Great Gods.*
*I am the Lord of Life, triumphant over Death.*
*Those who partaketh with me shall arise with me.*
*I am the Manifestor in matter of Those Whose Abode is in the*
*Invisible.*
*I am purified. I stand upon the Universe.*
*I am its Reconciler with the Eternal Gods.*
*I am the Perfecter of Matter,*
*And without me, the Universe is naught.*

Go to the West of the Altar facing East. Give the Projection Sign. Pick up the Rose and say, *"I invite all present to inhale with me the perfume of this rose as a symbol of elemental Air."* Smell the rose and replace it on the altar.

Pick up the Red Repast Candle and say, *"To feel with me the warmth of this candle flame, symbol of the Sacred Fire."* Take in the candle's warmth, then replace it.

Pick up the Paten and say, *"To eat with me this bread and salt as types of Earth."* Consume the bread, then replace the paten.

Pick up the Chalice of Wine. Say, *"And finally to drink with me this consecrated wine, the symbol of Elemental Water."* Make a cross[152] in the air with the chalice and consume the wine. Replace the chalice between the cross and the triangle.

## 5) GIVE A LICENSE TO DEPART:

*"I now release any spirits that may have been entrapped by this ceremony. Go in peace to your abodes and habitations with the blessing of Yeheshuah and Yehovashah, but be ye ready when ye are called."*

## 6) FINAL BANISHING RITUAL:
Repeat the LBRP as in Step 2 of the Opening Sequence.

---

152   Going from up, down, left, right. [Making the Cross over the altar, *not* over yourself. -ed.]

## 7) Declare the Temple Closed.

*"I now declare this temple duly closed. SO MOTE IT BE!"*

*~finis~*

Copyright © 2014 by Chic Cicero and Sandra Tabatha Cicero

# Offerings in Ceremonial Magick and African Traditional Religions
## (Ideas and Practices: Risks and Influences of Integrating ATR)

### Gilberto Strapazon
### (Swami Anand Prabuddha)

**Thanks!**
To all Great Masters who taught and helped me so much every day.
The choices were mine, but the lights were yours.

# INTRODUCTION

*My rebellion is positive, constructive, and creative.*
Gerd Ziegler, *Tarot: Mirror of the Soul*

The comments I write below will sometimes overlap with other magick areas, religions, and spiritual practices. We have good authors to explain many of the aspects and wonders of African Traditional Religious (ATR) practices. This work is about how things can go wrong and why. From the true ATR spirits and their Priests, Orishas, and Exus I have known, I ask wisdom and mercy.

## WE ARE A WORLD OF MANY WORLDS . . .

All magickal paths, as well as religions themselves, have their beauty, knowledge, wisdom, culture, and social aspects. People usually choose their paths because of family tradition, the local culture, personal interest, etc. The person identifies himself with that and has some sort of personal affinity. This means the choice is related to his/her personal life in some way.

But what happens when you welcome a completely strange tradition into your life? Practices that you do not have the slightest affinity to and are in no way a part of your personal beliefs. What if this has nothing to do with your outlook on life, ideals, and goals, as well as what is acceptable for your ethical and moral standards?

Think of the extent some simple acts may have in the long run. A different practice or new idea may have little impact in life, like trying a new food recipe. Others can have a much greater affect. But when we look into magick, it is associated with all different methods, tools, spirits, and correspondences. Many of them are related to cultural traditions. Let's take, for example, how color schema are not the same among various cultures. This is the same concerning elements, the use and meaning of tools, etc. What may be acceptable in one culture may be offensive in another. And most importantly, spirits and natural powers are not viewed the same way by each culture.

What is natural for us is different for others.

# Part I

The ATRs have many good things to offer; it's a fantastic area to explore. But many ATR-inspired procedures you may encounter are modified spells and promote the idea of cutting corners that is all too common within Western Magick Traditions. Much of this comes from the blind appropriation of African procedures to replace Western practices.

Before any work or study, you must ask yourself if the path you are choosing to explore is part of your personal culture. Does it make sense for you to become a member of a religion with its own rules — quite possibly an extremely different subculture than your own? Even the way you dispose your garbage may affect your life if that is a part of the dogma you receive.

I have survived after more than a decade and I'm deeply thankful for the help I received from many really skilled magicians and priests I found throughout the years.

## Background

I am a sorcerer and a ceremonial magician. During my years in the ATRs, I became a *Babalorixá* at *Candomble* (Father of Saint) in the line *Yorubá* (*Jeje* and *Oyo*). Additionally, I have some experience with Brazilian *Umbanda* and *Kimbanda*. I was glad that I had the opportunity to learn and receive good teachings from priests of Hoodoo, *Santeria*, and *Palo* among other like paths.

I desired to continue gathering more knowledge until I returned to my preferred areas of ceremonial magick. I kept to it throughout this time, despite attempts to force me to stop. This allowed me to see many common points related to how various traditional magick paths work.

I'm sure many ATR people will say, "But our line is different!" You will hear this too often. Each one has a personal opinion and viewpoint. Of course, each temple is different, as is each line. But many have similar qualities that can be identified.

Despite being from different lines, the responses I have heard to the idea of mixing ATR with anything foreign are always the same. And I'm sure the results of such mixing often can be the same, as I will explain in the following pages.

I'm glad and thankful for the good priests, the ones who are valuable and have honor. I'm sure most of them will understand my point of view within this work and realize this is not an attack against ATR, but just some notes to prevent people from making the same mistakes I, and many others, have made. The same may happen with people working within other traditions.

There are some basic things to know that would help one avoid a lot of suffering, though I had no one to tell me. I mean really basic things, nothing so spectacular, no deep secrets. Most are common sense but are often left unspoken. Perhaps discussing them is taboo due to fear, or maybe there is just too much mysticism. Perhaps discussing them would break an agreement of secrecy.

But I made no such agreement. In fact, I was sometimes prepared[153] by people who were themselves working under false pretenses. Still, I know many things are better kept secret to avoid people being harmed or, at times, because they are not advanced enough to have earned the knowledge. But if some basic concepts become clear, many people may have a better opportunity to learn and find the results they are after.

## Sources

When looking for information, to study or receive guidelines or ideas, it is desirable to have trustworthy and coherent sources. And, when we consult such sources about ATR, what do we find?

### There are differences between the many ATR lines, and this must be observed!

Look at a map of Africa. Each ATR line is the result of original practices from diverse regions across the continent. Each village had their own understanding and different practices. And many of those practices were a kind of secret *weapon* against their enemies, including neighbors or anyone the priests wanted to have under control.

---

153    To be "prepared" is to say one has been "initiatied" and/or "trained." - ed.

Coming to other countries, such practices were mixed again and formed new ones like Candomble. These resulted from mixing with local practices plus the resulting syncretism. For example Umbanda is a mix of African Tradition, Catholicism, and the native people's culture.

"The one and only truth" does not exist for ATR. Each of the ATR lines often have different and even opposite kinds of workings, chants, offerings, dates, places, etc. A sacred tree for one line is not the same for another. Can that conflict? Yes, and this happens a lot.

So, what happens? For each line there are *few reliable sources,* and then between those you will find different descriptions and practices about the same topics. And often each source claims to be the only right one. How many times have you seen someone reply that "this is the correct way"?

You may understand there's a big conflict over which are the "right" resources to get information because each has a different vision or goal. The search for trustworthy resources can be a problem for a client and even for an initiate, with a lot of doubts. Some initiates/priests, like many magicians, may just keep the secrets of the information they have. And often it is not appreciated if a member or client asks another source. The other temple may refuse to reply if they know you are already working at another place. It is seen as disrespectful to the main priest and even to the spirits of the temple where the initiated/client is working.

The best option you have is to look for more than one source before practicing something. If possible, have a second, third, or more opinions from different sources. When in doubt, be sure the additional source is from a different area and that it has no relations with the other. Often, within the same city, the different groups have some connection. Try to discover if this is so because they may share some ideas. You should try to seek out very different points of view.

## THE RISKS OF MIXING TRADITIONS

ATR has nothing related to Western Traditional Magick, Buddhism, Kemetic (Egyptian), Solomonic, etc.[154] But many mix these! Forget syncretism; the Orishas are not Catholic Saints nor are the Exus the same as Goetic demons.

---

154 This opinion may not be shared with other authors in this book. However, I do agree with the spirit of what this author is saying. Learning wisdom from other cultures is not the same as blindly appropriating elements from a foreign tradition you do not understand. - ed.

They do not have the same origin and do not share the same qualities and ways of acting.

With any syncretism I found, what was really acting with full control were the ATR spirits. They use the external aspect of other practices only at their convenience. These practices are different for each individual temple. You will hardly find two temples that have the same rites. Some will share aspects, but all the spirits and practices of the temple are under the guidance of (and controlled by) the main priest of the group. He is the one you must pay attention to. Forget the members! The main priest's character and personality are what set the direction in which the spirits will be developing and acting.

This is the same when working with these spirits yourself. It becomes very personal. Within ATR, each person has his own unique spirits that are not shared with others in the religion. Even when two or more practitioners have spirits of the same name, they are not the same spirit in practice. For example, the main priest has a specific spirit and many members of the temple have their own "versions" of that same spirit. All will be under the guidance and orders of the main priest, but as each person has their own definition of what that spirit is and their personal choices on what do with it, this affects how each spirit will be *"trained"* and grow.

There are many ATR lineages, but the spirits in those different lines are not the same *even if they share the same name*. They just share some qualities and a lot of "politically correct" texts. (People should pay more attention to literature describing opposite characteristics of the same spirit, side by side.)

Because of this, when someone that is not initiated lights a candle for an ATR spirit, he or she does not know what "version" of the spirit will come. Who will reply? From what tradition is the spirit? *Ketu, Jeju*, Santeria, Kimbanda, etc.? Most people never notice there are different nations, and each can be very different from one another.

With my ceremonial magic experience I feel comfortable evoking angels via different rituals. And guess what? The angels are always the same! I feel comfortable evoking a Goetic demon, even with a simplified root-work method, and guess what? The same demon is there! If I evoke Lucifer into my house via different conjurations, guess who is there every time?

I perform rituals from different grimoires and the spirits are the same. Some have more than one name, like the old Mesopotamian and Egyptian deities. But they will come, and they are always the same. In ceremonial magick rituals, it's possible that a strange event may happen, like a parasite or even some intrusive spirit of the dead. The need to cleanse, banish, and the like is necessary, but this will be during a ritual where the main guest is the one I called for and the procedures will be under their direction.

Working with trusted Western sources I have a better idea of limits and how to handle what may come. And if some problem happens, at least I know where I can find information about it.

Not so with ATR! You may be guided by experience and what you were able to learn from others, most of which is oral tradition. Mixing that with other systems may result in a *new* set of spirits being present — or more parasites. Different results will be produced just because some ingredient or tool receives a new meaning and purpose. An ATR spirit may cause problems if you use a white rose instead of a red. Or if you did not remove the stems.

Yes! Within some lines the spirits do not accept the roses' stems and it is offensive to them. If someone reads the instructions somewhere, and uses a complete rose the same way it would be used in witchcraft or ceremonial magick, that can be taken as offensive to some spirit. People will have absolutely no idea as to what is wrong and what may occur afterward . . . just because some small detail like this was overlooked.

Lighting a candle for *Yemanja* at the beach asking for blessings for family or a baby is usually alright. But lighting a candle because someone wants a love back can be harmful. What happens most often is the *Eguns* (spirits of dead ones) come first if the person is trying something not so "light" or simple. The Orisha refuses the offering and lets the lower spirits get it.

Therefore, the sources you find must be honest in their explanations of the characteristics of the spirits, so you will have a better idea of "what" is being called — who will be receiving that offering. Too often this is kept a secret, or a teacher will simply hide the information. They may say the spirit is the same but won't explain if the kind of offerings made in their line is something that would conflict with another line.

Now guess what may happen with such influences, used in a western traditional working? For example, what exactly are the spirits of "Kimbanda Goetia" manifested at the triangle or the scrying mirror? What may result from even a simple candle spell when mixed with such methods? What about the many oils used with the candles?

Remember, some of these spirits are looking for an activity they may recognize as an opportunity for free food. Even the good ones may act like undisciplined children. When opportunistic spirits find an entrance, this is one source for some magical wars, flames, arguments.

Some spirits feed from the confusion. They destroy the medium, the clients, temple, everything. They often will give fake information, invent charges against an innocent person just to create fights. This way they destroy the medium/priest, the client, and someone else.

Many magick wars are provoked by spirits just to control people and take what they can. When magically attacked, one just needs to know what spirit one is dealing with and make an offering to it. Of course the person who sent it will make offerings of his own, so the target must pay again to be free from the new problem. An alternate approach, the most used, is to always do offerings in advance "for protection." Ultimately, the spirit gets food from both sides. Yes, they betray and play both sides against each other.

The *Goetia* includes entire descriptions about what to do to force spirits to obey and also avoid lies. Often, I have read people's experiences who never needed to use those conjurations. Just being respectful and having coherence at both sides works most of the time.

Humans make choices and may ask for bad things. But when I see such occurrences with the cooperation or influence of spirits, this also demonstrates something important about the true nature of the "spirits" they work with.

One must learn to travel in those realms and still keep consistent and a person of integrity. You must be the owner of your life, not a slave. One of the great goals in magick is freedom. So, any practices that may lead to undesired compromises, or allow for secondary results that need a new work and another and another, must be used with caution.

ATR spirits are not angels, demons, nor like fairies. They are brute forces of nature, something elemental with steroids but without consciousness. They are linked with the lower astral area energies and spirits within those regions. According to their own mythos, some were humans who become Exus in the afterlife, so remember how close they are to our level.

## ONE NAME, MANY INDIVIDUALS

In ceremonial magick, the work is done with specific and individual spirits. If you evoke an angel, no matter which ritual you use, it is the same one you will always meet. Is he the same another individual will contact? The angelic spirits are always the same just because they are able to be present in multiple locations at once.[155]

In contrast, each ATR spirit may have the same name as others, because of their shared qualities, but each one is an *individual* spirit. So, different manifestations of that spirit in many places are not the same ATR spirit, but just have the same qualities, and they are often unaware of each other. Time and distance are different for spirits, so for example, said spirit, during a possession, may leave the medium for a fraction of a second, look or do something in another place, and come back without being noticed. This was not being consistently present in multiple locations. They can just do something in shorter time (within our perspective) when they want to. While they are only on the astral planes, they have a limited capability, as they do not have a physical settlement; their "home" is not on this plane.

Let's talk of the spirits who already have a medium or initiate, someone who will care and give a settlement[156] and become responsible for it. Traditionally this is done with some form of container — for instance a clay, ceramic, or metal bowl — plus some objects related to the spirit's aspects/qualities. Also a specific tree and other sacred objects can be used. Other lines may vary for sure.

This becomes a kind of temporary house where the spirit will try to grow. When they are "invited" to live in such settlements, it creates a connection with the initiate and starts the spirit "making." The initial commands are done (or overseen) by the temple priest. So they are under the command first of the temple priest, and then of the initiate.

Once begun, it is like creating a servitor, a thought form. Each has a "birth," building, then training, and everything the priest does when interacting will add parts of the new spirit's "personality." At the start, they are like children and must be guided. Because of this, the personal characteristics of the initiate and the temple will affect the resulting way the spirit will act.

This is not the same as a familiar spirit. A familiar is an already-existing spirit. He may vary in some things accordingly to the way you interact, but most often he will keep his original qualities for ages.

---

155   To be fair, even in the Western occult tradition there are those who view any summoned spirit as just one "version" of that spirit, connected to but not equal with a greater source/original. For instance, if both I and another magician summon the archangel Michael, we will each meet an entirely separate spirit named "Michael." Both of them would be an aspect of the greater universal Michael. Or some even suggest that the archangel merely sends subordinates to stand in for him. - ed.

156   Such as an altar or shrine. - ed.

Let's go back to compare with a servitor or thought form, which starts with an idea or a basic energy and grows accordingly with the commands received. Each ATR spirit is like an individual, but because of the process they become able to obtain what they need to stay alive and grow. Each spirit is like an individual that will learn and, with his development, can become either a corrupt one or a high one. The personality of the initiate and the priest who is with him/her will affect the process. All this may bring a different result when using any tool or process or method with that particular spirit. You must look for how the qualities developed in each one. Remember, only the name used by the spirit may be the same.

## Tools

The tools used in ceremonial magick most often do not have the same meaning and usage as they do in ATR, even if they have a similar format. Some tools used in ATR need to be consecrated in a special way so they will be accepted by the spirits. They are to be used for the specific practices of worshiping those spirits and to do agreeable things for them. The tool must be "their property" and can't be used in a different work. So the preparation of such tools is not for the magician, but first of all, they become property of the spirits.

Whereas with ceremonial magick most tools have a special meaning to command spirits, or to be used in the steps of a ritual or to store something. In ATR many tools are most used to prepare the offerings, like consecrated cooking utensils. This includes the sacrificial knives.

A blood sacrifice must be done only by a priest, who already has all the needed years and levels and received the training. He will use his/her own consecrated knife. The knife receives the blood of a sacrifice and/or special herbs are used. Then it spends some time resting in the settlements so it becomes property of the spirit.

In no way can a sacrifice be done without this proper tool. If for any reason the knife can't be used, and there's no other from another equivalent initiate, the priest will even cancel an entire event in order to avoid problems resulting from the use of a non-consecrated tool. It's a serious offense to that spirit.

There are a set of tools for Orishas and another set for the Exus. ATR spirits are easily offended by the use of anything that is not theirs. Becoming offended means the priest OR the client/initiate will be severely punished.

In ATR the tools become property of the spirits and are the only ones allowed to use them, be it a glass, a knife, all needed for direct working. A consecrated knife in ATR is used to sacrifice, while within ceremonial magick it is used because of the symbolism, correspondences, and as a commanding instrument. The ceremonial magician's tool will be consecrated too, but this is in order to empower it, to become charged with the higher energies for the practice of the ritual. In ATR, a tool is prepared to be the property of the spirits, and they become really offended if anything is not right.

## OFFERINGS

In ceremonial magick, we will give offerings in many ways: to show the spirits we are serious and in agreement, as a gift or payment, to give thanks for their work or as an exchange of energy, and also to feed such spirits. In ATR, the offering means the payment to the spirit. And it's always in advance. Pay first, receive the result later. Promises to pay later are not a good idea, but in times of real need it may work. Often then, it will be paid twice or more.

It is important to know that an offering in ATR is the main part of the ritual, and it often comprises the entire spell. Something like: prepare such food, place it in a specific location, and ask the spirit what you desire. So, there are offerings suitable for many situations.

For example, asking for the attention of a spirit who is the ruler of an area. A well-known offering is popcorn at the crossroads to ask for prosperity. Remember, this needs to be addressed for a specific spirit. It may be done for generic purposes, but even so there are specific places and times to do it.

Most offerings are really specific: the ingredients, the ways of doing it, and where it must be put — at the temple, crossroad, in the woods, a riverside, etc. This is, again, about feeding the spirits. A wrong offering most often is taken as an insult. Some Orishas and the Gypsy's spirits can receive a non-specific offering and even laugh about it. But many others find it an offense to ask for something without knowing who is called.

Is there some compassion for an individual who has done the offering without knowing what is wrong? Yes, but you need to consider who is doing the offering and what is being asked. It's safer with most spirits to request goals that already demand compassion, such as healing, care of children, help for a family in true need, and natural disasters. The spirits often do not pay attention to mistakes if you are an initiate or if you are giving something with a true heart.

But if the offering is to create a physical result or force something, like trying to get an ex-lover to return, force a result in a job, affect someone, and the like, there may be no such compassion. Beginners are frequent victims of their own lack of knowledge, preparation, and often laziness. This is another reason to repeat many times the need to study and follow known methods.

What can result from offending spirits of ATR? Think months, even years of troubles and serious diseases until another priest discovers what's really happening. I helped a lot of people who only lit a wrong color candle at the wrong place for some stupid reason.

Using a tool, but with someone's suggestion for an ATR method, may attract such negative forces, and the results can be very confusing or disturbing to say the least. This will cease only when the spirits receive more offerings, pleading, excuses, and cries for mercy because of something stupid. Remember, brute natural force, no conscience, and no morals. Think about water over acid or a match on gasoline.

In Western Traditional Magick, such things may result in some strange happenings, sounds, or other influences to show that was a bad choice. It is not very difficult to light a candle and explain or simply banish. But within ATR, this can result in disastrous results for a long time.

What problems may occur surrounding offerings if the wrong ATR spirit thinks you are working with them when you did not intend for them to? If you use an ATR method, those spirits may perceive it to be theirs. And they come very fast. If the circumstances of the ritual are not what they expect, they won't pay attention that the offering was for someone else. For instance, just enter a cemetery with an offering and many spirits will jump all over you.

## Practices with Other Reasons and Different Goals

Many practices of ATR do not have the same meaning as similar Western traditions. The most common are the *baths*. You will see them everywhere. The ATR instructions are to not wash your head with the herbs, salt, or other ingredients that you prepared. The exception is if you are initiated and the main temple priest will wash it using a special herb mixture in some events.

This is because the head is *property* of the Orishas. So, washing your head will break the connection or prevent them from becoming closer. There are even some ATR lines who prevent their members from washing their head in the sea (it's a salt bath). In such cases, anyone who has activity at sea will either be prohibited from doing it or must "acquire" special permission. Many lines see no problem with it, but some do have a rule for "never" crossing seven waves in sequence.

Imagine doing a Solomonic bath this way. You would be doing a partial bath, allowing space for another energy to affect the work. So, keep your normal bath from head to foot.

Other practices that have specific rules include work at the crossroads. ATR has meanings and specific classes of spirits for the corners, center, and if it is a "T" or "X" type crossroad. Another is to avoid walking at some hours or places.

Within the Solomonic grimoires, washing objects has one meaning: to consecrate and, as much as possible, align all energies according with the related correspondences.

In ATR, as told, this is done first to give it to the spirits as their *property*. To become an accepted tool for their use. That means they are in charge of how the tool is used and how the magick is done. Over time this will lead to changes even in your personal habits. What appears to be a simple idea given by the spirit, with time, will add with another simple suggestion, then another, and another — until the spirits are in control of all areas of your life. Some details as strange as the garbage can become too mystic and even sacred. But this is a part of the characteristics of some spirits.

How to dispose of the remains of rituals is equally interesting to observe. How many times do you find in the old grimoires instructions for what to do with the garbage? But in ATR, anything used in the ritual becomes property of the spirits. So it may need to be disposed in special ways.

A simple example: Do not allow a dirty used coffee cup to stay in the kitchen. This attracts the dead. Within ceremonial magick it is hard to think a dirty cup will attract demons. Most probably, lack of any organization will simply keep the spirits away.

Most magick practices may observe that some offerings should be done in a proper place. For example, working with water spirits is best to do near a river or lake. And just leave what remains there.

Within ATR, an offering, after the time required, must be disposed in some special way according to the type of spirit(s) involved. Some must be at a crossroad, others in the woods, others must be buried, and so on. Doing this wrong can result in the work having a negative/contrary result. A spirit of a different quality than the intended spirit may receive the remains. Or the places used to put such remains might be inhabited by dead spirits just waiting for their share. But there's more about the remains, even the wax of candles and cigarettes used during the rituals. Anything may have an important aspect.

Some practices use the offerings/sacrifices disposals for black magick. Just put it in the wrong place or add someone's name and that energy becomes contrary and may cause a lot of problems. So the wrong disposal can nullify or even destroy the results of any work.

It's the same with offering garbage instead of something good. The result: As the remains dissolve, so will that aspect in the life of the victim. Many corrupt priests do this with the temple's members and clients to assure control over their lives. Have you heard about someone who received such works, with good result in the beginning and soon a lot of problems occur? This is one possible reason for it.

Now, imagine a traditional Western Magick ritual, where the magicians work in such a way. What if the main ritual lost its importance because the leftovers became "special" and attracted attention? Have you ever heard of people doing a nice ritual and at the finish, or soon after, something darker or very strange happened? Or even after a well-done banishment something appears from nowhere? The ritual was closed, but the garbage was still there and was literally "prepared" to attract such energies because of the method used.

If someone tells you to keep the remainder of your dinner when you go to a restaurant, and you allow it to stay in the car with the windows opened, what may happen later? Might it attract cats, rats, dogs, some strange people? Usually in ceremonial magick, you go to a restaurant (ritual), have a nice dinner, say thanks to the chef, and then leave everything there. But in ATR, even cleaning up the leftovers involves practices that help maintain connections with the spirits.

## Hey, Why so Much Detail?

ATR practices have rules in place to avoid problems or, at the worst, offending the spirit. With too much detail, every aspect of your life may involve some type of risk. That becomes oppressive.

Details in Ceremonial Magick are part of a ritual, for a mental focus, consecration of the tools, preparing the space, study, etc. Details in ATR do concern the tools and ingredients, but they also include rules for even common aspects of life; so each day they make the initiate busy with more and more details. It could cause anything to become a source of potential problems. This is also an effective way to force the abandonment of other magick practices and lifestyles.

People changing their lives because of magick or religion is common. But in ATR there are cases where a person first had a life, a practice, a profession, and all that appears to be taken out.

*If the spirits you are working with do not give true wisdom, understanding of changes, and protection, something is very wrong.*

Many practices I worked with, during my years in ATR, were too often a source of conflict. That showed the spirits had some problem with it, and they tried fervently to interrupt my practices, to give full time and worship to something that was not my life interest. Really forcing situations! That was not what I asked for and stated clearly each time. That was not a "lesson toward my development." That was an admonition under penalty to force my obedience and servitude. This becomes slavery. This is not mutual respect — it's just a way to control the initiate.

So, my suggestion here is this: Be serious, but do not pay heed or grant the "self-proclaimed" importance to the details of your life the spirits might stress. Do not allow such control over your life. Starting with simple acts, in time they will even make you pray before flushing the toilet.

Being respectful with spirits means they have to respect you too. This is one reason we find in the grimoires conjurations to force reluctant spirits to obey.

*"No true spiritual ally, like a true friend in the land of the living, should treat you as a pet. Either they serve you or you're equals."*
*~ Gordon Finn*

# PART II

## APPROACHING THE MODERN TIMES

We see a lot of mixes in magick everywhere. Some are the results of modern practices presented by authors who study the area and have developed or adapted new working methods. Others think that being modern means being against the *"old obsolete methods."* We see this often; some are people who find it "too hard" to read a book, take some notes, and follow a method.

Many ATR priests express: *"the more you give the more you receive."* Well, it's not really about the amount you give. It's first of all the "quality" of the offering. If it's a sincere offering, the related work, the human part, is being justly rewarded.

The spirits feed off light, just energy. But the magician who is doing the work needs a lifetime of intense work and studies to learn to deal with each of these energies, and this deserves also a payment.

It's like comparing the work of an architect with the price of brick or the workers themselves. The brick can be cheap, but knowing how to use it and give the right instructions for the desired result, demands much time and sacrifice. And remember, with magick, we have no guarantees of result because of too many other aspects. The work is done for the good sake. So "give the most you can" means evaluate the effort and recognize to pay it accordingly. If the work is not valued, why should the result be? The spirits acting will observe this too.

ATR spirits do this a lot, as most others observe what is given, but with some differences. Some ATR original "spell recipes" appear to be really simple. Some type of flour, vegetables, oil, candles, and some drink. People who know a bit about ATR recognize such things easily. Those spells and offerings to ATR spirits are so simple they attract lots of people. Many magazines and websites have lots of them. And much of it does not cite what spirit will receive it, nor even that it is an ATR work. Once more, the mixing may catch a victim.

Those simple recipes may even be cited as "modern" by many who are uninformed just because of the few ingredients. Usually they are generic offerings. Some of them even give the name of what spirit will receive and the place it must be found, a crossroad, woods, or at a cemetery . . . Cemetery? A recipe can begin simple enough to prepare, but the next step adds another dimension and puts the person in direct hard contact with that force. A trap.

Most often, cemeteries can be the place of all kinds of dead ones. This is usually not fun. There's the sweet grandma who just slept, the criminal dead in a fight with the cops, an abused child, the victim of a disaster who is in suffering from his missing family, some really sick perverted ones, and all kinds of parasites and astral larvae who want to feed from that energy. And also, ATR spirits who use them as slave workers.

So pay attention about *where* an offering is given. The ingredients may be safe, but the place where it is to be given is a suggestion for a change in your ritual.

Some risks are found side by side. Most people are not aware of this when searching for books with complete recipes from ATR lines. They will find some basic recipes alongside others with the same goal but which require a lot of work and even some really difficult ingredients and personal sacrifice.

Now think, why are there so many spells to accomplish the same goal? Ok, this happens with Western Traditional Magick too. But instead of being a work for deep learning, a complex ATR work may produce spirits more ready to respond. And be claimed. Guess what they will ask for sometime later? A repetition of the simple spell or something complex? Months later a new event may take more effort.

So, the simple but unexplained recipe for an offering becomes a task of sacrifice for doing something more. With time, that becomes something one is forced to do: a tribute. Ask once, pay multiple times. And so, the spirits may have a new source of food.

## More and More

I started my occult studies some decades before this, and the way I've learned made possible many deep spiritual experiences and fantastic results. This happened a long time before any other formal magick study, using just meditation, working with nature, and calling spirits, angels, deities (not ATR) directly, without knowing a more formal evocation work or any other tradition. It was just me and the universe. And going into the woods and mountains, walking in parks and streets, I came to find a lot of spirits and nature forces ready to talk with me.

Since the beginning, I learned the *"being respectful"* approach before any other, and because of this, I received one of many important initiations. Even so, I got trapped and learned more in the hard way.

To me it was always natural to do some kind of offering, just being gentle. A flower, a candle, a simple nice gift like an incense stick is something you offer with heart. With time, I found very interesting works about offerings to angels and spirits. Like an act of sincere interest and payment for their work.

At Kemetic (Egyptian), Norse, Pagan practices, and others, we do offerings of milk, fruits, bread, even meat. Just simple sincere offerings. A work of hearth can do wonders! But where goes the sincere wrong offerings to ATR?

Again the words: offering, sacrifice, tribute.

And deal with brute natural forces.

What we found in most ceremonial magick classic works? Offerings of fruits, bread, cake, incense, a cup of drink, candles, drops of consecrated oil. And if meat is included, you can buy beef at the store and prepare it. No need to have all the work of learning to sacrifice a specific animal, clean it, and prepare.

We have found great sacrifices for deities and spirits in many cultures, in special ceremonies for great objectives. See the difference: sacrifice. Despite any offering being a kind of sacrifice, in ATR it does not have the same meaning or such deep work related with many other practices. The sacrifice is an act of personal work, of devotion, a big offering for something that really demands a lot of resources and to show the spirits you are doing your part so they must also do theirs to receive more.

So why do some people make hard sacrifices on other activities where a candle, frankincense, and oil would suffice? And what is asked or how is the process followed?

> *May this sacrifice which we find it proper to offer unto ye, noble and lofty beings, be agreeable and pleasing unto your desires; **be ye ready to obey us**, and ye shall receive greater ones.*
> *[The Greater Key of Solomon]*

Observe the phrase: "***be ye ready to obey us.***" Who is in charge of command? The magician is not under control nor asking mercy or "please may you accept this humble request and maybe help me?" Non-disciplined ATR spirits will work to gain control. And they will try to have control anyway. The sacrifice becomes a tribute demanded by a conqueror, an oppressor.

So, the magician must be careful to be firm, with wisdom, but respectful and be clear who is in charge. This is not asking for a favor, for mercy of any spirit.

> **There are many observations that grimoires do not compromise yourself with spirits. Be them angels or demons.**

So again, some "easy spells" we find are in practice creating a kind of unsolicited compromise for more.

How much is asked and how it is demanded are very important.

One of the first things I learned about ATR spirits in the 80's was that "the more you give, the more they want." I tried to observe this, but even so I was caught due to my compassion and discovered the hard way how many different ways you can be wronged.

Repeating: There were a lot of ATR initiates and priests who claim, "The more you give the more you receive." This is seen even in evangelic groups, as a practice so people think they have to give all to a "God" to receive something back. Is it a bargain? How much is needed? How much becomes abusive for both sides?

Sometimes an operation really needs a lot of material. But not always. What demands most is the knowledge and experience of the magician or priest.

ATR spirits' offerings are usually asking the same: a lot of food and drinks to the spirits. In some lines you have to spend most of your time in the kitchen, just cooking for spirits. And I may say, this can be a lot of time at the kitchen! And too many offerings can make such spirits lazy. Like someone who became fat and sedentary.

Magick has no guaranteed results. And lazy ATR spirits will just take the "easy" food and ask for more, but do nothing. Or even, create more problems to ask for more food.

I heard many times that the great secrets of learning Candomble (among others) is in the *kitchen*. The recipes, the way that it is done. Cook, cook, and cook. And what I saw was that each time more and more food is asked for, if they can take it. Serious temples have their well-defined dates and events. But even so, it is common to see how much food, quantity, and diversity are required. At the big events but also at any time. Again, some priests do such events as a way to get more resources and control the members and clients. And those spirits just receive that easily.

The main work goes to the kitchen not because of all the different offerings you will do. ATR has correspondences, but this varies a lot among different lines. What is sacred for one may be wrong to another. So they often just know what food each spirit likes more by oral tradition, and few explanations are found because that is "secret." Again, the trouble of finding truthful sources.

There are too many ATR secrets that nobody explains (or even knows). Many (in my honest opinion) are just a fantasy because many initiates also learned and used a lot of mixes. And still many come from ancient Africa, where such things were the *secret weapons* to do war against other groups.

Think, all this is about offerings. How does it relate to the Western Magick Tradition grimoires and other practices? Why let all this enter at the back door and corrupt ancient known practices?

Some offerings can be basic, if you really can't do better. Others need a lot. But often the result is that spirits want more and more. Even if they accept a humble offering, later they ask more as payment for the result of the previous paid work.

See, ATR works based on pay first, receive later. You can do a "thanks" offering for sure if you get happy with the results or knowledge you receive.

It's possible to do some work without the needed offerings and promise for a later payment. This is common in many religions like Catholicism. The spirit may even do what was asked but will claim for the payment really fast, and it is best to pay the promise with extra.

Sometimes a person may have a talk in a temple session, when the spirit uses a medium body. If the spirit states clearly nothing more is needed, it will be done. But anyways, some kind of "thanks" offering will be expected. A minimum of a public "thanks" (promotion and publicity) is expected.

Now think, with the current mixing between the traditions, this kind of thing is going to happen more on other magick paths. What if a ritual that started with the angels results in some strange events and a "new" kind of angel "appears" asking for more?

Most spirits in western traditional grimoires, as others, are really very old. Thousands of years and many civilizations. They have seen all aspects of human life. Do not worry that they will think you're a pervert or dumb; they have seen it all for thousands of years. So I expect few sudden changes in the way they act. Those spirits, angels and demons, really have a wide knowledge about us. They are not brute unconscious spirits.

I really worry about just mixing practices and working with spirits who appear to take more and more with really questionable results. They miss an important aspect: evolution. Because of the mixing of practices with ATR, I expect to see a new class of "spirits" coming around, a kind that tries to act (or mimic) the original but will later do what is expected from ATR spirits: ask for more food.

ATR contacts fantastic natural powers, to bond with for human development, but because of the lack of consciousness, the spirit gets the control. Too much depends on the awareness of their priests and their personal beliefs. With ATR there are more reasons why something might not work: They will just feed from the offerings and want more. Opportunists. For sure not all, but this happens most with Exus and the lower spirits. Some ATR spirits will do nothing or perform a bit and ask for more. Or, like working with angels, they will make things worse as a kind of "lesson."

Since their settlement, they have to receive discipline like children and be kept in safe bonds, otherwise they will try to take what they can, despite the way it happens.

Imagine now this happening over ceremonial magick rituals. An extreme example is someone being forced to do the last seven days of Abramelin, every year, including the previous preparation. If not done, you would receive a hard punishment after some time.

Why don't the spirits just take what they want, from anywhere, when they need it? Because this is a vital force to be taken from humans due to their connection with this plane, as they lived here before. Also, the one who does the offerings creates a link, like a door, where they can connect easily and so, gain access to the food they need.

**Remember, I'm writing about what may happen when working with brute nature forces, bad information sources, bad training, corrupt priests, lack of basic information. And this is what most people are likely to find. All this is just behind a lot of texts, shortcuts, and "magick spells" found anywhere. Much of that will lead to such events.**

Recognize some of that?

## REAL VS. FAKE SPIRITS

As in any area, a practitioner may find real and fake spirits. I found and lived with both. First, the fake spirits:

1) If you are an initiate of ATR or just mixing other magick areas with ATR practices, there's the need to see what spirit arrived and trust it. Many of these spirits, as the Eguns (dead ones) and *Kiumbas* (like an empty dead shell) are capable of mimicking other spirits. They learn and present themselves as Exus, Orishas, witch spirits, deities, angels, demons, whatever you may think. Such spirits can present themselves as Jesus, Saint Germain, The Pope, whatever they have received some information about. And such information may come from the priest/magician and the members/clients around.

In magick forums, ceremonial magick and witchcraft, I have read many comments from people who "cut corners" in their attempts at calling Goetic spirits, planetary, satanic, or anything else, resulting in such kinds of spirits — dead ones, kiumbas, or any parasites. A newbie tries at first to evoke a Demon King spirit, and the resulting troubles just show he received a lot of dead spirits or something worse at a lower level.

It's common for the "self-learning" new magicians to get into trouble because they attract a lot of such low-level spirits. When they try a basic demon banishment and discover that does nothing, the problems are just starting.

Second, the real ones:

2) With the real spirits, there are also problems because of corrupt priests and because a spirit might become "offended."

We see everywhere — on TV, videos, the internet, forums, magazines, and books — suggestions to do some "simple" work for money, love, etc. It appears to be as easy as just lighting a red candle to Pomba Gira at a crossroad or even (worst of all) inside the home. This is a sure way to become a future victim. Just using a candle in a different way, or adding some ingredient, changes the signals recognized by that spirit. People do not realize these principles and do not think each area is different. So they get burned.

The same idea applies even when the right process is followed. It's recognized by the ATR spirit as something proper to him. That's a signal, like a signature. Remember the "property idea." You use the signals, places, clothes, whatever is proper to some ATR spirit so they will come very fast. Remember, they have no conscious mind. So, what was a ritual for an ancient spirit instead attracts another one who does not know what's happening but may become very furious because the cup was not consecrated to him or the magician's T-shirt had an image of a rival force, etc.

Many modern magicians use music, as do most of us, and play, for example, J. S. Bach or Gothic Heavy Metal . . . but the resulting spirit of the ritual is an old style Orisha, who allows nothing except decent tribal drums. Of course, they become offended and make the magicians' lives worse. This is some of what mixing can do.

## BUT IF THE RITUAL IS FOR AN ANGEL/SPIRIT/DEMON, WHY DOES THIS HAPPEN?

Just because of the method, the tools, the preparation. The spirit found an opportunity through invitation. If you act like a lioness, why wouldn't lions arrive? I'm kidding, but you get the idea. What I have seen all this time in the practices in my country is that many ATR spirits act like vampires or parasites. And I have had no reason in all these years to think differently.

Once called (or self-invited), too often the spirits have the same approach: Even if the person is not initiated, the spirits will come again, multiple times later, and will cause different problems (before presenting again to you) to force you to "work for" (feed) them again. And often a spirit will suggest, "Hey, try X again; that worked last time." It's like "they have a solution." But you must pay again for "protection." "Hey, stupid, give us more food!"

This means that ritual didn't work at all. The magician or client, now a victim, was wronged — given a temporary result just for a new problem to arise later. To get more food, more worship, more sacrifices. This has become a tribute that recalls federal taxes. You didn't ask, but the bill is there every year. And they don't mind who you voted for!

Many of these spirits really become abusive and tend to take up more and more space. And once the door was opened, more will come. Give a finger and they want the arm. Just for your information, in the lines I know (Yorubá, Ketu, etc.) one former priest needed to have settlements for sixteen Orishas plus a lot of Exus. Guess how often one would need to be in the kitchen?

Maybe you are making offerings to angels, but if you mix in ATR this is not clear, so the method leaves space to attract undesired attention. All this can happen. It may take months or years. Each day, such forces will be closer, trying to get more, whispering suggestions, creating troubles, whatever to make you repeat that step and become under their control.

For sure, any spirit you have some kind of relationship with will, in time, be near again. Maybe you need something. They want to work with you. Usually the magician may "remember" or receive a signal from them and will just light a candle or do a simple offering of incense or a fruit. Just something simple like a "thanks, I know all you have done to help me."

You may have angels and demons around with nothing to do, so you may establish some order to keep them busy and that's okay. When not busy they can make some noise only. But the magician won't be forced to prepare a big party for a lot of people to eat.

On the other hand, the ATR spirits create the risk of a lot of them hanging around wanting to be fed. "Hey, we want a party and sacrifices!" So I get worried about offerings and grimoire traditions and others that do not have such in common within their origins. I see a risk of creating a new class of spirits, like food hunters.

## What You See Is Not Always What You Get

Any ATR spirit works with dead ones too. The Orishas have their legions of the dead and Exus under their orders. And each Exu (a kind of Orisha's messenger) uses the dead ones, so they have a personal group. Even the dead ones take the lower spirits among them to work too. Like a chain of natural force and death, all under a slavery relationship. The higher ones enslave the lower ones. Call an Exu and he/she will come with a personal group of dead ones. And some will try to stay.

If each spirit has dead spirits to work with, this means any reference to them, gestures, acts, words, methods, will attract them too. Even an image or a lit candle at home is the same as an open invitation.

## An Important Comment on Coherence

ATR spirits most often have dual aspects. I repeat: ATR spirits most often have dual aspects. Get it? ATR spirits most often have dual aspects.

Look for their descriptions. The same spirit who works for health can bring diseases. The same spirit who works at justice protects criminals. The family spirit creates discord. And so on. They are like humans and lived on this plane before.

Such spirits, even Orishas, usually named as "Saints," will consent to act on behalf of any side in a conflict, just because of the human qualities of the one who asked for it. So don't expect, for example, Xango (the Orisha related to justice) to help the person who is right. He will work for the one who does more for him, worships him, is stronger, and gives him food.

Using a mixing of practices, we'll see revenge spells to have Raphael make someone sick! But I'm sure the spirit of such a spell will not be Raphael, but another who mimics him.

There are a lot of texts about the Orishas with the characteristics of the people who they crown. Like strange astrological aspects. Good and bad aspects. The same Orisha who is a proud warrior and police protector will act to seduce and rape. What?!

It's not a surprise that spirits act in the opposite way they were expected to. Just because they have the two sides and no consciousness the results vary depending on the personal character of the initiate and if the offerings are the kind they expect (even if you never knew before) using the proper tools as they want. And if they are invoked (or self-invited) by a non-initiate, all they have is the person's thoughts, impressions, acts, offerings, and will work accordingly. Such spirits without a settlement lack discipline and will take anything to make (create) what they need to act.

Don't think all *Ilês* (ATR temples) use the right tools, either. Many don't, really. They do their mixes and also try to cut corners. So the bad results are often ignored, or they do not pay attention to that. When things go bad, be ready to hear, "this is a lesson" or "shut up and accept it." When I see someone say this, to me it just means *slavery and submission*. I'm glad we have good priests. You don't need to give all your life for nothing.

## THINK

I worked in many spiritual and magick areas and have my personal preferences. Even with the background I have, I had a lot of years in ATR. And during that time I was cheated and wronged on occasions. But I did my best to learn about and follow other cultures with a better understanding. This helped me to keep my own faith, my own work, and continue to study and learn more.

The offering is a great part of magick, and there are good instructions about them within the proper texts. Before trying modern or different methods, pay attention for the source and act wisely. A magician must work with power, wisdom, and evolution.

# CONTRIBUTORS

## Aaron Leitch

Aaron Leitch has been a scholar and spiritual seeker for nearly three decades. He is a member of the Hermetic Order of the Golden Dawn, the Gentlemen for Jupiter, and the academic Societas Magica. His writings cover such varied fields as ancient Middle Eastern religion and mythology, Solomonic mysticism, shamanism, Neoplatonism, Hermeticism and Alchemy, Traditional Wicca and Neopaganism, The Hermetic Order of the Golden Dawn, Thelema, Angelology, Qabalah, Enochiana, African Diaspora Religions, Hexcraft and Hoodoo folk traditions, Psychology and Consciousness Expansion, Cyberspace and Virtual Reality, and modern social commentary. He is the author of *Secrets of the Magickal Grimoires*, *The Angelical Language: Vols. I* and *II*, and *The Essential Enochian Grimoire*. Visit Aaron online at kheph777.tripod.com and aaronleitch.wordpress.com

## Chic Cicero & Sandra Tabatha Cicero

Charles "Chic" Cicero was born in Buffalo, New York. An early love of music, particularly of the saxophone, resulted in Chic's many years of experience as a lead musician in several jazz, blues, and rock ensembles, working with many famous performers in the music industry. Chic's interest in Freemasonry and the Western Esoteric Tradition resulted in research articles on Rosicrucianism and the Knights Templar, printed in such publications as *Ars Quatuor Coronatorum* and the *1996–2000 Transactions of the Metropolitan College of the SRIA*. Chic is a member of several Masonic, Martinist, and Rosicrucian organizations. He is a Past Grand Commander of the Grand Commandery of Knights Templar in Florida (2010–2011). He was also a close personal friend and confidant of Dr. Israel Regardie. Having established a Golden Dawn temple in 1977, Chic was one of the key people who helped Regardie to resurrect a legitimate, initiatory branch of the Hermetic Order of the Golden Dawn in the United States in the early 1980s. He met his wife and co-author, Sandra Tabatha Cicero, shortly thereafter.

Sandra "Tabatha" Cicero was born in rural Wisconsin. Her areas of interest include drawing, painting, poetry, theater, dance, and printmaking. A lifelong fascination with the creative arts has served to inspire her work in the magical world. After graduating from the University of Wisconsin-Milwaukee with a Bachelor's Degree in Fine Arts in 1982, Tabatha worked as an entertainer, typesetter, editor, commercial artist, and computer graphics illustrator. In 2009 she obtained an Associate in Science degree in Paralegal Studies.

Tabatha is a member of several Martinist and Rosicrucian organizations. She met her husband and co-author Charles "Chic" Cicero in the early 1980s, and the Golden Dawn system of magic has been her primary spiritual focus ever since. Tabatha spent five years working on the paintings for The Golden Dawn Magical Tarot which she began at the encouragement of Israel Regardie.

Both Chic and Tabatha are Chief Adepts of the Hermetic Order of the Golden Dawn as re-established by Israel Regardie (www.hermeticgoldendawn. org). The Hermetic Order of the Golden Dawn, of which Chic is the G.H. Imperator and Tabatha is the G.H. Cancellaria, is an international Order with temples in several countries. Tabatha is also the Supreme Magus (Imperatrix) of the Societas Rosicruciana in America (www.sria.org). Chic and Tabatha share an enthusiasm for Ceremonial Magic and the Hermetic arts. Their books, which are published by Llewellyn, include *The Golden Dawn Magical Tarot* (kit), *Secrets of a Golden Dawn Temple*, *The Essential Golden Dawn*, *Tarot Talismans*, *The Babylonian Tarot*, and *Self-Initiation into the Golden Dawn Tradition*. They have also edited and annotated new editions of Israel Regardie's classics *The Middle Pillar*, *The Tree of Life*, *A Garden of Pomegranates*, and *The Philosopher's Stone*.

## Brother Moloch

Brother Moloch began his foray into the murky world of Sorcery and the Occult back on November 17, 1987. Since that day, he has studied under a couple of highly competent and well-respected spiritual teachers. Moloch also trains his own students and apprentices. Also an author of several Occult texts, such as *Pragmatic Magics*, Moloch has taught various subjects at metaphysical gatherings and given in-store lectures on topics such as sorcery and evocation of spirits. He has also been a friend to the media and given both radio and newspaper interviews over the years. Moloch was formally initiated into Haitian Vodu on March 4, 2009. Visit Brother Moloch online at www. molochsorcery.com.

## Bryan Garner (Frater Ashen Chassan F.:N.:F.:)

Bryan is a practicing occultist and grimoric traditionalist who has been involved in traditional forms of Western Ceremonial Magic for over fifteen years. His passions center on closely reproducing experiments from the Solomonic magical texts and exploring their effectiveness. He takes a serious and straightforward approach to the study of historic forms of magic and spirit communication. He is the author of *Gateways Through Stone and Circle*, a manual of evocation of the planetary intelligences and co-author of *The Holy Guardian Angel*. Continuously immersing himself in occult practice, Bryan aims to discover what the limits of traditional forms of magical ritual are.

## JASON MILLER (INOMINANDUM)

Jason Miller's interest in the occult was sparked by a series of psychic experiences he had when he was just five years old. He took up the practice of both High Magick and Hoodoo Rootworking while still a teenager, learning how ceremonial and folk magick can work together and complement each other.

He has been involved with a number of orders and groups over the years, always seeking the quintessence of the arte. He has traveled to New Orleans to study Hoodoo, Europe to study Witchcraft and Ceremonial Magick, and Nepal to study Tantra. Miller is a member of the Chthonic Ouranian Temple and the Sangreal Sodality, as well as an initiated Tantrika in the Nyingma and Bon lineages of Tibet.

He is the author of *Protection & Reversal Magick: A Witch's Defense Manual* and the Strategic Sorcery blog. He is also a regular contributor to *Behutet* magazine. Miller lives with his wife and on the New Jersey shore, where he practices and teaches magick professionally.

## ZADKIEL

Zadkiel has practiced spirit-based magic (Solomonic and otherwise) for over twenty years. He taught workshops for many years on medieval astrology, medieval magic, spirit magic, and similar subjects, and eight years ago began the initiatory process in Lukumi (Cuban-style Orisha worship, often erroneously referred to as *Santeria*). In 2011, he was initiated to the role of *babalawo* and now practices as a divination priest of Ifa. He is currently working on his addiction to parenthetical asides (as you can see in his article).

## DENISE ALVARADO

Denise Alvarado is a New Orleans born, native Creole raised in the unique culture of New Orleans, Louisiana, and has studied indigenous healing traditions from a personal and academic perspective for over four decades. She has a M.S. in Professional Psychology from Walden University and a B.A. in Cultural Anthropology from Northern Arizona University. An independent researcher, Denise is a member of the American Anthropological Association and the Association of Indigenous Anthropologists as well as several special interest groups, including Anthropology of Childhood and Children Interest Group (ACCIG), Digital Anthropologies Interest Group (DAIG), and Interest Group on NGOs and Nonprofits (IGNN). She is Editor in Chief of *Hoodoo & Conjure* magazine, as well as a series of books that focus on folk magic traditions from the American South.

Denise's activities include cultural and spiritual consulting, assessment, and training for individuals and organizations. She is regularly consulted by film makers and production companies about New Orleans Voodoo and Hoodoo and southern folk magic traditions. She has consulted with Scotland Yard on the issue of African Ju Ju and human trafficking, the History Channel on New Orleans Voodoo, and with the production company for the Sci-Fi channel Raw TV on paranormal phenomenon. Her artwork has appeared on National Geographic's *Taboo*, *Blue Bloods*, *The Originals*, and *The Vampire Diaries*.

Denise was the recipient of Walden University's Fellowship in Research and Applications for Social Change, 2008–2009, with her research "The Native American Wellness Scale (NAWS): The Development of an Intertribal Quality of Life Measure for Native American and Indigenous Populations." She developed the first culturally appropriate quality-of-life instrument for use among Native American populations.

Denise lives the life she writes about and researches, giving her a unique participant observation perspective to her work.

BOOKS AUTHORED: *The Voodoo Doll Spellbook*, *The Voodoo Hoodoo Spellbook*, *Voodoo Dolls in Magick and Ritual*, *Hoodoo and Conjure Quarterly*, *Hoodoo and Conjure New Orleans*, *Hoodoo and Conjure New Orleans 2014*, *Hoodoo Almanac* (2012, 2013, 2014, and 2015) (with Dean and Pustanio), *Workin' in da Boneyard*, *105 Spiritual Baths for Every Occasion*, and *The Day of the Dead Handbook*.

# Rufus Opus

Rufus Opus is a professional Hermetic magician and teacher of the esoteric arts. He has authored several eBooks on the practical application of Hermetic Principles and teaches the Red Work series of courses, an in-depth study of the process of the alchemical Great Work. With over twenty years of training and practice, RO is a firm believer that magical study should result in tangible, practical manifestations of a better life, not only for the magician, but for everyone they come into contact with. For more information, see his blog at http://headforred.blogspot.com.

## NICK FARRELL

Nick Farrell was born in the UK and raised in New Zealand. At the age of four he suffered from a series of night-time terrors. He saw things that were particularly frightening. He knew they were not dreams, but they appeared real. These visions lasted until he was seventeen when he bought his first set of Tarot cards and suddenly found himself in a Golden Dawn offshoot called Builders of the Adytum. Nick started to read everything he could find on the Golden Dawn and Magic. Nick moved to Hawkes Bay where he hooked up with the former members of the last surviving temple of the Golden Dawn, Whare Ra. In particular he joined the Order of the Table Round, which was a side order of the now defunct Whare Ra temple. He moved to the UK to join Dolores Ashcroft-Nowicki's Servants of the Light School and found himself being trained by David Goddard. In 1997 he joined the Hermetic Order of the Golden Dawn forming a Temple of that Group in Nottingham. Around that time Nick wrote his first book, *Making Talismans*, which has turned out to be an esoteric classic. He moved to Sofia in Bulgaria where he wrote *Magical Pathworking*, *The Druidic Order of Pendragon* (with Colin Robertson), *Gathering the Magic*, and *Egyptian Shaman*. He also began to work with the artist Harry Wendrich and his wife Nicola on the Golden Dawn Temple Tarot deck. In 2007 he wrote his first novel *When a Tree Falls*, which is an occult fantasy based on his silly and at times black sense of humor. In 2008 he moved to Rome where he wrote two more books on the Golden Dawn, *King Over the Water* and *Mathers' Last Secret*. Later that year he established the Magical Order of the Aurora Aurea, which is a traditional Golden Dawn based order and already has five temples worldwide and a thriving correspondence course. During the day he makes money as a journalist for online technology magazines including *Techeye* and *Fudzilla*.

## SAM WEBSTER

Sam Webster, M.Div., Mage, hails from the Bay Area and has taught magick publicly since 1984. He graduated from Starr King School for the Ministry at the Graduate Theological Union in Berkeley in 1993. He is now a Ph.D. candidate at the University of Bristol, UK, studying Pagan history under Prof. Ronald Hutton. He is an Adept of the Golden Dawn, a cofounder of the Chthonic-Ouranian Templar order, and an initiate of Wiccan, Druidic, Buddhist, Hindu, and Masonic traditions. His work has been published in a number of journals such as *Green Egg* and *Gnosis*, and 2010 saw his first book, *Tantric Thelema*, establishing the publishing house Concrescent Press (http://Concrescent.net). He is now a columnist at *The Wild Hunt*. He founded the Open Source Order of the Golden Dawn (http://OSOGD.org) in 2001, the Pantheon Foundation (http://PantheonFoundation.org/) in 2013, and serves the Pagan community principally as a priest of Hermes. Contact Sam at samwebster11@gmail.com.

## GILBERTO STRAPAZON (SWAMI ANAND PRABUDDHA)

Gilberto Strapazon is a writter, student, and sorcerer with experience in meditation, tarot, witchcraft, Freemasonry, Golden Dawn FOM (a Brazilian independent branch), and Kemetic (Egyptian) traditions. He also spent eleven years practicing the Candomble religion. Afterward, he moved back to his preferred area of ceremonial magick — working mainly with the teachings of the Solomonic and other grimoires.

Gilberto started as a writer in 1986, focusing on human interaction with computers and developing an understanding of the evolution of people, companies, and spiritual development. He has published some independent works and created tales of fantastic fiction.

CPSIA information can be obtained
at www.ICGtesting.com
Printed in the USA
BVHW07s1630210518
516872BV00007B/633/P